NEW JERSEY STATUTES

TITLE 3B
ADMINISTRATION OF ESTATES
DECEDENTS AND OTHERS

2020 EDITION

Revised on January 21, 2020

By West Hartford Legal Publishing

NEW JERSEY LEGISLATURE

Table of Contents

Title 3B. Administration of Estates——Decedents and Others 5

    Chapter 1. Definitions and General Provisions 5

    Chapter 2. Superior and Surrogate's Courts; General Jurisdiction 7

    Chapter 3. Wills 8

    Chapter 4. Trusts; Testamentary Additions 15

    Chapter 5. Intestacy 16

    Chapter 6. Uniform Simultaneous Death Law 19

    Chapter 7. Decedent's Intentional Death; Effect 19

    Chapter 8. Right to Elective Share by Surviving Spouse 20

    Chapter 9. Disclaimers of Transfers by Will; Under Powers of Testamentary Appointment or by Intestate Succession 22

    Chapter 10. Personal Representatives 25

    Chapter 11. Trusts and Trustees 29

    Chapter 12. Minors and Incapacitated Persons 35

    Chapter 12A. Kinship Legal Guardianship 49

    Chapter 13. Guardianship of Veterans 56

    Chapter 13A. Conservators 59

    Chapter 14. Fiduciaries 62

    Chapter 15. Bonds and Sureties 75

    Chapter 16. Inventories 79

    Chapter 17. Accounting 80

    Chapter 18. Commissions 81

    Chapter 19. Principal and Income [Repealed] 85

    Chapter 19B. Uniform Principal and Income Act 85

    Chapter 20. Investments 94

    Chapter 21. Transfer of Property Out of State 98

    Chapter 22. Rights and Remedies of Creditors of Decedents 98

    Chapter 23. Distributive Shares and Devises 102

    Chapter 24. Apportionment of New Jersey Estate and Federal Taxes 106

    Chapter 25. Exoneration of Property Subject to Mortgage or Security Interest 108

    Chapter 26. Absentees 108

Chapter 27. Absence for Five Years 108

Chapter 28. Dower and Curtesy 109

Chapter 29. Repealer 110

Chapter 30. Uniform Transfer on Death Security Registration Act 111

Chapter 31. Uniform Trust Code 113

Title 3B. Administration of Estates——Decedents and Others

Chapter 1. Definitions and General Provisions

§ 3B:1-1. Definitions A to H

As used in this title, unless otherwise defined:

"Administrator" includes general administrators of an intestate and unless restricted by the subject or context, administrators with the will annexed, substituted administrators, substituted administrators with the will annexed, temporary administrators and administrators pendente lite.

"Beneficiary," as it relates to trust beneficiaries, includes a person who has any present or future interest, vested or contingent, and also includes the owner of an interest by assignment or other transfer and as it relates to a charitable trust, and includes any person entitled to enforce the trust.

"Child" means any individual, including a natural or adopted child, entitled to take by intestate succession from the parent whose relationship is involved and excludes any individual who is only a stepchild, a resource family child, a grandchild or any more remote descendant.

"Claims" include liabilities whether arising in contract, or in tort or otherwise, and liabilities of the estate which arise at or after the death of the decedent, including funeral expenses and expenses of administration, but does not include estate or inheritance taxes, demands or disputes regarding title to specific assets alleged to be included in the estate.

"Cofiduciary" means each of two or more fiduciaries jointly serving in a fiduciary capacity.

"Descendant" of an individual means all of his progeny of all generations, with the relationship of parent and child at each generation being determined by the definition of child contained in this section and parent contained in N.J.S.3B:1-2.

"Devise," when used as a noun, means a testamentary disposition of real or personal property and when used as a verb, means to dispose of real or personal property by will.

"Devisee" means any person designated in a will to receive a devise. In the case of a devise to an existing trust or trustee, or to a trustee of a trust described by will, the trust or trustee is the devisee and the beneficiaries are not devisees.

"Distributee" means any person who has received property of a decedent from his personal representative other than as a creditor or purchaser. A trustee is a distributee only to the extent of a distributed asset or increment thereto remaining in his hands. A beneficiary of a trust to whom the trustee has distributed property received from a personal representative is a distributee of the personal representative.

"Domestic partner" means a domestic partner as defined in section 3 of P.L.2003, c.246 (C.26:8A-3).

"Domiciliary foreign fiduciary" means any fiduciary who has received letters, or has been appointed, or is authorized to act as a fiduciary, in the jurisdiction in which the decedent was domiciled at the time of his death, in which the ward is domiciled or in which is located the principal place of the administration of a trust.

"Estate" means all of the property of a decedent, minor or incapacitated individual, trust or other person whose affairs are subject to this title as the property is originally constituted and as it exists from time to time during administration.

"Fiduciary" includes executors, general administrators of an intestate estate, administrators with the will annexed, substituted administrators, substituted administrators with the will annexed, guardians, substituted guardians, trustees, substituted trustees and, unless restricted by the subject or context, temporary administrators, administrators pendente lite, administrators ad prosequendum, administrators ad litem and other limited fiduciaries.

"Governing instrument" means a deed, will, trust, insurance or annuity policy, account with the designation "pay on death" (POD) or "transfer on death" (TOD), security registered in beneficiary form with the designation "pay on death" (POD) or "transfer on death" (TOD), pension, profit-sharing, retirement or similar benefit plan, instrument creating or exercising a power of appointment or a power of attorney, or a dispositive, appointive, or nominative instrument of any similar type.

"Guardian" means a person who has qualified as a guardian of the person or estate of a minor or incapacitated individual pursuant to testamentary or court appointment, but excludes one who is merely a guardian ad litem.

"Heirs" means those persons, including, but not limited to, the surviving spouse, the domestic partner and the descendants of the decedent, who are entitled under the statutes of intestate succession to the property of a decedent.

§ 3B:1-2. Definitions I to Z

"Incapacitated individual" means an individual who is impaired by reason of mental illness or intellectual disability to the extent that the individual lacks sufficient capacity to govern himself and manage his affairs.

The term incapacitated individual is also used to designate an individual who is impaired by reason of physical illness or disability, chronic use of drugs, chronic alcoholism, or other cause (except minority) to the extent that the individual lacks sufficient capacity to govern himself and manage the individual's affairs.

The terms incapacity and incapacitated refer to the state or condition of an incapacitated individual as hereinbefore defined.

"Intellectual disability" means a significant subaverage general intellectual functioning existing concurrently with deficits in adaptive behavior which are manifested during the development period.

"Issue" of an individual means a descendant as defined in N.J.S.3B:1-1.

"Joint tenants with the right of survivorship" means co-owners of property held under circumstances that entitle one or more to the whole of the property on the death of the other or others, but excludes forms of co-ownership in which the underlying ownership of each party is in proportion to that party's contribution.

"Local administration" means administration by a personal representative appointed in this State.

"Local fiduciary" means any fiduciary who has received letters in this State and excludes foreign fiduciaries who acquire the power of local fiduciary pursuant to this title.

"Minor" means an individual who is under 18 years of age.

"Nonresident decedent" means a decedent who was domiciled in another jurisdiction at the time of his death.

"Parent" means any person entitled to take or who would be entitled to take if the child, natural or adopted, died without a will, by intestate succession from the child whose relationship is in question and excludes any person who is a stepparent, resource family parent, or grandparent.

"Per capita." If a governing instrument requires property to be distributed "per capita," the property is divided to provide equal shares for each of the takers, without regard to their shares or the right of representation.

"Payor" means a trustee, insurer, business entity, employer, government, governmental agency or subdivision, or any other person authorized or obligated by law or a governing instrument to make payments.

"Person" means an individual or an organization.

"Per Stirpes." If a governing instrument requires property to be distributed "per stirpes," the property is divided into as many equal shares as there are: (1) surviving children of the designated ancestor; and (2) deceased children who left surviving descendants. Each surviving child is allocated one share. The share of each deceased child with surviving descendants is divided in the same manner, with subdivision repeating at each succeeding generation until the property is fully allocated among surviving descendants.

"Personal representative" includes executor, administrator, successor personal representative, special administrator, and persons who perform substantially the same function under the law governing their status. "General personal representative" excludes special administrator.

"Representation; Per Capita at Each Generation." If an applicable statute or a governing instrument requires property to be distributed "by representation" or "per capita at each generation," the property is divided into as many equal shares as there are: (1) surviving descendants in the generation nearest to the designated ancestor which contains one or more surviving descendants; and (2) deceased descendants in the same generation who left surviving descendants, if any. Each surviving descendant in the nearest generation is allocated one share. The remaining shares, if any, are combined and then divided in the same manner among the surviving descendants of the deceased descendants, as if the surviving descendants who were allocated a share and their surviving descendants had predeceased the designated ancestor.

"Resident creditor" means a person domiciled in, or doing business in this State, who is, or could be, a claimant against an estate.

"Security" includes any note, stock, treasury stock, bond, mortgage, financing statement, debenture, evidence of indebtedness, certificate of interest or participation in an oil, gas, or mining title or lease or in payments out of production under the title or lease, collateral, trust certificate, transferable share, voting trust certificate or, in general, any interest or instrument commonly known as a security or as a security interest or any certificate of interest or participation, any temporary or interim certificate, receipt or certificate of deposit for, or any warrant or right to subscribe to or purchase, any of the foregoing.

"Stepchild" means a child of the surviving, deceased, or former spouse who is not a child of the decedent.

"Successor personal representative" means a personal representative, other than a special administrator, who is appointed to succeed a previously appointed personal representative.

"Successors" means those persons, other than creditors, who are entitled to real and personal property of a decedent under a decedent's will or the laws governing intestate succession.

"Testamentary trustee" means a trustee designated by will or appointed to exercise a trust created by will.

"Testator" includes an individual and means male or female.

"Trust" includes any express trust, private or charitable, with additions thereto, wherever and however created. It also includes a trust created by judgment under which the trust is to be administered in the manner of an express trust. "Trust" excludes other constructive trusts, and it excludes resulting trusts, guardianships, personal representatives, trust accounts created under the "Multiple-party Deposit Account Act," P.L.1979, c.491 (C.17:16I-1 et seq.), gifts to minors under the "New Jersey Uniform Gifts to Minors Act," P.L.1963, c.177 (C.46:38-13 et seq.), or the "New Jersey Uniform Transfers to Minors Act," R.S.46:38A-1 et seq., business trusts providing for certificates to be issued to beneficiaries, common trusts, security arrangements, liquidation trusts, and trusts for the primary purpose of paying debts, dividends, interest, salaries, wages, profits, pensions or employee benefits of any kind, and any arrangement under which a person is nominee or escrowee for another.

"Trustee" includes an original, additional or successor trustee, whether or not appointed or confirmed by court.

"Ward" means an individual for whom a guardian is appointed or an individual under the protection of the court.

"Will" means the last will and testament of a testator or testatrix and includes any codicil and any testamentary instrument that merely appoints an executor, revokes or revises another will, nominates a guardian, or expressly excludes or limits the right of a person or class to succeed to property of the decedent passing by intestate succession.

§ 3B:1-3. Devolution of property upon death

Upon the death of an individual, his real and personal property devolves to the persons to whom it is devised by his will or to those indicated as substitutes for them in cases involving lapse, renunciation, or other circumstances affecting the devolution of testate estates, or in the absence of testamentary disposition, to his heirs, or to those indicated as substitutes for them in cases involving renunciation or other circumstances affecting devolution of intestate estates, subject to rights of creditors and to administration.

§ 3B:1-4. Contractual arrangements relating to death

A contract to make a will or devise, or not to revoke a will or devise, or to die intestate, if executed after September 1, 1978, can be established only by (1) provisions of a will stating material provisions of the contract; (2) an express reference in a will to a contract and extrinsic evidence proving the terms of the contract; or (3) a writing signed by the decedent evidencing the contract. The execution of a joint will or mutual wills does not create a presumption of a contract not to revoke the will or wills.

§ 3B:1-5. Effect upon vested rights and remedies

The repeal of any sections, acts or parts of acts by the enactment of this title shall not affect any right now vested in any person pursuant to any sections, acts or parts of acts so repealed, nor any remedy where an action or proceeding thereunder has been instituted and is pending on the effective date of this title.

§ 3B:1-6. Law governing rights, duties and powers of fiduciaries

The provisions of this title shall govern the rights, duties and powers of successors and fiduciaries relating to the administration of all estates except that the validity and propriety of all acts done by a fiduciary and all rights established in successors prior to September 1, 1978, shall be determined under the law as then in effect.

§ 3B:1-7. Exclusion of property passing to a testamentary trustee other than by devise from rights of personal representative or creditors of decedent

Property passing to a testamentary trustee other than by devise shall not be subject to rights of, powers of or to administration by a personal representative or to rights of creditors to any extent beyond that to which it would otherwise be if the testamentary trust was an inter vivos trust.

§ 3B:1-8. Application of title to wills

The provisions of this title shall apply to any wills of decedents dying on or after September 1, 1978.

§ 3B:1-8.1. Applicability of act

The provisions of P.L.2004, c. 132 and P.L.2005, c.160 (C.3B:1-8.1 et al.) shall apply to any decedent dying on or after February 27, 2005.

§ 3B:1-9. Effect of fraud and evasion

Whenever fraud has been perpetrated in connection with any proceeding or in any statement filed under this title or if fraud is used to avoid or circumvent the provisions or purposes of this title, any person injured thereby may obtain appropriate relief against the perpetrator of the fraud or restitution from any person (other than a bona fide purchaser or lender) benefitting from the fraud, whether innocent or not. Any proceeding must be commenced within 2 years after the discovery of the fraud, but no proceeding may be brought against one not a perpetrator of the fraud later than 5 years after the time of commission of the fraud. This section has no bearing on remedies relating to fraud practiced on a decedent during his lifetime which affects the succession of his estate.

Chapter 2. Superior and Surrogate's Courts; General Jurisdiction

§ 3B:2-1. Jurisdiction of Superior Court not affected

The provisions of this title are not intended and shall not be so construed as in any way to affect, impair or limit the original general jurisdiction of the Superior Court given to it by the Constitution.

§ 3B:2-2. General authority of Superior Court as to probate matters

The Superior Court shall have full authority to hear and determine all controversies respecting wills, trusts and estates, and full authority over the accounts of fiduciaries, and also authority over all other matters and things as are submitted to its determination under this title.

§ 3B:2-3. Jurisdiction of Superior Court over surrogate's proceedings

The Superior Court shall have jurisdiction to hear and determine disputes or doubts arising before the surrogate or in the surrogate's court of a county, to review any order, determination or judgment of the surrogate or the surrogate's court of a county and upon the review to hear and determine the matter, and to grant relief from or to direct the entry of, as of a former time, any order, determination or judgment of the surrogate or the surrogate's court of a county.

§ 3B:2-4. Proceedings in Superior Court on order to show cause

The Superior Court, in any proceeding by or against fiduciaries or other persons, may proceed in a summary manner.

§ 3B:2-5. Disputes or doubts in proceedings before the surrogate

In the event of any dispute or doubt arising before the surrogate or in the surrogate's court, neither the surrogate nor the court shall take any further action therein, except in accordance with the order of the Superior Court.

§ 3B:2-6. Oath; affidavit; deposition or proof

Any oath, affidavit, deposition or proof required to be made or taken in any proceeding before a surrogate, the surrogate's court or in the Superior Court, or necessary or proper to be used before the surrogate or the court, may be made and taken before the surrogate or before any individual authorized by law to administer oaths. Qualifications of executors and administrators and acceptances of trusteeships and guardianships may be taken as provided by the rules of the Supreme Court.

§ 3B:2-7. Issuance of subpoenas by surrogate

A surrogate may issue process of subpoenas to any person within the State to appear and give evidence in any matter pending before the surrogate's court.

§ 3B:2-8. Penalty for failure to obey subpoena

Any person subpoenaed as a witness by a surrogate, who does not appear pursuant thereto, or appearing refuses to be sworn or give evidence, without reasonable cause assigned, shall, for every such default or refusal, be subject to a fine of not more than $50.00, as the surrogate's court issuing the subpoena shall by judgment determine proper to impose. The fine, when collected, shall be paid to the county.

In default of the payment of a fine so imposed, the surrogate's court by its judgment may commit the witness to the county jail of the county until it is paid or he is sooner discharged.

The judgment of the surrogate's court imposing a fine or committing a witness to jail shall be reviewable by the Superior Court in the same manner as other judgments of the court are reviewed.

Chapter 3. Wills

§ 3B:3-1. Individuals competent to make a will and appoint a testamentary guardian

Any individual 18 or more years of age who is of sound mind may make a will and may appoint a testamentary guardian.

§ 3B:3-2. Execution; witnessed wills; writings intended as wills.

a. Except as provided in subsection b. and in N.J.S.3B:3-3, a will shall be:
(1) in writing;
(2) signed by the testator or in the testator's name by some other individual in the testator's conscious presence and at the testator's direction; and
(3) signed by at least two individuals, each of whom signed within a reasonable time after each witnessed either the signing of the will as described in paragraph (2) or the testator's acknowledgment of that signature or acknowledgment of the will.
b. A will that does not comply with subsection a. is valid as a writing intended as a will, whether or not witnessed, if the signature and material portions of the document are in the testator's handwriting.
c. Intent that the document constitutes the testator's will can be established by extrinsic evidence, including for writings intended as wills, portions of the document that are not in the testator's handwriting.

§ 3B:3-2.1. Creation, maintenance of will registry; fees

a. The Secretary of State shall create and maintain a will registry in which a testator or his attorney may register information regarding the testator's will. The information contained in such registry shall include the name of the person making the will, the date the will was made, and sufficient identification of the location of the will at the time of registration. The registry shall not contain a copy of the will.
b. The fee for registration of a will shall be $10.00, which shall be deposited by the Secretary of State in the General Fund.
c. The existence or nonexistence of a registration for a particular will shall not be considered as evidence in any proceeding relating to such will, and the failure to file information about a will in the will registry shall not be a factor in determining the validity of the will.
d. The fee for application to the Secretary of State to conduct a search of the registry shall be $10.00, which shall be deposited by the Secretary of State in the General Fund. Only interested persons and their representatives may conduct a search of the registry. As used in this act, 'interested persons' means children, spouses, potential heirs, devisees, fiduciaries, creditors, beneficiaries and any others having a property right in or claim against a trust estate or the estate of a decedent which may be affected by the proceeding.
e. The Secretary of State shall not be liable for the accuracy of the representation of the person conducting a search of the registry or for the accuracy of the information contained in the registry.

§ 3B:3-2.2. Regulations

The Secretary of State shall promulgate regulations pursuant to the provisions of the "Administrative Procedure Act," P.L. 1968, c. 410 (C. 52:14B-1 et seq.) to effectuate the provisions of this act.

§ 3B:3-3. Writings intended as wills

Although a document or writing added upon a document was not executed in compliance with N.J.S.3B:3-2, the document or writing is treated as if it had been executed in compliance with N.J.S.3B:3-2 if the proponent of the document or writing establishes by clear and convincing evidence that the decedent intended the document or writing to constitute: (1) the decedent's will; (2) a partial or complete revocation of the will; (3) an addition to or an alteration of the will; or (4) a partial or complete revival of his formerly revoked will or of a formerly revoked portion of the will.

§ 3B:3-4. Making will self-proved at time of execution

Any will executed on or after September 1, 1978 may be simultaneously executed, attested, and made self-proved, by acknowledgment thereof by the testator and affidavits of the witnesses, each made before an officer authorized pursuant to R.S. 46:14-6.1 to take acknowledgments and proofs of instruments entitled to be recorded under the laws of this State, in substantially the following form:

I, _____ the testator, sign my name to this instrument this .... day of _____ 20 _____, and being duly sworn, do hereby declare to the undersigned authority that I sign and execute this instrument as my last will and that I sign it willingly (or willingly direct another to sign for me), that I execute it as my free and voluntary act for the purposes therein expressed, and that I am 18 years of age or older, of sound mind, and under no constraint or undue influence.

Testator

We, _____, the witnesses, sign our names to this instrument, and, being duly sworn, do hereby declare to the undersigned authority that the testator signs and executes this instrument as the testator's last will and that the testator signs it willingly (or willingly directs another to sign for him), and that each of us, in the presence and hearing of the testator, hereby signs this will as witness to the testator's signing, and that to the best of our knowledge the testator is 18 years of age or older, of sound mind, and under no constraint or undue influence.

Witness

Witness

The State of _____

County of _____

Subscribed, sworn to and acknowledged before me by _____, the testator and subscribed and sworn to before me by _____ and _____, witnesses, this _____ day of _____

(Signed) _____

(Official capacity of officer)

§ 3B:3-5. Making will self-proved subsequent to time of execution

A will executed in compliance with N.J.S. 3B:3-2 may at any time subsequent to its execution be made self-proved by the acknowledgment thereof by the testator and the affidavits of the witnesses, each made before an officer authorized pursuant to R.S. 46:14-6.1 to take acknowledgments and proofs of instruments entitled to be recorded under the laws of this State, attached or annexed to the will in substantially the following form:

The State of

County of

We, , and , the testator and the witnesses, respectively, whose names are signed to the attached or foregoing instrument, being duly sworn, do hereby declare to the undersigned authority that the testator signed and executed the instrument as his last will and that the testator had signed willingly (or willingly directed another to sign for the testator), and that he executed it as the testator's free and voluntary act for the purposes therein expressed, and that each of the witnesses, in the presence and hearing of the testator, signed the will as witness and that to the best of his knowledge the testator was at that time 18 years of age or older, of sound mind and under no constraint or undue influence.

Testator

Witness

Witness

Subscribed, sworn to and acknowledged before me by, the testator, and subscribed and sworn to before me by and, witnesses, this day of.

(Signed)

(Official capacity of officer)

§ 3B:3-6. Validating acknowledgment

An acknowledgment to make a will self-proved taken on or after September 1, 1978, but before October 11, 1979, pursuant to R.S. 46:14-6, R.S. 46:14-7 or R.S. 46:14-8 to make a will self-proved under N.J.S. 3B:3-4 or N.J.S. 3B:3-5 is a valid acknowledgment, notwithstanding that the certificate of acknowledgment does not have the officer's official seal affixed thereto.

§ 3B:3-7. Who may witness a will

Any individual generally competent to be a witness may act as a witness to a will and to testify concerning execution thereof.

§ 3B:3-8. Will not invalidated if signed by interested witness

A will or any provision thereof is not invalid because the will is signed by an interested witness.

§ 3B:3-9. Laws determining valid execution of will

A written will is validly executed if executed in compliance with N.J.S. 3B:3-2 or N.J.S. 3B:3-3 or its execution was in compliance with the law of the place where it was executed, or with the law of the place where at the time of execution or at the time of death the testator was domiciled, had a place of abode or was a national.

§ 3B:3-10. Incorporation by reference

Any writing in existence when a will is executed may be incorporated by reference if the language of the will manifests this intent and describes the writing sufficiently to permit its identification.

§ 3B:3-11. Identifying devise of tangible personal property by separate writing

A will may refer to a written statement or list to dispose of items of tangible personal property not otherwise specifically disposed of by the will, other than money. To be admissible under this section as evidence of the intended disposition, the writing must be either in the handwriting of the testator or be signed by the testator and must describe the items and the devisees with reasonable certainty. The writing may be referred to as one to be in existence at the time of the testator's death; it may be prepared before or after the execution of the will; it may be altered by the testator after its preparation; and it may be a writing which has no significance apart from its effect upon the dispositions made by the will.

§ 3B:3-12. Acts and events of independent significance

A will may dispose of property by reference to acts and events which have significance apart from their effect upon the dispositions made by the will, whether they occur before or after the execution of the will or before or after the testator's death. The execution or revocation of a will of another individual is such an event.

§ 3B:3-13. Revocation by writing or by act

A will or any part thereof is revoked:

a. By the execution of a subsequent will that revokes the previous will or part expressly or by inconsistency; or

b. By the performance of a revocatory act on the will, if the testator performed the act with the intent and for the purpose of revoking the will or part or if another individual performed the act in the testator's conscious presence and by the testator's direction. For purposes of this subsection, "revocatory act on the will" includes burning, tearing canceling, obliterating or destroying the will or any part of it. A burning, tearing or cancelling is a "revocatory act on the will," whether or not the burn, tear, or cancellation touched any of the words on the will.

(1) If a subsequent will does not expressly revoke a previous will, the execution of the subsequent will wholly revokes the previous will by inconsistency if the testator intended the subsequent will to replace rather than supplement the previous will.

(2) The testator is presumed to have intended a subsequent will to replace rather than supplement a previous will if the subsequent will makes a complete disposition of the testator's estate. If this presumption arises and is not rebutted by clear and convincing evidence, the previous will is revoked; only the subsequent will is operative on the testator's death.

(3) The testator is presumed to have intended a subsequent will to supplement rather than replace a previous will if the subsequent will does not make a complete disposition of the testator's estate. If this presumption arises and is not rebutted by clear and convincing evidence, the subsequent will revokes the previous will only to the extent the subsequent will is inconsistent with the previous will; each will is fully operative on the testator's death to the extent they are not inconsistent.

§ 3B:3-14. Revocation of probate and non-probate transfers by divorce or annulment; revival by remarriage to former spouse

a. Except as provided by the express terms of a governing instrument, a court order, or a contract relating to the division of the marital estate made between the divorced individuals before or after the marriage, divorce or annulment, a divorce or annulment:

(1) revokes any revocable:

(a) dispositions or appointment of property made by a divorced individual to his former spouse in a governing instrument and any disposition or appointment created by law or in a governing instrument to a relative of the divorced individual's former spouse;

(b) provision in a governing instrument conferring a general or special power of appointment on the divorced individual's former spouse, or on a relative of the divorced individual's former spouse; and

(c) nomination in a governing instrument of a divorced individual's former spouse or a relative of the divorced individual's former spouse to serve in any fiduciary or representative capacity; and

(2) severs the interests of the former spouses in property held by them at the time of the divorce or annulment as joint tenants with the right of survivorship or as tenants by the entireties, transforming the interests of the former spouses into tenancies in common. In the event of a divorce or annulment, provisions of a governing instrument are given effect as if the former spouse and relatives of the former spouse disclaimed all provisions revoked by this section or, in the case of a revoked nomination in a fiduciary or representative capacity, as if the former spouse and relatives of the former spouse died immediately before the divorce or annulment. If provisions are revoked solely by this section, they are revived by the divorced individual's remarriage to the former spouse or by the revocation, suspension or nullification of the divorce or annulment. No change of circumstances other than as described in this section and in N.J.S.3B:7-1 effects a revocation or severance.

A severance under paragraph (2) of subsection a. does not affect any third-party interest in property acquired for value and in good faith reliance on an apparent title by survivorship in the survivor of the former spouse unless a writing declaring the severance has been noted, registered, filed, or recorded in records appropriate to the kind and location of the property which are relied upon, in the ordinary course of transactions involving such property, as evidence of ownership.

b. For purposes of this section: (1) "divorce or annulment" means any divorce or annulment, or other dissolution or declaration of invalidity of a marriage including a judgment of divorce from bed and board; (2) "governing instrument" means a governing instrument executed by the divorced individual before the divorce or annulment; (3) "divorced individual "includes an individual whose marriage has been annulled; and (4) "relative of the divorced individual's former spouse" means an individual who is related to the divorced individual's former spouse by blood, adoption or affinity and who, after the divorce or annulment, is not related to the divorced individual by blood, adoption or affinity.

c. This section does not affect the rights of any person who purchases property from a former spouse for value and without notice, or receives a payment or other item of property in partial or full satisfaction of a legally enforceable obligation, which the former spouse was not entitled to under this section, but the former spouse is liable for the amount of the proceeds or the value of the property to the person who is entitled to it under this section.

d. A payor or other third party making payment or transferring an item of property or other benefit according to the terms of a governing instrument affected by a divorce or annulment is not liable by reason of this section unless prior to such payment or transfer it has received at its home or principal address written notice of a claimed revocation, severance or forfeiture under this section.

§ 3B:3-15. Revival of revoked will

a. Except as otherwise provided in N.J.S. 3B:3-14 or as provided in subsections b., c. and d. of this section, a revoked will or codicil shall not be revived except by reexecution or by a duly executed codicil expressing an intention to revive it.

b. If a subsequent will that wholly revoked a previous will is thereafter revoked by a revocatory act described in N.J.S. 3B:3-13, the previous will remains revoked unless it is revived. The previous will is revived if there is clear and convincing evidence from the circumstances of the revocation of the subsequent will or from the testator's contemporary or subsequent declarations that the testator intended the previous will to take effect as executed.

c. If a subsequent will that partly revoked a previous will is thereafter revoked by a revocatory act described in N.J.S. 3B:3-13, a revoked part of the previous will is revived unless there is clear and convincing evidence from the circumstances of the revocation of the subsequent will or from the testator's contemporary or subsequent declarations that the testator did not intend the revoked part to take effect as executed.

d. If a subsequent will that revoked a previous will in whole or in part is thereafter revoked by another, later will, the previous will remains revoked in whole or in part, unless it or its revoked part is revived. The previous will or its revoked part is revived to the extent it appears from the terms of the later will that the testator intended the previous will to take effect.

§ 3B:3-16. Methods of altering will

No devise in, or clause of a will may be altered, except by another will or codicil or other writing declaring the alteration executed in the manner in which wills are required by law to be executed.

§ 3B:3-17. Probate of will and grant of letters

The surrogates of the several counties or the Superior Court may take depositions to wills admit the same to probate, and grant thereon letters testamentary or letters of administration with the will annexed.

§ 3B:3-18. Necessity to probate will to transfer property or nominate executor

To be effective to prove the transfer of any property or to nominate an executor, a will must be admitted to probate.

§ 3B:3-19. Proof required to probate will

A will executed as provided in N.J.S. 3B:3-2 may be admitted to probate by the surrogate upon the proof of one of the attesting witnesses or by some other individual having knowledge of the facts relating to the proper execution of the will by the testator and its attestation by one of the witnesses.

A will executed and acknowledged in the manner provided in N.J.S. 3B:3-4, or N.J.S. 3B:3-5 may be admitted to probate by the surrogate without further affidavit, deposition or proof.

A writing intended as a will may be admitted to probate only in the manner provided by the Rules Governing the Courts of the State of New Jersey.

§ 3B:3-20. Probate of a will of testator who died in military service or within 2 years of discharge

When a resident of this State dies while a member of the armed forces of the United State or within 2 years from the date of his discharge from the armed forces and no witness to his will is available in this State to prove the will, either because of death, incapacity, nonresidence, absence, or for any other reason, the will shall be admitted to probate upon proof of the signature of the testator by any two individuals, provided the will was validly executed as provided in N.J.S. 3B:3-9, and the will would have been admitted to probate if the witnesses were dead.

§ 3B:3-21. Probate of will where witnesses are in service in time of war

When the only living subscribing witness or witnesses, to the will of a resident of this State, is not or are not available in this State to prove the will, because of absence from the State while in the armed forces of the United States or of any ally of the United States, or while in the merchant marine, in time of war or national emergency, the will shall be admitted to probate upon proof of the signatures of the witnesses to the will, provided the will would then have been admitted to probate if the witnesses were dead.

§ 3B:3-22. Time for probate of will; preliminary filing

No will shall be admitted to probate until after 10 days from the death of the testator; but the complaint and other papers in any action for the probate of a will may be filed, and the depositions of the witnesses thereto and the qualification of the executor or administrator with the will annexed may be taken at any time subsequent to the death of the testator and before the will is admitted to probate.

§ 3B:3-23. Proof of execution required in contested probate action

If an issue as to the execution of a will arises in a contested probate action, the testimony of at least one of the attesting witnesses, if within the State, competent and able to testify, is required. Other evidence is admissible as to the due execution of a will.

§ 3B:3-24. Where a will of a resident is to be probated; effect of failure to probate

The will of any individual resident within any county of this State at his death may be admitted to probate in the surrogate's court of the county or in the Superior Court. If the will of any individual resident within the State at his death is probated outside the State, it shall be without effect unless or until probate is granted within the State.

§ 3B:3-25. Filing probate record with surrogate of any county

When a will devising real estate has been duly admitted to probate by the Superior Court, any person interested therein may file with the surrogate of any county a certified copy of the will, the complaint or application for probate, the proofs, the judgment or order for probate and the letters testamentary issued thereon. The surrogate shall thereupon record them which record, or a certified copy thereof, shall be received in evidence in any cause involving the title to real estate in that county as if the will had been originally admitted to probate before the surrogate.

§ 3B:3-26. Probate of will of nonresident probated in another state or country

When the will of any individual not resident in this State at his death shall have been admitted to probate in any state of the United States or other jurisdiction or country, the surrogate's court of any county may admit it to probate for any purpose and issue letters thereon, provided the will is valid under the laws of this State.

§ 3B:3-27. Recording of will of nonresident probated in another state or country

A copy of any will or of the record of any will of a decedent not resident in this State at his death, admitted to probate in any state of the United States or other jurisdiction or country, and of the certificate or judgment for probate, and if title to real estate of the decedent depends on the conveyance by an executor, administrator with the will annexed, substituted administrator with the will annexed, trustee or substituted trustee, of the record of the grant of letters testamentary thereon, or of administration, or substitutionary administration, with the will annexed, or of a copy of the letters, attested and certified pursuant to the rules of the Supreme Court or, if it be a record of any state of the United States, exemplified and authenticated according to the act of Congress, heretofore or hereafter filed and recorded in the office of the surrogate of any county in this State, shall have the same force and effect in respect to all real estate whereof the testator died seized, as if the will had been admitted to probate and the letters aforesaid had been issued in this State, provided it appears either from the deposition in the record or the attestation clause, or by a deposition taken under a commission or otherwise, that the will is valid under the laws of this State.

All conveyances of the real estate heretofore or hereafter made by any executor, administrator with the will annexed, substituted administrator with the will annexed, trustee, substituted trustee, or the survivor or survivors of them, or by any devisee or persons claiming under the devisee shall be as valid as if the will had been admitted to probate and letters aforesaid had been issued in this State.

Certified copies of the will, deposition, judgment for probate and letters, or of the record thereof, shall be received in evidence in all the courts of this State.

§ 3B:3-28. Probate of will of nonresident decedent where property situated in New Jersey

Where the will of any individual not resident in this State at his death has not been admitted to probate in the state, jurisdiction or country in which he then resided and no proceeding is there pending for the probate of the will, and he died owning real estate situate in any county of this State or personal property, or evidence of the ownership thereof, situate therein at the time of probate, the Superior Court or the surrogate's court may admit the will to probate and grant letters thereon.

§ 3B:3-28.1. Probate of will of nonresident where laws of decedent's domicile are discriminatory

Where the will of any individual who is not resident in this State at the time of his death has not been admitted to probate in the state in which he resided and no proceeding is there pending for the probate of the will, the Superior Court may admit the will to probate and grant letters thereon if the laws of that state discriminate against residents of New Jersey either as a beneficiary or as a fiduciary.

§ 3B:3-29. Order to compel production of purported will

The Superior Court shall have jurisdiction to compel discovery as to the existence or whereabouts of any paper purporting to be a will of any decedent who died a resident of the county, which has not been offered for probate, and to require the paper to be lodged with the surrogate of the county for probate.

§ 3B:3-30. Allowances by Superior Court to spouse or children pending contest over probate of will

If a contest is pending over the probate of any paper purporting to be a will, the Superior Court may, on application by the widow or widower of the decedent, by any of decedent's children, or by any children of any of decedent's deceased children, order the person having the custody of the decedent's estate to pay out of the income of the estate, pending the contest, an allowance for the support and maintenance of the widow, widower, child or children as the court may deem just; and any further allowance out of the income, or, if need be, out of the corpus, of the estate as may be necessary to meet the expenses incurred or to be incurred in conducting the contest.

To entitle a widow or widower to the benefit of this section the applicant must have been ceremonially married to the decedent and been living with him or her as his or her spouse at decedent's death.

§ 3B:3-31. Judgment for probate; conclusive effect on title to real property after 7 years

Where judgment has been or shall be entered by any surrogate's court in this State or Superior Court of the State, admitting to probate the will of any individual whether or not a resident of the State at his death and 7 years have elapsed after the judgment, the judgment unless set aside, shall, as to all matters adjudicated thereby, be conclusive upon the title to real estate.

§ 3B:3-32. Requirement of survival by 120 hours; exceptions; survivorship with respect to future interests

a. Except as provided in subsections b. and c., for purposes of construing a will, trust agreement, or other governing instrument, an individual who is not established by clear and convincing evidence to have survived an event, including the death of another individual, by 120 hours is deemed to have predeceased the event.

b. If it is not established by clear and convincing evidence that one of two co-owners with right of survivorship survived the other co-owner by 120 hours, one-half of the property passes as if one had survived by 120 hours and one-half as if the other had survived by 120 hours.

c. If there are more than two co-owners and it is not established by clear and convincing evidence that at least one of them survived the others by 120 hours, the property passes in the proportion that one bears to the whole number of co-owners.

d. The 120 hour survival requirement of subsections a., b. and c. shall not apply if: (1) the will, trust agreement, or other governing instrument, contains some language applicable to the event dealing explicitly with simultaneous deaths or deaths in a common disaster, or requiring survival for a stated time period; (2) application would cause a non-vested property interest or power of appointment to be invalid under a rule against perpetuities concerning an interest created prior to the enactment of P.L. 1999, c. 159 (effective on July 8, 1999); or (3) it is established by clear and convincing evidence that application to multiple governing instruments would result in an unintended failure or duplication of a disposition.

e. For purposes of this section, "co-owners with right of survivorship" includes joint tenants, tenants by the entireties, and other co-owners of property or accounts held under circumstances that entitle one or more to the whole of the property or account on the death of the other or others.

To the extent this section is inconsistent with the "Uniform Simultaneous Death Law" (N.J.S. 3B:6-1 et seq.), the provisions of this section shall apply.

§ 3B:3-33. Choice of law as to meaning and effect of wills; testator's intention; rules of construction

The meaning and legal effect of a disposition in a will, trust or other governing instrument shall be determined by the local law of a particular state selected in the will, trust or other governing instrument, unless the application of that law is contrary to the provisions relating to the elective share described in N.J.S. 3B:8-1 et seq. or any other public policy of this State otherwise applicable to the disposition.

§ 3B:3-33.1. Testator's intention; settlor's intention; rules of construction applicable to wills, trusts and other governing instruments

a. The intention of a testator as expressed in his will controls the legal effect of his dispositions, and the rules of construction expressed in N.J.S. 3B:3-34 through N.J.S. 3B:3-48 shall apply unless the probable intention of the testator, as indicated by the will and relevant circumstances, is contrary.

b. The intention of a settlor as expressed in a trust, or of an individual as expressed in a governing instrument, controls the legal effect of the dispositions therein and the rules of construction expressed in N.J.S. 3B:34 through N.J.S. 3B:3-48 shall apply unless the probable intent of such settlor or of such individual, as indicated by the trust or by such governing instrument and relevant circumstances, is contrary. For purposes of this Title, when construing each of these rules of construction the word "testator" shall include but not be limited to a settlor or a creator of any other governing instrument; the word "will" shall include a trust or other governing instrument; the word "devise" shall include any disposition in a trust or other governing instrument; and the word "devisee" shall include a beneficiary of a trust or other governing instrument.

§ 3B:3-34. Will construed to pass all property of testator including after-acquired property

Unless a will expressly provides otherwise, it is construed to pass all property the testator owns at death including property acquired after the execution of the will, and all property acquired by the estate after the testator's death.

§ 3B:3-35. Anti-lapse; deceased devisee; class gifts

If a devisee who is a grandparent, stepchild or a lineal descendant of a grandparent of the decedent is dead at the time of the execution of the governing instrument, fails to survive the decedent, or is treated as if he predeceased the decedent, any descendants of the deceased devisee who survives the decedent by 120 hours take by representation in place of the deceased devisee. One who would have been a devisee under a class gift if he had survived the decedent is treated as a devisee for purposes of this section whether his death occurred before or after the execution of the governing instrument. For purposes of this section, a "stepchild" means a child of the surviving, deceased or former spouse who is not a child of the decedent.

§ 3B:3-36. Failure of testamentary provision; residuary devise to two or more residuary devisees; death of one or more before testator

Except as provided in N.J.S. 3B:3-35:

a. a devise, other than a residuary devise, that fails for any reason becomes a part of the residue.

b. if the residue is devised to two or more persons, unless a contrary intention shall appear by the will, the share of a residuary devise that fails for any reason passes to the other residuary devisee, or to other residuary devisees in proportion to the interest of each in the remaining part of the residue.

§ 3B:3-37. Residuary devise to two or more residuary devisees; death of one or more before testator

When a residuary devise shall be made to two or more persons by the will of any testator, unless a contrary intention shall appear by the will, the share of any residuary devisees dying before the testator and not saved from the lapse by N.J.S. 3B:3-35, or not capable of taking effect because of any other circumstance or cause, shall go to and be vested in the remaining residuary devisees, if any there be, and if more than one, then to the remaining residuary devisees in proportion to their respective shares in the residue.

§ 3B:3-38. Construction of words "die without issue" or "die without descendants"

In a devise of real or personal property the words "die without issue" or "die without descendants" or "die without lawful issue" or "die without lawful descendants" or "have no issue" or "have no descendants" or other words which may import a want or failure of issue or descendants of an individual in his lifetime, or at his death, or an indefinite failure of his issue or descendants, shall be construed to mean a failure of issue or descendants at the death of the individual, unless a contrary intention shall otherwise appear by the will.

§ 3B:3-39. Construction when "heirs and assigns" omitted from devise; fee passed

When a devise of real estate within this State to any devisee omits the words "heirs and assigns" and the will contains no expressions indicating an intent to devise only an estate for life, or the real estate is not further devised after the death of the devisee, the devise shall be deemed to pass an estate in fee simple to the devisee as if the real estate had been devised to the devisee and to his heirs and assigns forever.

§ 3B:3-40. Words importing estate in fee not to prevent further devise

In any devise of real or personal property set forth in a will, the giving to one person of an indeterminate or other interest in the property or an estate in fee therein or absolute ownership thereof, together with a power, absolute or otherwise, to dispose of the property, shall not be construed to render void a limitation over of the property to another person which is to take effect in the event that the first named devisee shall not have disposed of the property during his lifetime. In all those cases, the testator's intent shall be given effect.

§ 3B:3-41. Issue and descendants to take by representation

Where under any governing instrument provision is made for the benefit of issue and descendants and no contrary intention is expressed, the issue or descendants shall take by representation.

§ 3B:3-42. Increase in securities, accessions

a. If a testator executes a will that devises securities and the testator then owned securities that meet the description in the will, the devise includes additional securities owned by the testator at death to the extent the additional securities were acquired by the testator after the will was executed as a result of the testator's ownership of the described securities and are securities of any of the following types:
(1) securities of the same organization acquired by reason of action initiated by the organization or any successor, related, or acquiring organization, excluding any acquired by exercise of purchase options;
(2) securities of another organization acquired as a result of a merger, consolidation, reorganization, or other distribution by the organization or any successor, related, or acquiring organization; or
(3) securities of the same organization acquired as a result of a plan of reinvestment.
b. Distributions in cash declared and payable as of a record date before death with respect to a described security, whether paid before or after death, are not part of the devise.

§ 3B:3-43. Nonademption of specific devise; sale by or payment of condemnation award or insurance proceeds to guardian of testator or agent

If specifically devised property is sold or mortgaged by a guardian for a testator, or by an agent acting within the authority of a durable power of attorney for an incapacitated individual, or if a condemnation award, insurance proceeds or recovery for injury to the property are paid to a guardian for a testator or such agent as a result of condemnation, fire or casualty, the specific devisee has the right to a general pecuniary devise equal to the net sale price, the amount of the unpaid loan, the condemnation award, the insurance proceeds or the recovery. This section does not apply if subsequent to the sale, mortgage, condemnation, casualty, or recovery the guardianship is terminated or the durable power of attorney is revoked by the testator and the testator survives by 1 year the judgment terminating the guardianship or such revocation. The right of the specific devisee under this section is reduced by any right he has under N.J.S. 3B:3-44.

§ 3B:3-44. Specific devise; right of devisee after sale, condemnation, casualty loss or foreclosure

A specific devisee has the right to the remaining specifically devised property in the testator's estate at death and:
a. Any balance of the purchase price (together with any security interest) owing from a purchaser to the testator at death by reason of sale of the property;
b. Any amount of a condemnation award for the taking of the property unpaid at death;
c. Any proceeds unpaid at death on fire or casualty insurance on, or other recovery for injury to, the property; and

d. Property owned by testator at his death as a result of foreclosure, or obtained in lieu of foreclosure, of the security for a specifically devised obligation.

§ 3B:3-45. Exercise of power of appointment

a. Unless the terms of a will, trust, or other governing instrument expressly provide otherwise, whenever such will, trust, or other governing instrument grants a power of appointment to another person, who as the power holder is authorized to further dispose of the property amongst appointees selected by the power holder, that power holder, other than a power holder acting in the capacity of a trustee or other fiduciary, shall be deemed authorized to exercise the power of appointment to create less than absolute interests for the benefit of one or more permissible appointees of the power, including interests in trust and the creation of new powers of appointment, whether general or limited, exercisable by the one or more appointees. A direction in the will, trust, or governing instrument that property subject to a power of appointment be distributed "to" an appointee, or to an appointee "outright," "in fee simple," "absolutely," "forever," or any other term, phrase, or statement of similar import, shall not be deemed to evidence the intent of the testator, settlor, or creator of the governing instrument to prohibit the exercise of a power of appointment to create less than absolute interests, including interests in trust.

b. A general residuary clause in a will, or a will making general disposition of all of the testator's property, does not exercise a power of appointment held by the testator unless specific reference is made to the power or there is some other indication of intention to include the property subject to the power.

§ 3B:3-46. Ademption by satisfaction

a. Property which a testator gave in his lifetime to a person is treated as a satisfaction of a devise to that person in whole or in part, only if the will provides for deduction of the lifetime gift, or the testator declares in a contemporaneous writing that the value of the gift is to be deducted from the value of the devise or is in satisfaction of the devise, or the devisee acknowledges in writing that the gift is in satisfaction of the devise or that its value is to be deducted from the value of the devise.

b. For purpose of partial satisfaction, property given during lifetime is valued as of the time the devisee came into possession or enjoyment of the property or as of the time of death of the testator, whichever occurs first.

c. If the devisee fails to survive the testator, in the case of a substituted devise or a devise saved from lapse, the gift is treated as a full or partial satisfaction of the devise, as appropriate, unless the testator's contemporaneous writing provides otherwise.

§ 3B:3-47. Penalty clause for contesting will

A provision in a will purporting to penalize any interested person for contesting the will or instituting other proceedings relating to the estate is unenforceable if probable cause exists for instituting proceedings.

§ 3B:3-48. Construction of generic terms included in class gift terminology

a. Adopted individuals and individuals born out of wedlock, and their respective descendants if appropriate to the class, are included in class gifts and other terms of relationship in accordance with the rules for intestate succession. Terms of relationship that do not differentiate relationships by the half blood from those by the whole blood, such as "brothers," "sisters," "nieces," or "nephews," are construed to include both types of relationships.

b. In addition to the requirements of subsection a., in construing a donative disposition by a transferor who is not the natural parent, an individual born to the natural parent is not considered the child of that parent unless the individual lived while a minor as a regular member of the household of that natural parent or of that parent's parent, brother, sister, spouse or surviving spouse.

c. In addition to the requirements of subsection a., in construing a dispositive provision by a transferor who is not the adoptive parent, an adopted individual is not considered the child of the adoptive parent unless the adopted individual lived while a minor, either before or after the adoption, as a regular member of the household of the adoptive parent.

§ 3B:3-49. Effect of final order of court of another state admitting will to probate or determining validity or construction

A final order of a court of another state admitting a will to probate or determining the validity or construction of a will made in a proceeding involving notice to and an opportunity for contest by all interested persons must be accepted as determinative by the courts of this State if it includes, or is based upon, a finding that the decedent was domiciled at his death in the state where the order was made.

Chapter 4. Trusts; Testamentary Additions

§ 3B:4-1. Short title

This chapter shall be known and may be cited as the "New Jersey Testamentary Additions to Trusts Law."

§ 3B:4-2. Devise to trustee of trust created other than by testator's will

A will may validly devise property to the trustee of a trust established or a trust which will be established: (1) during the testator's lifetime by the testator, or by the testator and some other person, or by some other person including a funded or unfunded life insurance trust, although the settlor has reserved any or all rights of ownership of the insurance contracts, or (2) at the testator's death by the testator's devise to the trustee, if the trust is identified in the testator's will, and its terms are set forth in a written instrument, other than a will, executed before, concurrently with, or after the execution of the testator's will or in another individual's will, executed before, concurrently with or after the execution of the testator's will, if that other individual has predeceased the testator, regardless of the existence, size, or character of the corpus of the trust.

§ 3B:4-3. Devise not invalidated because trust is amendable or revocable

A devise made as provided in N.J.S. 3B:4-2 shall not be invalid because the trust is amendable or revocable, or because the trust was amended after the execution of the will or the testator's death.

§ 3B:4-4. Administration of trust

Unless the testator's will provides otherwise, property devised to a trust described in N.J.S. 3B:4-2 shall not be deemed to be held under a testamentary trust of the testator, but shall become a part of the trust to which it is devised and shall be administered and disposed of in accordance with the provisions of the governing instrument setting forth the terms of the trust, including any amendments thereto made before or after the testator's death.

§ 3B:4-5. Lapse of devise

Unless the testator's will provides otherwise, a revocation or termination of the trust before the testator's death causes the devise to lapse.

Chapter 5. Intestacy

§ 3B:5-1. Requirement that heir survive decedent by 120 hours

For the purposes of intestate succession an individual who is not established by clear and convincing evidence to have survived the decedent by 120 hours is deemed to have predeceased the decedent. This section is not to be applied where its application would result in a taking of intestate estate by the State.

§ 3B:5-2. Intestate estate

a. Any part of the decedent's estate not effectively disposed of by his will passes by intestate succession to the decedent's heirs as prescribed in N.J.S. 3B:5-3 through N.J.S. 3B:5-14, except as modified by the decedent's will.
b. A decedent by will may expressly exclude or limit the right of an individual or class to succeed to property of the decedent passing by intestate succession. If that individual or member of that class survives the decedent, the share of the decedent's intestate estate to which that individual or class would have succeeded passes as if that individual or each member of that class had disclaimed his intestate share.

§ 3B:5-3. Intestate share of decedent's surviving spouse or domestic partner

The intestate share of the surviving spouse or domestic partner is:
a. The entire intestate estate if:
(1) No descendant or parent of the decedent survives the decedent; or
(2) All of the decedent's surviving descendants are also descendants of the surviving spouse or domestic partner and there is no other descendant of the surviving spouse or domestic partner who survives the decedent;
b. The first 25% of the intestate estate, but not less than $50,000.00 nor more than $200,000.00, plus three-fourths of any balance of the intestate estate, if no descendant of the decedent survives the decedent, but a parent of the decedent survives the decedent;
c. The first 25% of the intestate estate, but not less than $50,000.00 nor more than $200,000.00, plus one-half of the balance of the intestate estate:
(1) If all of the decedent's surviving descendants are also descendants of the surviving spouse or domestic partner and the surviving spouse or domestic partner has one or more surviving descendants who are not descendants of the decedent; or
(2) If one or more of the decedent's surviving descendants is not a descendant of the surviving spouse or domestic partner.

§ 3B:5-4. Intestate shares of heirs other than surviving spouse or domestic partner

Any part of the intestate estate not passing to the decedent's surviving spouse or domestic partner under N.J.S.3B:5-3, or the entire intestate estate if there is no surviving spouse or domestic partner, passes in the following order to the individuals designated below who survive the decedent:
a. To the decedent's descendants by representation;
b. If there are no surviving descendants, to the decedent's parents equally if both survive, or to the surviving parent, except as provided in section 4 of P.L.2009, c.43 (C.3B:5-14.1);
c. If there are no surviving descendants or parent, to the descendants of the decedent's parents or either of them by representation;
d. If there is no surviving descendant, parent or descendant of a parent, but the decedent is survived by one or more grandparents, half of the estate passes to the decedent's paternal grandparents equally if both survive, or to the surviving paternal grandparent, or to the descendants of the decedent's paternal grandparents or either of them if both are deceased, the descendants taking by representation; and the other half passes to the decedent's maternal relatives in the same manner; but if there is no surviving grandparent, or descendant of a grandparent on either the paternal or the maternal side, the entire estate passes to the decedent's relatives on the other side in the same manner as the half;
e. If there is no surviving descendant, parent, descendant of a parent, or grandparent, but the decedent is survived by one or more descendants of grandparents, the descendants take equally if they are all of the same degree of kinship to the decedent, but if of unequal degree those of more remote degree take by representation;
f. If there are no surviving descendants of grandparents, then the decedent's step-children or their descendants by representation.

§ 3B:5-5.1. Diligent inquiry by fiduciary to find heirs

If it appears to a fiduciary administering an intestate estate that there may be individuals whose names or addresses are unknown who may be entitled to participate in the distribution of the estate, the fiduciary shall make a diligent inquiry, under the circumstances, to identify and locate the individuals. The actions taken by a fiduciary shall be those that have some reasonable likelihood of finding the individuals and are reasonable in cost compared with the amount of the distribution involved.

§ 3B:5-6. Determining representation

a. As used in this section:
(1) "Deceased descendant," "deceased parent," or "deceased grandparent" means a descendant, parent or grandparent who either predeceased the decedent or is deemed to have predeceased the decedent under N.J.S. 3B:5-1.
(2) "Surviving descendant" means a descendant who neither predeceased the decedent nor is deemed to have predeceased the decedent under N.J.S. 3B:5-1.
b. If, under N.J.S. 3B:5-4, a decedent's intestate estate or part thereof passes "by representation" to the decedent's descendants, the estate or part thereof is divided into as many equal shares as there are: (1) surviving descendants in the generation nearest to the decedent which contains one or more surviving descendants; and (2) deceased descendants in the same generation who left surviving descendants, if any. Each surviving descendant in the nearest generation is allocated one share. The remaining shares, if any, are combined and then divided in the same manner among the surviving descendants of the deceased descendants as if the surviving descendants who were allocated a share and their surviving descendants had predeceased the decedent.
c. If, under section c. or d. of N.J.S. 3B:5-4, a decedent's intestate estate or a part thereof passes "by representation" to the descendants of the decedent's deceased parents or either of them or to the descendants of the decedent's deceased paternal or maternal grandparents or either of them, the estate or part thereof is divided into as many equal shares as there are: (1) surviving descendants in the generation nearest the deceased parents or either of them, or the deceased grandparents or either of them, that contains one or more surviving descendants; and (2) deceased descendants in the same generation who left surviving descendants, if any. Each surviving descendant in the nearest generation is allocated one share. The remaining shares, if any, are combined and then divided in the same manner among the surviving descendants of the deceased descendants as if the surviving descendants who were allocated a share, and their surviving descendants had predeceased the decedent.

§ 3B:5-7. Relatives of the half blood

Relatives of the half blood inherit the same share they would inherit if they were of the whole blood.

§ 3B:5-8. After born heirs

An individual in gestation at a particular time is treated as living at that time if the individual lives 120 hours or more after birth.

§ 3B:5-9. Adopted child

If, for the purposes of intestate succession, a relationship of parent and child must be established to determine succession by, through or from an individual, the relationships and rights of a minor adopted child shall be those as provided in section 14 of P.L. 1977, c. 367 (C. 9:3-50), and the relationships and rights of an adopted adult shall be as provided in N.J.S. 2A:22-3.

§ 3B:5-10. Establishment of parent-child relationship

If, for the purposes of intestate succession, a relationship of parent and child must be established to determine succession by, through, or from an individual, in cases not covered by N.J.S. 3B:5-9, an individual is the child of the individual's parents regardless of the marital state of the individual's parents, and the parent and child relationship may be established as provided by the "New Jersey Parentage Act," P.L. 1983, c. 17 (C. 9:17-38 et seq.). The parent and child relationship may be established for purposes of this section regardless of the time limitations set forth in subsection b. of section 8 of P.L. 1983, c. 17 (C. 9:17-45).

§ 3B:5-11. Debt to decedent

A debt owed to a decedent is not charged against the intestate share of any individual except the debtor. If the debtor fails to survive the decedent, the debt is not taken into account in computing the intestate share of the debtor's descendants.

§ 3B:5-12. Aliens not disqualified; individuals related to decedent through two lines

a. An individual is not disqualified to take as an heir because he or an individual through whom he claims is or has been an alien.
b. An individual who is related to the decedent through two lines of relationship is entitled to only a single share based on the relationship that would entitle the individual to the larger share.

§ 3B:5-13. Advancements.

a. If an individual dies intestate as to all or a portion of his estate, property the decedent gave during the decedent's lifetime to an individual who, at the decedent's death, is an heir is treated as an advancement against the heir's intestate share only if: (1) the decedent declared in a contemporaneous writing or the heir acknowledged in writing that the gift is an advancement; or (2) the decedent's contemporaneous writing or the heir's written acknowledgment otherwise indicates that the gift is to be taken into account in computing the division and distribution of the decedent's intestate estate.
b. For purposes of subsection a., property advanced is valued as of the time the heir came into possession or enjoyment of the property or as of the time of the decedent's death, whichever occurs first.
c. If the recipient of the property fails to survive the decedent, the property is not taken into account in computing the division and distribution of the decedent's intestate estate, unless the decedent's contemporaneous writing or the heir's written acknowledgment provides otherwise.

§ 3B:5-14. Tenancy in common; marriage and domestic partnership settlements

Property descending and distributable under this article to two or more persons shall devolve upon them as tenants in common. Nothing in this article shall be construed or taken to make void or in any way to affect any marriage settlement or settlement concerning a domestic partnership.

§ 3B:5-14.1. "Minor" defined; loss of right to intestate succession by parent, certain circumstances

a. As used in this section, "minor" means a person under the age of 18 years.

b. A parent of a decedent shall lose all right to intestate succession in any part of the decedent's estate and all right to administer the estate of the decedent if:

(1) The parent refused to acknowledge the decedent or abandoned the decedent when the decedent was a minor by willfully forsaking the decedent, failing to care for and keep the control and custody of the decedent so that the decedent was exposed to physical or moral risk without proper and sufficient protection, or failing to care for and keep the control and custody of the decedent so that the decedent was in the care, custody and control of the State at the time of death;

(2) The parent was convicted of committing any of the following crimes against the decedent:

(a) N.J.S.2C:14-2, Sexual Assault.

(b) N.J.S.2C:14-3, Criminal Sexual Contact.

(c) N.J.S.2C:24-4, Endangering Welfare of Children;

(3) The parent was convicted of an attempt or conspiracy to murder the decedent; or

(4) The parent abused or neglected the decedent, as defined in subsection c. of section 1 of P.L.1974, c.119 (C.9:6-8.21), and the abuse or neglect contributed to the decedent's death.

c. If a parent is disqualified from taking a distributive share in the estate of a decedent under this section, the estate shall be distributed as though the parent predeceased the decedent.

§ 3B:5-15. Entitlement of spouse or domestic partner; premarital will

a. If a testator's surviving spouse married the testator after the testator executed the testator's will, or if a testator's domestic partner formed a domestic partnership with the testator after the testator executed the testator's will, the surviving spouse or domestic partner is entitled to receive, as an intestate share, no less than the value of the share of the estate the surviving spouse or domestic partner would have received if the testator had died intestate, unless:

(1) it appears from the will or other evidence that the will was made in contemplation of the testator's marriage to the surviving spouse or in contemplation of the testator's formation of a domestic partnership with the domestic partner;

(2) the will expresses the intention that it is to be effective notwithstanding any subsequent marriage or domestic partnership; or

(3) the testator provided for the spouse or domestic partner by transfer outside the will and the intent that the transfer be in lieu of a testamentary provision is shown by the testator's statements or is reasonably inferred from the amount of the transfer or other evidence.

b. In satisfying the share provided by this section, devises made by the will to the testator's surviving spouse or domestic partner, if any, are applied first, and other devises shall abate ratably and in proportion to their respective interests therein.

c. Notwithstanding any other provision of law to the contrary, this section shall apply only to wills executed on or after September 1, 1978.

§ 3B:5-16. Omitted children

a. Except as provided in subsection b., if a testator fails to provide in his will for any of his children born or adopted after the execution of his will, the omitted after-born or after-adopted child receives a share in the estate as follows;

(1) If the testator had no child living when he executed the will, an omitted after-born or after-adopted child receives a share in the estate equal in value to that which the child would have received had the testator died intestate, unless the will devised all or substantially all of the estate to the other parent of the omitted child or to a trust primarily for the benefit of that other parent and that other parent survives the testator and is entitled to take under the will.

(2) If the testator had one or more children living when he executed the will, and the will devised property or an interest in property to one or more of the then-living children, an omitted after-born or after-adopted child is entitled to share in the testator's estate as follows:

(a) the portion of the testator's estate in which the omitted after-born or after-adopted child is entitled to share is limited to devises made to the testator's then-living children under the will.

(b) the omitted after-born or after-adopted child is entitled to receive the share of the testator's estate, as limited in subparagraph (a), that the child would have received had the testator included all omitted after-born and after-adopted children with the children to whom devises were made under the will and had given an equal share of the estate to each child.

(c) to the extent feasible, the interest granted an omitted after-born or after-adopted child under this section must be of the same character, whether equitable or legal, present or future, as that devised to the testator's then-living children under the will.

(d) in satisfying a share provided by this paragraph, devises to the testator's children who were living when the will was executed abate ratably. In abating the devises of the then-living children, the court shall preserve to the maximum extent possible the character of the testamentary plan adopted by the testator.

b. Neither subsection a. (1) nor subsection a. (2) applies if:

(1) it appears from the will that the omission was intentional; or

(2) the testator provided for the omitted after-born or after-adopted child by transfer outside the will and the intent that the transfer be in lieu of a testamentary provision is shown by the testator's statements or is reasonably inferred from the amount of the transfer or other evidence.

c. If at the time of execution of the will the testator fails to provide in his will for a living child solely because he believes the child to be dead, the child is entitled to a share in the estate as if the child were an omitted after-born or after-adopted child.

d. The share provided by subsection a. (1) shall be taken from devisees under the will ratably and in proportion to their respective interests therein.

Chapter 6. Uniform Simultaneous Death Law

§ 3B:6-1. Short title

This chapter shall be known and may be cited as the "Uniform Simultaneous Death Law."

§ 3B:6-2. Disposition of property of persons dying simultaneously

Where the title to property or the devolution thereof depends upon priority of death and there is no sufficient evidence that the persons have died otherwise than simultaneously, the property of each person shall be disposed of as if he had survived, except as provided otherwise in this chapter.

§ 3B:6-3. Division of property, two or more beneficiaries

Where two or more beneficiaries are designated to take successively by reason of survivorship under another person's disposition of property and there is no sufficient evidence that these beneficiaries have died otherwise than simultaneously, the property thus disposed of shall be divided into as many equal portions as there are successive beneficiaries and these portions shall be distributed respectively to those who would have taken in the event that each designated beneficiary had survived.

§ 3B:6-4. Division of property, joint tenants or tenants by the entirety

Where there is no sufficient evidence that two joint tenants or tenants by the entirety have died otherwise than simultaneously, the property so held shall be distributed one-half as if one had survived and one-half as if the other had survived. If there are more than two joint tenants and all of them have so died, the property thus distributed shall be in the proportion that one bears to the whole number of joint tenants.

§ 3B:6-5. Distribution of proceeds of life or accident policies

Where the insured and the beneficiary in a policy of life or accident insurance have died and there is no sufficient evidence that they have died otherwise than simultaneously, the proceeds of the policy shall be distributed as if the insured had survived the beneficiary.

§ 3B:6-6. Chapter not to apply in certain cases

This chapter shall not apply to a devolution of property of a decedent under a will or upon intestacy, where the law provides that in order to take on the devolution, a person shall survive the decedent by 120 hours, living trusts, deeds, or contracts of insurance, wherein provision has been made for distribution of property different from the provisions of this chapter.

§ 3B:6-7. Construction and interpretation

This chapter shall be so construed and interpreted as to effectuate its general purpose to make uniform the law in those states which enact it.

Chapter 7. Decedent's Intentional Death; Effect

§ 3B:7-1.1. Effect of intentional killing on intestate succession, wills, trusts, joint assets, life insurance and beneficiary designations

a. An individual who is responsible for the intentional killing of the decedent forfeits all benefits under this title with respect to the decedent's estate, including an intestate share, an elective share, an omitted spouse's, domestic partner's or child's share, exempt property and a family allowance. If the decedent died intestate, the decedent's intestate estate passes as if the killer disclaimed his share.

b. The intentional killing of the decedent:

(1) revokes any revocable (a) disposition or appointment of property made by decedent to the killer in a governing instrument and any disposition or appointment created by law or in a governing instrument to a relative of the killer, (b) provision in a governing instrument conferring a general or special power of appointment on the killer or a relative of the killer, and (c) nomination in a governing instrument of the killer or a relative of the killer, nominating or appointing the killer or a relative of the killer to serve in any fiduciary or representative capacity; and

(2) severs the interests of the decedent and the killer in property held by them at the time of the killing as joint tenants with the right of survivorship or as tenants by the entireties, transforming the interests of the decedent and killer into tenancies in common.

c. For purposes of this chapter: (1) "governing instrument" means a governing instrument executed by the decedent; and (2) "relative of the killer" means an individual who is related to the killer by blood, adoption or affinity and who is not related to the decedent by blood or adoption or affinity.

§ 3B:7-1.2. Effect of revocation

Provisions of a governing instrument are given effect as if the killer or relative of the killer disclaimed all provisions revoked by this chapter or, in the case of a revoked nomination in a fiduciary or representative capacity, as if the killer or relative of the killer predeceased the decedent.

§ 3B:7-5. Other acquisitions of property by decedent's killer

Any other acquisition of property or interest by the decedent's killer or by a relative of the killer not covered by this chapter shall be treated in accordance with the principle that a killer or a relative of a killer cannot profit from the killer's wrongdoing.

§ 3B:7-6. Effect of final judgment of conviction

A final judgment of conviction establishing responsibility for the intentional killing of the decedent is conclusive for purposes of this chapter. In the absence of such a conviction the court may determine by a preponderance of evidence whether the individual was responsible for the intentional killing of the decedent for purposes of this chapter.

§ 3B:7-7. Rights of purchasers; protection of payors and other third parties.

This chapter does not affect the rights of any person who, before rights under this chapter have been adjudicated, purchases from the killer for value and without notice or receives a payment or other item of property in partial or full satisfaction of a legally enforceable obligation which the killer would have acquired except for this chapter, but the killer is liable for the amount of the proceeds or the value of the property. A payor or other third party making payment or transferring an item of property or other benefit according to the terms of a governing instrument affected by an intentional killing is not liable by reason of this chapter unless prior to such payment or transfer it has received at its home office or principal address written notice of a claimed forfeiture or revocation under this chapter.

Chapter 8. Right to Elective Share by Surviving Spouse

§ 3B:8-1. Elective share of surviving spouse or domestic partner of person dying domiciled in this State; conditions

If a married person or person in a domestic partnership dies domiciled in this State, on or after May 28, 1980, the surviving spouse or domestic partner has a right of election to take an elective share of one-third of the augmented estate under the limitations and conditions hereinafter stated, provided that at the time of death the decedent and the surviving spouse or domestic partner had not been living separate and apart in different habitations or had not ceased to cohabit as man and wife, either as the result of judgment of divorce from bed and board or under circumstances which would have given rise to a cause of action for divorce or nullity of marriage to a decedent prior to his death under the laws of this State.

§ 3B:8-2. Elective share of surviving spouse or domestic partner of person dying not domiciled in this State

If a married person or person in a domestic partnership not domiciled in this State dies, the right, if any, of the surviving spouse or domestic partner to take an elective share in property in this State is governed by the law of the decedent's domicile at death.

§ 3B:8-3. Meaning of "augmented estate"

The "augmented estate" means the estate reduced by funeral and administration expenses, and enforceable claims, to which is added the value of property transferred by the decedent at any time during marriage, or during a domestic partnership, to or for the benefit of any person other than the surviving spouse or domestic partner, to the extent that the decedent did not receive adequate and full consideration in money or money's worth for the transfer, if the transfer is of any of the following types:

a. Any transfer made after May 28, 1980, under which the decedent retained at the time of his death the possession or enjoyment of, or right to income from, the property;

b. Any transfer made after May 28, 1980, to the extent that the decedent retained at the time of his death a power, either alone or in conjunction with any other person, to revoke or to consume, invade or dispose of the principal for his own benefit;

c. Any transfer made after May 28, 1980, whereby property is held at the time of decedent's death by decedent and another with right of survivorship;

d. Any transfer made, after May 28, 1980, if made within 2 years of death of the decedent, to the extent that the aggregate transfers to any one donee in either of the years exceed $3,000.00.

§ 3B:8-4. Valuing property transferred

Property transferred in the manner set forth in N.J.S. 3B:8-3 is valued as of the decedent's death except that property given irrevocably to a donee during the lifetime of the decedent is valued as of the date the donee came into possession or enjoyment of the property if that occurs first.

§ 3B:8-5. Transfers excluded

Any transfer of property shall be excluded from the augmented estate under N.J.S. 3B:8-3, if made with the written consent or joinder of the surviving spouse or domestic partner. There shall also be excluded from the augmented estate any life insurance, accident insurance, joint annuity or pension payable to a person other than the surviving spouse or domestic partner.

§ 3B:8-6. Other property to be included in augmented estate

There shall also be included in the augmented estate:

a. The value of property owned by the surviving spouse or domestic partner at the time of, or as a result of, the decedent's death to the extent that the property is derived from the decedent by means other than by testate or intestate succession without a full consideration in money or money's worth; and

b. The value of the property described in subsection a. hereof which has been transferred by the surviving spouse or domestic partner at any time during marriage or domestic partnership without a full consideration in money or money's worth to any person other than the decedent which would have been includable in the spouse's or domestic partner's augmented estate if the surviving spouse or domestic partner had predeceased the decedent.

Income earned by included property prior to the decedent's death is not treated as property derived from the decedent.

§ 3B:8-7. Property derived from decedent

For the purposes of N.J.S. 3B:8-6, property derived from the decedent includes, but is not limited to, any beneficial interest of the surviving spouse or domestic partner in a trust created by the decedent during his lifetime, any property appointed to the spouse or domestic partner by the decedent's exercise of a general or special power of appointment also exercisable in favor of others than the spouse or domestic partner, any proceeds of insurance, including accidental death benefits on the life of the decedent attributable to premiums paid by him, any lump sum immediately payable and the commuted value of the proceeds of annuity contracts under which the decedent was the primary annuitant attributable to premiums paid by him, the commuted value of amounts payable after the decedent's death under any public or private pension, disability compensation, death benefit or retirement plan, exclusive of the Federal Social Security system, by reason of service performed or disabilities incurred by the decedent, the value of the share of the surviving spouse or domestic partner resulting from rights in community property acquired in any other state formerly owned with the decedent and the value of any rights of dower and curtesy. Premiums paid by the decedent's employer, his partner, a partnership of which he was a member, or his creditors, are deemed to have been paid by the decedent.

§ 3B:8-8. Valuation of property derived from decedent

For the purposes of valuing property derived from the decedent as provided in N.J.S. 3B:8-6:

a. Property owned by the spouse or domestic partner at the decedent's death is valued as of the date of decedent's death; and

b. Property transferred by the spouse or domestic partner is valued at the time the transfer became irrevocable, or at the decedent's death, whichever occurs first.

§ 3B:8-9. Presumption as to property owned or previously transferred by spouse or domestic partner at decedent's death

Property owned by the surviving spouse or domestic partner as of the decedent's death, or previously transferred by the surviving spouse or domestic partner, is presumed to have been derived from the decedent except to the extent that any party in interest establishes that it was derived from another source.

§ 3B:8-10. Waiving right to an elective share

The right of election of a surviving spouse or domestic partner and the rights of the surviving spouse or domestic partner may be waived, wholly or partially, before or after marriage before, on or after May 28, 1980, by a written contract, agreement or waiver, signed by the party waiving after fair disclosure. Unless it provides to the contrary, a waiver of "all rights" (or equivalent language) in the property or estate of a present or prospective spouse or domestic partner or a complete property settlement entered into after or in anticipation of separation, divorce or termination of a domestic partnership is a waiver of all rights to an elective share by each spouse or domestic partner in the property of the other and a renunciation by each of all benefits which would otherwise pass to him from the other by intestate succession or by virtue of the provisions of any will executed before the waiver or property settlement.

§ 3B:8-11. Who may exercise the right to take an elective share

The right of election to take an elective share by a surviving spouse or domestic partner may be exercised only during his lifetime. In the case of a surviving spouse or domestic partner for whom the court has appointed a guardian to manage his estate, the right of election may be exercised only by order of the court making the appointment after finding that the election is necessary to provide adequate support of the surviving spouse or domestic partner during his probable life expectancy.

§ 3B:8-12. Filing complaint for elective share; extension of time

The surviving spouse or domestic partner may elect to take his elective share in the augmented estate by filing a complaint in the Superior Court within 6 months after the appointment of a personal representative of the decedent's estate. The court may, before the time for election has expired and upon good cause shown by the surviving spouse or domestic partner, extend the time for election upon notice to persons interested in the estate and to distributees and recipients of portions of the augmented estate whose interests will be adversely affected by the taking of the elective share.

§ 3B:8-13. Notice of hearing

The surviving spouse or domestic partner shall give notice of the time and place set for hearing to persons interested in the estate and to the distributees and recipients of portions of the augmented estate whose interests will be adversely affected by the taking of the elective share.

§ 3B:8-14. Withdrawal of demand for an elective share

The surviving spouse or domestic partner may withdraw his demand for an elective share at any time before entry of a final judgment by the court.

§ 3B:8-15. Fixing amount of elective share; payment of elective share

The court shall determine the amount of the elective share and shall order its payment from the assets of the augmented estate or by contribution as appears appropriate in the manner as hereinafter set forth in this chapter. If it appears that a fund or property included in the augmented estate has not come into the possession of the personal representative, or has been distributed by the personal representative, the court nevertheless shall fix the liability of any person who has any interest in the fund or property or who has possession thereof, whether as trustee or otherwise. The proceeding may be maintained against fewer than all persons against whom relief could be sought, but no person is subject to contribution in any greater amount than he would have been if relief had been secured against all persons subject to contribution.

§ 3B:8-16. Enforcing judgment

The judgment of the court made pursuant to N.J.S. 3B:8-15 may be enforced as other judgments are enforced by law.

§ 3B:8-17. Value of surviving spouse's or domestic partner's interest in any life estate.

In an action for an elective share, the electing spouse's or domestic partner's total or proportional beneficial interest in any life estate in real or personal property or in any trust shall be valued at one-half of the total value of the property or trust or of the portion of the property or trust subject to the life estate.

§ 3B:8-18. Satisfaction of elective share

The amount of the surviving spouse's or domestic partner's elective share shall be satisfied by applying:
a. The value of all property, estate or interest therein, owned by the surviving spouse or domestic partner in his own right at the time of the decedent's death from whatever source acquired, or succeeded to by the surviving spouse or domestic partner as a result of decedent's death notwithstanding that the property, estate or interest or part thereof, succeeded to by the surviving spouse or domestic partner as the result of decedent's death has been renounced by the surviving spouse or domestic partner;
b. The value of the property described in subsection b. of N.J.S. 3B:8-6, and
c. The remaining property of the augmented estate is so applied that liability for the balance of the elective share of the surviving spouse or domestic partner is equitably apportioned among the recipients of the augmented estate in proportion to the value of their interests therein.

§ 3B:8-19. Persons subject to contribution

Only original transferees from, or appointees of, the decedent and their donees, to the extent the donees have the property or its proceeds, are subject to the contribution to make up the elective share of the surviving spouse or domestic partner. A person liable to contribution may choose to give up the property transferred to him or to pay its value as fixed in the manner provided in N.J.S. 3B:8-4.

Chapter 9. Disclaimers of Transfers by Will; Under Powers of Testamentary Appointment or by Intestate Succession

§ 3B:9-1. Definitions

As used in this chapter:
a. A "present interest" is one to take effect in immediate possession, use or enjoyment without the intervention of a preceding estate or interest or without being dependent upon the happening of any event or thing;
b. A "future interest" is one to take effect in possession, use or enjoyment dependent upon the termination of an intervening estate or interest or the happening of any event or thing;
c. A "devisee" means any person designated in a will to receive a devise, but does not mean a trustee or trust designated in a will to receive a devise;
d. The "effective date" is the date on which a property right vests, or a contract right arises, even though the right is subject to divestment;
e. "Joint property" is property that is owned by two or more persons with rights of survivorship and includes a tenancy by the entirety, a joint tenancy, a joint tenancy with rights of survivorship and a joint life estate with contingent remainder in fee. For purposes of this chapter, joint property is deemed to consist of a present interest and a future interest. The future interest is the right of survivorship;
f. "Joint tenant" is the co-owner of joint property.

§ 3B:9-2. Disclaimer of an interested party

a. Any person who is an heir, or a devisee or beneficiary under a will or testamentary trust, or appointee under a power of appointment exercised by a will or testamentary trust, including a person succeeding to a disclaimed interest, may disclaim in whole or in part any property or interest therein, including a future interest, by delivering and filing a disclaimer under this chapter.
b. Any person who is a grantee, donee, surviving joint tenant, surviving party to a P.O.D. account or a trust deposit account, person succeeding to a disclaimed interest, beneficiary under a nontestamentary instrument or contract, appointee under a power of appointment exercised by a nontestamentary instrument, or a beneficiary under an insurance policy, may disclaim in whole or in part any such property or interest therein by delivering, and if required by N.J.S. 3B:9-7, by filing, a written disclaimer under this chapter.

c. A surviving joint tenant may disclaim as a separate interest any property or interest therein devolving to him by right of survivorship without regard to the extent, if any, the surviving joint tenant contributed to the creation of the joint property interest.

d. A disclaimer may be of a pecuniary or a fractional share, expressed as either a percentage or dollar amount, specific property or any limited interest or estate.

§ 3B:9-3. Requirements of a disclaimer

a. A disclaimer shall be in writing, signed and acknowledged by the person disclaiming, and shall:

(1) Describe the property, interest, power or discretion disclaimed;

(2) If the property interest disclaimed is real property, identify the municipality and county in which the real property is situated; and

(3) Declare the disclaimer and the extent thereof.

b. The disclaimer shall be made within the time prescribed by section 68 of P.L. 2004, c. 132 (C. 3B:9-4.2).

§ 3B:9-4. Disclaimer by a fiduciary of an interest in property

a. A fiduciary or agent acting on behalf of a principal within the express, general or implied authority of a power of attorney, may disclaim property or any interest therein.

b. Except as provided in subsection c. of this section, such disclaimer shall not be effective unless, prior thereto, the fiduciary or agent has been authorized to disclaim by the court having jurisdiction over the fiduciary or the principal after finding that such disclaimer is advisable and will not materially prejudice the rights of: (1) creditors, devisees, heirs or beneficiaries of the estate; (2) beneficiaries of the trust; or (3) the minor, the incapacitated individual, the conservatee or the principal for whom such fiduciary or agent acts.

c. If the governing instrument expressly authorizes the fiduciary or the agent to disclaim, the disclaimer by the fiduciary or agent shall be effective without court authorization.

§ 3B:9-4.1. Disclaimer by a fiduciary of a power of discretion

a. Any fiduciary, including an agent acting on behalf of a principal within the implied or general authority of a power of attorney, may disclaim any power or discretion held by such fiduciary in a fiduciary capacity. Unless the governing instrument specifically authorizes the fiduciary to disclaim such power or discretion without obtaining court authorization to do so, the disclaimer by the fiduciary shall not be effective unless, prior thereto, such fiduciary has been authorized to disclaim by the court having jurisdiction over the fiduciary after finding that it is advisable and will not materially prejudice the rights of: (1) devisees, heirs, or beneficiaries of the decedent; (2) the minor, the incapacitated individual, the conservatee, or the principal; or (3) the beneficiaries of the trust.

b. Unless expressly authorized by the court or by the governing instrument:

(1) Any disclaimer under this section shall be personal to the fiduciary so disclaiming and shall not constitute a disclaimer by a co-fiduciary or a successor or substituted fiduciary of such power or discretion;

(2) No disclaimer shall affect the rights of: (a) devisees, heirs or beneficiaries of the decedent; (b) the minor, the incapacitated individual, the conservatee, or the principal; or (c) the beneficiaries of the trust.

§ 3B:9-4.2. Time for disclaiming

a. The disclaimer of an interest in property may be delivered, and if required by this chapter filed, at any time after the effective date of the governing instrument, or in the case of an intestacy, at any time after the death of the intestate decedent, and must be delivered, and if required by this chapter filed, before the right to disclaim is barred by N.J.S.3B:9-9. With respect to joint property, the barring of the right to disclaim the present interest does not bar the right to disclaim the future interest.

b. The disclaimer of a power or discretion by a fiduciary, including an agent acting on behalf of a principal within the implied or general authority of a power of attorney, in a fiduciary capacity may be made at any time, before or after exercise.

§ 3B:9-6. Delivering and filing disclaimer

a. The disclaimer of an interest by an intestate heir, or a person who is a devisee or beneficiary under a will or a testamentary trust or who is an appointee under a power of appointment exercised by a will or testamentary trust, including a person succeeding to a disclaimed interest, shall be filed in the office of the surrogate or clerk of the Superior Court in which proceedings have been commenced or will be commenced for the administration of the estate of the decedent or deceased donee of the power of appointment. A copy of the disclaimer shall also be delivered to any personal representative, or other fiduciary of the decedent or to the donee of the power or to the holder of the legal title to which the interest relates. The fiduciary shall promptly notify the person or persons who take the disclaimed interest, although any such failure to provide the notice required herein shall not affect the validity of the disclaimer.

b. The disclaimer of an interest in property, other than property passing under or pursuant to a will or testamentary trust shall be delivered to the fiduciary, payor or other person having legal title to or possession of the property or interest disclaimed or who is entitled thereto in the event of disclaimer. Any fiduciary, payor or other person having title to or possession of the property or interest who receives such disclaimer shall promptly notify the person or persons who take the disclaimed interest, although any such failure to provide the notice required herein shall not affect the validity of the disclaimer.

c. In the case of a disclaimer by a fiduciary of a power or discretion:

(1) If such disclaimer is made after court authorization, the fiduciary shall deliver a copy to such person or persons and in such manner as shall be directed by the court; or

(2) If such disclaimer is made without court authorization pursuant to N.J.S. 3B:9-4(a), the fiduciary shall deliver a copy to all co-fiduciaries, but if there are none, then to all persons whose property interests are affected by the disclaimer.

d. In the case of a will or testamentary trust or power of appointment under a will or testamentary trust, if real property or any interest therein is disclaimed, the surrogate or clerk of the Superior Court, as the case may be, shall forthwith forward a copy of the disclaimer for filing in the office of the clerk or register of deeds and mortgages of the county in which the real property is situated. In the case of a nontestamentary instrument or contract, if real property or any interest therein is disclaimed, the original thereof shall be filed in the office of the clerk or register of deeds and mortgages of the county in which the real property is situated.

e. For the purposes of this section, delivery may be effected: (1) in person; (2) by registered or certified mail; or (3) by another means which is reasonably likely to accomplish delivery.

§ 3B:9-7. Recording of disclaimer where real property or interest therein is disclaimed

Each county clerk or register of deeds and mortgages shall provide a book to be entitled "Disclaimers," so arranged that he may record therein:

a. The name of the disclaimant;
b. The name of the decedent or the name of the donee of the power of appointment, the name of the trustee or other person having legal title to, or possession of, the property or interest disclaimed or entitled thereto in the event of disclaimer or the name of the donee of the power of appointment;
c. The location of the property;
d. The file number of the county clerk's office or the office of register of deeds and mortgages indorsed upon each disclaimer filed;
e. The date of filing the disclaimer.

The county clerk or the register of deeds and mortgages shall maintain in the record an alphabetical index of the names of all disclaimants stated in any disclaimer file, and also keep in his office for public inspection, all disclaimers so filed therein.

§ 3B:9-8. Effect of disclaimer

A disclaimer acts as a nonacceptance of the disclaimed interest, rather than as a transfer of the disclaimed interest. The disclaimant is treated as never having received the disclaimed interest. Unless a governing instrument otherwise provides, the property or interest disclaimed devolves:

a. As to a present interest:
(1) in the case of an intestacy, a will, a testamentary trust or a power of appointment exercised by a will or testamentary trust, as if the disclaimant had predeceased the decedent or, if the disclaimant is designated to take under a power of appointment exercised by a will or testamentary instrument, as if the disclaimant had predeceased the donee of the power. If by law or under the will or testamentary trust the descendants of the disclaimant would take the disclaimant's share by representation were the disclaimant to predecease the decedent, then the disclaimed interest devolves by representation to the descendants of the disclaimant who survive the decedent; and
(2) in the case of a nontestamentary instrument or contract, other than a joint property interest, as if the disclaimant had died before the effective date of the instrument or contract. If by law or under the nontestamentary instrument or contract the descendants of the disclaimant would take the disclaimant's share by representation were the disclaimant to predecease the effective date of the instrument, then the disclaimed interest devolves by representation to the descendants of the disclaimant who survive the effective date of the instrument.
(3) in the case of joint property created by a will, testamentary trust or non-testamentary instrument: (a) if the disclaimant is the only living owner, the disclaimed interest devolves to the estate of the last to die of the other joint owners; or (b) if the disclaimant is not the only living owner, the disclaimed interest devolves equally to the living joint owners, or all to the other living owner, if there is only one living owner.

b. As to a future interest:
(1) In the case of a will or testamentary trust or a power of appointment exercised by a will or testamentary trust, as if the disclaimant had died before the event determining that the taker of the property or interest is finally ascertained and his interest is vested; and
(2) In the case of a nontestamentary instrument or contract, as if the disclaimant had died before the event determining that the taker of the property or interest had become finally ascertained and the taker's interest is vested; and
(3) Notwithstanding the foregoing, a future interest that is held by the disclaimant who also holds the present interest and which takes effect at a time certain, such as a fixed calendar date or the disclaimant's attainment of a certain age, is not accelerated by the disclaimer and continues to take effect at the time certain.

c. Except as provided in subsection b. of this section, a disclaimer relates back for all purposes to the date of death of the decedent or the donee of the power or the effective date of the nontestamentary instrument or contract.

§ 3B:9-9. Bar of right to disclaim

Bar of right to disclaim.

a. The right of an individual to disclaim property or any interest therein is barred by:
(1) an assignment, conveyance, encumbrance, pledge or transfer of the property or interest or a contract therefor; or
(2) a written waiver of the right to disclaim; or
(3) an acceptance of the property or interest or a benefit under it after actual knowledge that a property right has been conferred; or
(4) a sale of the property or interest that was seized under judicial process before the disclaimer is made; or

(5) the expiration of the permitted applicable perpetuities period; or
(6) a fraud on the individual's creditors as set forth in the "Uniform Fraudulent Transfer Act" (R.S.25:2-20 et seq.).
b. The disclaimant shall not be barred from disclaiming all or any part of the balance of the property where the disclaimant has received a portion of the property and there still remains an interest which the disclaimant is yet to receive.
c. A bar to the right to disclaim a present interest in joint property does not bar the right to disclaim a future interest in that property.
d. The right to disclaim may be barred to the extent provided by other applicable statutory law.

§ 3B:9-10. Binding effect of disclaimer or waiver
The disclaimer or written waiver of the right to disclaim a property interest shall be binding upon the disclaimant or the individual waiving and all individuals claiming by, through or under him.

§ 3B:9-11. Spendthrift provision not to affect right to disclaim
The right to disclaim a property interest exists notwithstanding any limitation on the interest of the disclaimant in the nature of a spendthrift provision or similar restriction or any restriction or limitation on the right to disclaim a property interest contained in the governing instrument.

§ 3B:9-12. Right to disclaim, etc.; under other law not abridged
Right to disclaim, etc.; under other law not abridged. This chapter does not abridge the right of an individual to waive, release, disclaim or renounce property or an interest therein under any other statute or law.

§ 3B:9-13. Extension of time to disclaim interest existing on February 28, 1980
a. An interest in property existing on February 28, 1980, as to which, if a present interest, the time for filing a disclaimer under this chapter has not expired, or if a future interest, the interest has not become indefeasibly vested or the taker finally ascertained, may be disclaimed within 9 months after February 28, 1980.
b. An interest in property existing on the effective date of this chapter as amended and supplemented by P.L.2004, c.132 (C.3B:3-33.1 et al.) as to which the right to disclaim has not been barred by prior law may be disclaimed at any time before the right to disclaim is barred by N.J.S.3B:9-9.

§ 3B:9-14. Federal law
The provisions of this chapter, as amended and supplemented by P.L. 2004, c. 132 (C. 3B:3-33.1 et al.) are not intended to enlarge, limit, modify or otherwise affect the federal requirements for a qualified disclaimer under 26 U.S.C. § 2518 or 26 U.S.C. § 2046.

Chapter 10. Personal Representatives
Article 1. Administration

§ 3B:10-1. Grant of letters of administration
The surrogate's court of the county in which a decedent resided at the time of his death, or the Superior Court, may grant letters of general administration on the estate of the decedent.

§ 3B:10-2. To whom letters of administration granted
If any person dies intestate, administration of the intestate's estate shall be granted to the surviving spouse or domestic partner of the intestate, if he or she will accept the administration, and, if not, or if there be no surviving spouse or domestic partner, then to the remaining heirs of the intestate, or some of them, if they or any of them will accept the administration, and, if none of them will accept the administration, then to any other person as will accept the administration.
If the intestate leaves no heirs justly entitled to the administration of his estate, or if his heirs shall not claim the administration within 40 days after the death of the intestate, the Superior Court or surrogate's court may grant letters of administration to any fit person applying therefor.

§ 3B:10-3. When spouse, partner in a civil union, or domestic partner entitled to assets without administration
Where the total value of the real and personal assets of the estate of an intestate will not exceed $50,000, the surviving spouse, partner in a civil union, or domestic partner upon the execution of an affidavit before the Surrogate of the county where the intestate resided at his death, or, if then nonresident in this State, where any of the assets are located, or before the Superior Court, shall be entitled absolutely to all the real and personal assets without administration, and the assets of the estate up to $10,000 shall be free from all debts of the intestate. Upon the execution and filing of the affidavit as provided in this section, the surviving spouse, partner in a civil union, or domestic partner shall have all of the rights, powers and duties of an administrator duly appointed for the estate. The surviving spouse, partner in a civil union, or domestic partner may be sued and required to account as if he had been appointed administrator by the Surrogate or the Superior Court. The affidavit shall state that the affiant is the surviving spouse, partner in a civil union, or domestic partner of the intestate and that the value of the intestate's real and personal assets will not exceed $50,000, and shall set forth the residence of the intestate at his death, and specifically the nature, location and value of the intestate's real and personal assets. The affidavit shall be filed and recorded in the office of such Surrogate or, if the proceeding is before the Superior Court, then in the office of the clerk of that court. Where the affiant is domiciled outside this State, the Surrogate may authorize in writing that the affidavit be executed in the affiant's domicile before any of the officers authorized by R.S.46:14-6.1 to take acknowledgments or proofs.

§ 3B:10-4. When heirs entitled to assets without administration

Where the total value of the real and personal assets of the estate of an intestate will not exceed $20,000 and the intestate leaves no surviving spouse, partner in a civil union, or domestic partner, and one of his heirs shall have obtained the consent in writing of the remaining heirs, if any, and shall have executed before the Surrogate of the county where the intestate resided at his death, or, if then nonresident in this State, where any of the intestate's assets are located, or before the Superior Court, the affidavit herein provided for, shall be entitled to receive the assets of the intestate of the benefit of all the heirs and creditors without administration or entering into a bond. Upon executing the affidavit, and upon filing it and the consent, he shall have all the rights, powers and duties of an administrator duly appointed for the estate and may be sued and required to account as if he had been appointed administrator by the Surrogate or the Superior Court.

The affidavit shall set forth the residence of the intestate at his death, the names, residences and relationships of all of the heirs and specifically the nature, location and value of the real and personal assets and also a statement that the value of the intestate's real and personal assets will not exceed $20,000.

The consent and the affidavit shall be filed and recorded, in the office of the Surrogate or, if the proceeding is before the Superior Court, then in the office of the clerk of that court. Where the affiant is domiciled outside this State, the Surrogate may authorize in writing that the affidavit be executed in the affiant's domicile before any of the officers authorized by R.S.46:14-6.1 to take acknowledgments or proofs.

§ 3B:10-6. Acts of administrator before notice of will

Lawful acts performed in good faith by an administrator before notice of a will and purchases or transfers made by him in good faith before notice shall remain valid and shall not be impeached or altered by an executor upon probate of the will.

Nothing in this section shall be construed to relieve the administrator of any liability to the executor under the will for property unadministered or maladministered.

§ 3B:10-7. Ancillary administration on estate of nonresident intestate

Where a nonresident dies intestate seized of real property or possessed of personal property in this State, or where the evidence of his personal property shall be in the hands of any resident of this State, the surrogate's court of the county wherein any of the real or personal property or evidence thereof, is situate, or the Superior Court, shall, in an action upon satisfactory proof of intestacy, issue letters of administration upon the estate of the nonresident to the administrator of his estate or, on notice to the administrator as the court shall require, to any person who would be entitled to administration if the intestate had been a resident at his death.

§ 3B:10-8. Administration by creditor of nonresident decedent

If a personal representative of a nonresident decedent fails to apply in this State for letters testamentary or of administration within 60 days next after the death of the decedent and there is real or personal property of the decedent within this State, or the evidence thereof in the hands of a resident of this State, the surrogate's court of a county wherein the real property, or personal property or evidence, is situate, or the Superior Court, may, in an action by any person resident or nonresident, alleging himself to have a debt or legal claim against the decedent which by the law of this State survives against his representatives, issue letters of administration, with the will annexed or otherwise as the case may require, to some fit person to be designated by the court.

§ 3B:10-9. Record of appointment of personal representative; evidentiary effect

If any person shall desire to have the appointment of a personal representative appointed in another state recorded in this State for the purpose of manifesting the authority of the personal representative to release or discharge real estate in this State from any mortgage, judgment, other lien or encumbrance which was held by his decedent the surrogate of the county wherein the real estate is situate, or the clerk of the Superior Court, may, upon the presentation to him of an exemplified copy of the record of the appointment of the personal representative, record and file the exemplified copy in his office, and the record or certified copies thereof shall be received as evidence in all courts of this State.

§ 3B:10-10. Executor de son tort

Whereas it is sometimes practiced to the defrauding of creditors, that persons who are entitled to the administration of the estate of an intestate will not accept administration, but suffer or procure the administration to be granted to others of indigent circumstances, from whom they, or others, by their means, by deeds of gifts, or by letters of attorney, obtain the estate of the intestate into their hands, and are not subject to the payment of the debts of the intestate, and so the creditors cannot have or recover their just debts and demands; therefore, if any person shall obtain, receive and have, any property or debts of an intestate, or a release or other discharge of any debt or duty due the intestate, upon any fraud as herein provided, without valuable consideration as shall amount to the value of the property or debts, or near thereabouts except it be in or towards satisfaction of some just debt, of the value of the same property or debts, to him owing by the intestate at the time of his decease, the person shall be charged and chargeable as executor of his own wrong so far only, as all the property and debts coming to his hands, or whereof he is released or discharged by the administrator, will satisfy. However he shall not be charged for those just debts, contracted without fraud and upon a good consideration, which are owing to him by the intestate at the time of his decease, nor for payments made by him which lawful executors or administrators ought to pay.

§ 3B:10-11. Administration ad prosequendum on death by wrongful act

The surrogate's court of the county wherein an intestate resided at his death, or, if the intestate resided outside the State, the surrogate's court of the county wherein the accident resulting in death occurred, or the Superior Court, may grant letters of administration ad prosequendum to the person entitled by law to general administration. An administrator ad prosequendum shall not be required to give bond.

§ 3B:10-12. Temporary administration

The Superior Court may grant administration ad litem, temporary administration, administration pendente lite, or any form of limited administration.

§ 3B:10-13. Duty to apply in this State for original letters of administration

When an intestate is resident in any county of New Jersey at his death, it shall be the duty of the heir or any other person desiring original letters of administration upon his estate to make application therefor to the surrogate of that county or to the Superior Court of this State.

Any person having knowledge of the grant in a foreign jurisdiction of original letters of administration upon the estate of a person dying resident in any county of New Jersey, shall give information thereof to the Superior Court.

The court may direct the clerk of the court to issue and have served subpenas or an order to show cause requiring the appearance before it, at a specified time, of any persons having any interest in the estate, and commanding them to abide the order of the court. The matter of the grant of letters of administration shall be wholly within the jurisdiction of the court.

Article 2. Executors

§ 3B:10-14. Appointment of debtor as executor; debt not discharged

The appointment of a debtor as executor shall not, unless otherwise expressed in the will, be construed to discharge the executor from payment of the debt, but the debt shall be considered an asset in the hands of the executor and shall be accounted for in the same manner as any other part of the decedent's estate.

Article 3. Substituted Administrators

§ 3B:10-15. Appointment of substituted administrators

When a sole or sole surviving or remaining executor or administrator, with or without the will annexed, dies or is removed or discharged by the court after qualifying and entering upon the duties of his office but before the completion thereof, the vacancy so created shall, except as hereinafter provided, be filled by the appointment of a fit person to exercise the vacated office. The person so appointed shall be nominated substituted administrator with the will annexed or substituted administrator, as the case may be.

§ 3B:10-16. Decedent's will to be observed

Where administration is granted with the will annexed, the will of the decedent therein expressed shall be observed and performed.

§ 3B:10-17. Manner in which appointment shall be made

The appointment shall be made by the issuance of letters of substitutionary administration, with or without the will annexed as the case may be, by the surrogate's court or the Superior Court in the manner and upon the conditions prescribed for granting letters of administration to the first administrators in other cases.

§ 3B:10-18. When appointment unnecessary

The appointment of a substituted administrator shall not be required if the unadministered assets of the intestate or testator consist of money on deposit in a bank, trust company or savings and loan association not exceeding $1,000.00, in which event it shall be lawful for the Superior Court, in an action brought by any party in interest, to authorize the bank, trust company or savings and loan association to distribute to the persons entitled by law to receive the assets. Payments made pursuant to the authority of this section shall release the bank, trust company or savings and loan association from any claim of, or liability to, any person interested in the estate.

Article 4. Personal Representatives; Duties and Powers

§ 3B:10-19. Commencement of duties and powers of a personal representative

The duties and powers of a personal representative commence upon his appointment. The powers of a personal representative relate back in time to give acts by the person appointed which are beneficial to the estate occurring prior to appointment the same effect as those occurring thereafter.

§ 3B:10-20. Ratification of prior acts

A personal representative may ratify and accept acts on behalf of the estate done by others where the acts would have been proper for a personal representative.

§ 3B:10-21.1. Appointment of person to control funeral, disposition of remains

§ 3B:10-22. Priority among letters

A person to whom general letters of appointment are issued first has exclusive authority under the letters until his appointment is terminated or modified. If, through error, general letters of appointment are afterwards issued to another, the first appointed personal representative may recover any property of the estate in the hands of the personal representative subsequently appointed, but the acts of the latter done in good faith before notice of the first letters are not void for want of validity of appointment.

§ 3B:10-23. Duty of personal representative to settle and distribute estate

A personal representative is under a duty to settle and distribute the estate of the decedent in accordance with the terms of any probated and effective will and applicable law, and as expeditiously and efficiently as is consistent with the best interests of the estate. He shall use the authority conferred upon him by law, the terms of the will, if any, and any order in proceedings to which he is a party for the best interests of successors to the estate.

§ 3B:10-24. Liability for acts of administration or distribution

A personal representative shall not be surcharged for acts of administration or distribution if the conduct in question was authorized at the time. Subject to other obligations of administration, a probated will is authority to administer and distribute the estate according to its terms. An order of appointment of a personal representative is authority to distribute apparently intestate assets to the heirs of the decedent if, at the time of distribution, the personal representative is not aware of a pending proceeding to probate a will or to determine heirs, a proceeding to vacate an order entered in an earlier proceeding to probate a will, a formal proceeding questioning his appointment or fitness to continue. Nothing in this section affects the duty of the personal representative to administer and distribute the estate in accordance with the rights of claimants and others interested in the estate.

§ 3B:10-25. Standing to sue and be sued

Except as to proceedings which do not survive the death of the decedent, a personal representative of a decedent domiciled in this State at his death has the same standing to sue and be sued in the courts of this State and the courts of any other jurisdiction as his decedent had immediately prior to death.

§ 3B:10-26. Standards of care to be observed

Except as otherwise provided by the terms of a decedent's will, the personal representative shall observe the standards in dealing with the estate assets that would be observed by a prudent man dealing with the property of another, and if the personal representative has special skills or is named personal representative on the basis of representations of special skills or expertise, he is under a duty to use those skills.

§ 3B:10-27. Right to possession of property transferred in fraud of creditors

The right to possession of property transferred in fraud of creditors recovered for the benefit of creditors is exclusively in the personal representative.

§ 3B:10-28. Expeditious settlement and distribution

A personal representative shall proceed expeditiously with the settlement and distribution of a decedent's estate and do so without adjudication, order, or direction of a court, but he may invoke the jurisdiction of a court, in proceedings authorized by law to resolve questions concerning the estate or its administration.

§ 3B:10-29. Possession and control of estate

Except as otherwise provided by a decedent's will, every personal representative has a right to, and shall take possession or control of, the decedent's property, except that any tangible personal property may be left with or surrendered to the person presumptively entitled thereto unless or until, in the judgment of the personal representative, possession of the property by him will be necessary for purposes of administration. The request by a personal representative for delivery of any property possessed by an heir or devisee is conclusive evidence, in any action against the heir or devisee for possession thereof, that the possession of the property by the personal representative is necessary for purposes of administration. The personal representative shall pay taxes on, and take all steps reasonably necessary for the management, protection and preservation of, the estate in his possession. He may maintain an action to recover possession of property or to determine the title thereto.

§ 3B:10-30. Power over title to property

Until termination of his appointment a personal representative has the same power over the title to property of the estate that an absolute owner would have, in trust however, for the benefit of the creditors and others interested in the estate. This power may be exercised without notice, hearing, or order of court.

§ 3B:10-30.1. Voluntary discharge of personal representative for an estate.

a.
(1) Following appointment by the Surrogate's Court, whenever a personal representative for an estate is unwilling or unable to perform the duties and powers of a personal representative, that personal representative may seek to be voluntarily discharged from the further performance of the duties and powers of the office by filing for voluntary discharge with the Surrogate's Court of the county which granted the personal representative's letters. Any application for voluntary discharge shall be consented to by all parties in interest to the estate that is under the administration of the personal representative seeking to be discharged.
(2) Nothing in this section concerning the voluntary discharge of a personal representative through an application filed with the Surrogate's Court shall prohibit a personal representative from instead filing a discharge action with the Superior Court pursuant to N.J.S.3B:14-18 et seq.
b. The voluntary discharge filing shall include the following:
(1) A request for discharge, made in accordance with Rules of Court adopted by the Supreme Court, which contains the following information:
(a) the name of the personal representative seeking to be discharged, and the representative's address where future pleadings involving the estate can be served;
(b) the name and address of every party in interest to the estate, and a description of that party's interest;
(c) an affirmation by the personal representative that every party in interest to the estate listed in the form pursuant to subparagraph (b) of this paragraph has consented to the voluntary discharge of the personal representative, accompanied by the written, notarized

consent of every party in interest, or that of any party in interest under disability whose consent is provided by the party's guardian or other legal representative;

(d) an affirmation by the personal representative, if applicable, that every party in interest to the estate listed in the form pursuant to subparagraph (b) of this paragraph has consented to waiving the additional requirement, set forth in subsection c. of this section, that the personal representative file a verified final account with the Chancery Division, Probate Part for adjudication, showing the true condition of the estate, in order to release any sureties on the personal representative's bond, accompanied by the written, notarized consent of every party in interest, or that of any party in interest under disability whose consent is provided by the party's guardian or other legal representative. This consent and the consent presented pursuant to subparagraph (c) of this paragraph, whereby every party in interest has agreed to the voluntary discharge of the personal representative, may be included in the same notarized document; and

(e) a statement that the personal representative's voluntary discharge is not intended to impair the rights of any party in interest or creditor of the estate; and

(2) Along with the request for discharge and any accompanying documents, an application completed by another person to be appointed a successor or substitute personal representative for the estate.

c.

(1) The personal representative filing for voluntary discharge with the Surrogate's Court shall also file a verified final account showing the true condition of the estate with a verified complaint in the Chancery Division, Probate Part for adjudication, unless every party in interest to the estate listed in the Personal Representative Voluntary Discharge Form pursuant to subparagraph (b) of paragraph (1) of subsection b. of this section has consented in a written, notarized document to waiving this additional requirement and this consent accompanies the discharge form in lieu of any filing for a final account of the estate with the Chancery Division, Probate Part.

(2) Any sureties on the bond of a personal representative who files for voluntary discharge with the Surrogate's Court shall not be released until a final judgment has been rendered on the verified final account of the estate, unless the additional requirement for the final account was waived by the consent of every party in interest.

(3) Notwithstanding any consent by every party in interest to waive the requirement of a verified final account of an estate, a creditor of that estate whose interest has not been satisfied may petition the Superior Court for an accounting of the estate.

d.

(1) A personal representative shall be discharged from the further performance of the duties and powers of the office, and the personal representative's letters revoked, upon the approval of the personal representative's voluntary discharge filing by the Surrogate's Court; except the personal representative shall account for and pay over the money and assets with which the personal representative is chargeable by virtue of the office to the successor or substitute personal representative.

(2) A personal representative who is voluntarily discharged from the office pursuant to an approved voluntary discharge filing shall not be entitled to any statutory commissions relating to the performance of the duties and powers of that office.

§ 3B:10-31. Powers and duties of successor representative

A successor personal representative has the same power and duty as the original personal representative to complete the administration and distribution of the estate, as expeditiously as possible, but he shall not exercise any power expressly made personal to the executor named in the will.

§ 3B:10-32. Powers of surviving copersonal representative

Unless the terms of the will otherwise provide, every power exercisable by copersonal representatives may be exercised by the one or more remaining after the appointment of one or more is terminated, and if one of two or more nominated as copersonal representatives is not appointed, those appointed may exercise all the powers incident to the office.

Chapter 11. Trusts and Trustees

Article 1. General Provisions

§ 3B:11-1. Creator's reserved interest in trust alienable subject to creditors' claims

a. The right of any creator of a trust to receive either the income or the principal of the trust or any part of either thereof, presently or in the future, shall be freely alienable and shall be subject to the claims of his creditors, notwithstanding any provision to the contrary in the terms of the trust.

b. A trustee's discretionary authority to pay trust income or principal to the creator of such trust in an amount equal to the income taxes on any portion of the trust principal chargeable to the creator shall not be considered to be a right of the trust creator to receive trust income or principal within the meaning of subsection a. of this section. The trust creator shall not be considered to have the right to receive income or principal of the trust solely because the trustee is authorized under the trust instrument or any other provision of law to pay or reimburse the creator for any tax on trust income or trust principal that is payable by the creator under the law imposing such tax or to pay any such tax directly to the taxing authorities. No creditor of a trust creator shall be entitled to reach any trust property based on the discretionary powers described in this subsection.

§ 3B:11-2. Letters of trusteeship under a will

A testamentary trustee or substituted testamentary trustee, before exercising the authority vested in him by virtue of any will admitted to probate by the Superior Court, or any surrogate's court of this State, shall obtain letters of trusteeship from that court.

§ 3B:11-3. Trustees construed to be joint tenants

All estates heretofore or hereafter granted or devised to trustees shall be construed to have vested and to vest an estate of joint tenancy in the trustees.

When a trustee is removed a conveyance or devise from the removed trustee to the old and new trustees or to the new trustees shall vest in the old and new trustees or the new trustees an estate in joint tenancy, notwithstanding any want of unity.

When a trustee dies or resigns or his office becomes vacant for any cause, and a new trustee is appointed, the surviving trustees, if any there be, and the new trustees shall hold the trust estate as joint tenants, and a conveyance of a right and interest in the trust estate from the surviving trustees, to the new trustee shall vest in all the trustees an estate in joint tenancy, notwithstanding any want of unity.

When a new, additional or substituted trustee is appointed by a court of competent jurisdiction or becomes such by operation of the terms of a will or other instrument or by operation of law, title to the trust assets shall forthwith vest in all the trustees in office including the new, additional or substituted trustee as joint tenants.

§ 3B:11-4. Effect to be given consent by holders of general powers of appointment upon beneficiaries

For the purpose of granting consent or approval with regard to the acts or accounts of a fiduciary or trustee, including relief from liability or penalty for failure to post bond, or to perform other duties, and for purposes of consenting to modification or termination of a trust or to deviation from its terms, the sole holder or all coholders of a presently exercisable general power of appointment, including one in the form of a power of amendment or revocation, are deemed to act for beneficiaries to the extent that the interests of the beneficiaries as objects, takers in default, or otherwise are subject to the power. As used in this section, a presently exercisable general power of appointment is one which enables the power holder to presently draw absolute ownership to himself.

§ 3B:11-4.1. Limitations on powers of trustees; applicability; "interested party" defined

a. The following powers conferred by a governing instrument upon a trustee in his or her capacity as a trustee shall not be exercised by that trustee:

(1) The power to make discretionary distributions of either principal or income to or for the benefit of the trustee, the trustee's estate, or the creditors of either, unless either:

(a) limited by an ascertainable standard relating to the trustee's health, education, support or maintenance, within the meaning of 26 U.S.C. §§ 2041 and 2514; or

(b) exercisable by the trustee only in conjunction with another person having a substantial interest in the property subject to the power which is adverse to the interest of the trustee within the meaning of 26 U.S.C. § 2041(b) (1) (C) (ii);

If a trustee is prohibited by paragraph (1) of this subsection from exercising a power conferred upon the trustee, the trustee nevertheless may exercise that power but shall be limited to distributions for the trustee's health, education, support or maintenance to the extent otherwise permitted by the terms of the trust.

(2) The power to make discretionary distributions of either principal or income to satisfy any of the trustee's personal legal obligations for support or other purposes;

(3) The power to make discretionary allocations in the trustee's personal favor of receipts or expenses as between income and principal, unless such trustee has no power to enlarge or shift any beneficial interest except as an incidental consequence of the discharge of such trustee's fiduciary duties;

(4) The power to exercise any of the powers proscribed in this subsection with regard to an individual other than the trustee to the extent that such individual could exercise a similar prohibited power in connection with a trust that benefits the trustee.

b. Unless otherwise prohibited by the provisions of subsection a. of this section, a trustee may exercise a power described in that subsection in favor of someone other than the trustee, the trustee's estate, or the creditors of either.

c. If a governing instrument contains a power proscribed under subsection a. of this section the following shall apply:

(1) If the power is conferred on two or more trustees, it may be exercised by the trustee or trustees who are not so prohibited as if they were the only trustee or trustees; or

(2) If there is no trustee in office who can exercise such power upon application of any interested party, a court of competent jurisdiction shall appoint a trustee to exercise such power or, except as provided in subsection d. of this section, a successor trustee who would not be disqualified shall be appointed to exercise the power that the other trustees cannot exercise in accordance with the provisions of the trust instrument as if the office of trustee were vacant.

d. No beneficiary of a trust, in an individual, trustee or other capacity, may appoint, or remove and appoint, a trustee who is related or subordinate to the beneficiary within the meaning of 26 U.S.C. § 672(c) unless:

(1) the trustee's discretionary power to make distributions to or for such beneficiary is limited by an ascertainable standard relating to the beneficiary's health, education, support or maintenance as set forth in subsection a. of this section;

(2) the trustee's discretionary power may not be exercised to satisfy any of such beneficiary's legal obligations for support or other purposes; and

(3) the trustee's discretionary power may not be exercised to grant to such beneficiary a general power to appoint property of the trust to the beneficiary, the beneficiary's estate or the creditors thereof within the meaning of 26 U.S.C. § 2041.

This subsection d. shall not apply if the appointment of the trustee by the beneficiary may be made only in conjunction with another person having a substantial interest in the property of the trust, subject to the power, which is adverse to the exercise of the power in favor of the beneficiary within the meaning of 26 U.S.C. § 2041(b) (1) (C) (ii).

e. The provisions of this section shall not apply during the time that a trust remains revocable or amendable by the grantor.

f. This section applies to:
(1) Any trust created under a governing instrument executed 90 days or more after the effective date of this act, unless the governing instrument expressly provides that this act does not apply; and
(2) Any trust created under a governing instrument executed before 90 days after the effective date of this act, unless all interested parties affirmatively elect on or before three years after the effective date by a written declaration signed by or on behalf of each interested party and delivered to the trustee, not to be subject to the application of this act. In the case of a testamentary trust, such declarations shall be filed with the clerk of the court in which the will was admitted to probate.
g. In this section the term "interested party" means:
(1) Each trustee then serving; and
(2) Each person having an interest in income or principal whom it would be necessary to join as a party in a proceeding for the judicial settlement of a trustee's account or, if such a person has not attained majority or is otherwise incapacitated, the person's legal representative under applicable law or the person's agent under a durable power of attorney that is sufficient to grant such authority.

Article 2. Additional or Substitute Trustees [Repealed July 17, 2016]

§ 3B:11-5. Trustee's death or failure to act; appointment of new trustee by court; powers [Repealed]

§ 3B:11-6. Vacancy in trusteeship upon discharge or removal [Repealed]

§ 3B:11-7. Powers of new, substituted or additional trustees [Repealed]

Article 3. Charitable Trusts

§ 3B:11-8. Short title

This article shall be known and may be cited as the "Charitable Trust Law of 1971."

§ 3B:11-9. Definitions

As used in this article:
a. "Code" means the Internal Revenue Code of 1954 as amended;
b. "Private foundation trust" means a charitable trust which is a private foundation described in section 509(a) of the code, including each nonexempt charitable trust described in section 4947(a)(1) of the code which is treated as a private foundation;
c. "Split-interest trust" means a nonexempt split-interest trust described in section 4947(a)(2) of the code, but only to the extent that section 508(e) of the code is applicable to the nonexempt split-interest trust under section 4947(a)(2) of the code;
d. "Trust instrument" means a will, deed, agreement, court order, or other instrument pursuant to which money or other property is entrusted to a fiduciary, and also means the certificate of incorporation of a nonprofit corporation administering a charitable foundation trust;
e. "Trustee" means every fiduciary administering a trust instrument, and includes a corporation which is a private charitable foundation administering a private foundation trust;
f. "Trust" means private foundation trusts and split-interest trusts.

§ 3B:11-10. Provision included in trust instruments governing nonprofit corporations administering private foundation trusts

Notwithstanding any provision to the contrary contained in any law of this State or in any trust instrument, and except as otherwise provided in N.J.S. 3B:11-12, each trust instrument governing a nonprofit corporation administering a private foundation trust shall, by virtue of this article, and without any further act by any person or persons, be deemed to include the following:
"This corporation shall make distributions at times and in a manner as not to subject it to tax under section 4942 of the Internal Revenue Code of 1954 as amended, and shall not engage in any act of self-dealing as defined in section 4941 of the code, and shall not retain any excess business holdings as defined in section 4943 of the code, and shall not make any investments as defined in section 4944 of the code, and shall not make any taxable expenditure which would subject it to tax under section 4945 of the code."

§ 3B:11-11. Provision included in trust instruments governing split-interest trusts or private foundation trusts

Notwithstanding any provision to the contrary contained in any law of this State or in any trust instrument, and except as otherwise provided in N.J.S. 3B:11-12, each trust instrument governing a split-interest trust or a private foundation trust other than one as described in N.J.S. 3B:11-10, shall, by virtue of this article and without any further act by any person or persons, be deemed to include the following:
"Distributions of this trust shall be made at times and in a manner as not to subject the trust to tax under section 4942 of the Internal Revenue Code of 1954, as amended, and shall not engage in any act of self-dealing as defined in section 4941 of the code, and shall not retain any excess business holdings as defined in section 4943 of the code, and shall not make any investment as defined in section 4944 of the code, and shall not make any taxable expenditure which would subject it to tax under section 4945 of the code."

§ 3B:11-12. Execution of instrument stating certain provisions not applicable to trust; filing

The trustee or trustees of any trust may, without judicial proceedings, execute an instrument stating that the provisions of N.J.S. 3B:11-10 or N.J.S. 3B:11-11, as the case may be, shall not be applicable to the trust, and upon filing a copy thereof in the office of the Secretary of State of this State, the provisions of N.J.S. 3B:11-10 or N.J.S. 3B:11-11, as the case may be, shall not apply to the trust.

§ 3B:11-13. Construction of article

This article shall be so construed as to enable split-interest trusts and private foundation trusts to qualify for the maximum tax exemptions available to those trusts under the Internal Revenue Code of 1954 as amended.

§ 3B:11-14. Power of courts or Attorney General not impaired by article

Nothing in this article shall impair the power conferred by law upon the courts or the Attorney General of this State with respect to any trust subject to the provisions of this article.

§ 3B:11-15. Application of article

This article shall apply to all trusts, as defined herein, whether created before or after December 13, 1971.

§ 3B:11-16. Pooled trust accounts

Prepaid funeral expense moneys used to fund a prepaid funeral agreement may be deposited into a pooled trust account in a federally insured State or federally chartered bank, savings bank or savings and loan association pursuant to a written trust agreement the beneficiaries of which shall be the purchasers or intended funeral recipients. Any such trust agreement shall assure that the following terms and conditions are clearly and conspicuously disclosed in writing to purchasers and intended funeral recipients prior to the acceptance of any moneys by the trustees:

a. The right to immediately withdraw on demand any moneys plus accrued interest paid into the trust, except as provided in section 1 of P.L.1991, c.502 (C.2A:102-16.1).
b. The right to receive periodic statements not less than once per year reflecting the amount of principal and accrued interest, if any, in the trust.
c. The amount or rate of commissions to be taken.
d. The identity and location of the trustees.
e. The location of the trust agreement and the conditions under which it may be examined.

All such trust agreements entered into by a provider on or after the effective date of this 1993 amendatory and supplementary act shall comply with the provisions set forth in sections 1 through 13 of P.L.1993, c.147 (C.45:7-82 to 45:7-94).

§ 3B:11-17. Trustees' commission

The trustees of a pooled trust fund established pursuant to section 1 of this act for the benefit of not less than 200 purchasers or intended funeral recipients shall be entitled to a commission of not more than 1% per annum of the corpus of the trust fund. The trustees of a pooled trust fund for the benefit of less than 200 purchasers or intended funeral recipients shall not be entitled to any commission. All expenses incurred in the administration of such a trust or the services rendered thereby shall be deducted from income received by the trustees and in no event shall the trustees invade the corpus of the trust funds.

§ 3B:11-18. Report; rules, regulations

The Commissioner of Banking shall determine whether, among pooled trust funds established pursuant to this act, adequate competition exists with respect to interest rate yield and commissions or fees charged during the one year period following the effective date of this act. No later than one year after the effective date of this act the commissioner shall report to the Legislature his findings and any recommendations he may have to provide for greater competition among pooled trust funds.

The commissioner shall adopt rules and regulations pursuant to the "Administrative Procedure Act," P.L. 1968, c. 410 (C. 52:14B-1 et seq.) as may be necessary to effectuate the purposes of this section.

Article 4. Community Trusts

§ 3B:11-19. Short title

This act shall be known and may be cited as the "New Jersey Community Trust for Persons with Severe Chronic Disabilities Act."

§ 3B:11-20. Findings

The Legislature finds that it is in the public interest to encourage activities by voluntary associations and private citizens which will supplement and augment those services provided by local, State, and federal government agencies in discharge of their responsibilities toward individuals with severe chronic disabilities. The Legislature further finds that, as a result of changing social, economic, and demographic trends, families of persons with severe chronic disabilities are increasingly aware of the need for a vehicle by which they can assure ongoing individualized personal concern for a severely disabled family member who may survive his parents or other family members, and provide for the efficient management of small legacies or trust funds to be used for the benefit of such a disabled person. In a number of other states voluntary associations have established foundations or trusts intended to be responsive to these concerns. Therefore, a study of the experience in other states suggests that New Jersey would benefit by the enactment of enabling legislation expressly authorizing the formation of community trusts in accordance with criteria set forth by statute and administered by the Secretary of State. These community trusts permit the pooling of resources contributed by families or persons with philanthropic intent, along with the reservation of portions of these funds for the use and benefit of designated beneficiaries.

§ 3B:11-21. Purposes, policies

This act shall be liberally construed and applied to promote its underlying purposes and policies, which are among others to:
a. encourage the orderly establishment of community trusts for the benefit of persons with severe chronic disabilities;

b. ensure that community trusts are administered properly and that the managing boards of the trusts are free from conflicts of interest, except that an unpaid member of the managing board of a nonprofit corporation provider shall not be deemed to be in conflict as a member of the managing board of a trust;
c. facilitate sound administration of trust funds for persons with severe chronic disabilities by allowing family members and others to pool resources in order to make professional management investment more efficient;
d. provide parents of persons with severe chronic disabilities peace of mind in knowing that a means exists to ensure that the interests of their children who have severe chronic disabilities are properly looked after and managed after the parents die or become incapacitated;
e. help make guardians available for persons with severe chronic disabilities who are incapacitated, when no other family member is available for this purpose;
f. encourage the availability of private resources to purchase for persons with severe chronic disabilities goods and services that are not available through any governmental or charitable program and to conserve these resources by limiting purchases to those which are not available from other sources;
g. encourage the inclusion, as beneficiaries of community trusts, of persons who lack resources and whose families are indigent, in a way that does not diminish the resources available to other beneficiaries whose families have contributed to the trust; and
h. remove the disincentives which discourage parents and others from setting aside funds for the future protection of persons with severe chronic disabilities by ensuring that the interests of beneficiaries in community trusts are not considered assets or income which would disqualify them from any governmental or charitable entitlement program with an economic means test.

§ 3B:11-22. Definitions

As used in P.L.1985, c.424 (C.3B:11-19 et seq.):
a. "Beneficiary" means any person with a severe chronic disability who has qualified as a member of the community trust program and who has the right to receive those services and benefits of the community trust program as provided in P.L.1985, c.424.
b. "Board" means the board of trustees or the group of persons vested with the management of the business and affairs of a corporation, formed for the purpose of managing a community trust, irrespective of the name by which the group is designated.
c. "Community trust" means a nonprofit organization which offers the following services:
(1) administration of special trust funds for persons with severe chronic disabilities;
(2) follow-along services;
(3) guardianship for persons with severe chronic disabilities who are incapacitated, when no other immediate family member or friend is available for this purpose; and
(4) advice and counsel to persons who have been appointed as individual guardians of the persons or estates of persons with severe chronic disabilities.
d. "Follow-along services" means those services offered by community trusts which are designed to insure that the needs of each beneficiary are being met for as long as may be required and may include periodic visits to the beneficiary and to the places where the beneficiary receives services, participation in the development of individualized plans being made by service providers for the beneficiary, and other similar services consistent with the purposes of P.L.1985, c.424.
e. "Severe chronic disability" means a physical or mental impairment which is expected to give rise to a long-term need for specialized health, social, and other services, and which makes the person with that impairment dependent upon others for assistance to secure these services.
f. "Trustee" means any member of the board of a corporation, formed for the purpose of managing a community trust, whether that member is designated as a trustee, director, manager, governor, or by any other title.
g. "Surplus trust funds" means funds accumulated in the trust from contributions made on behalf of an individual beneficiary, which, after the death of the beneficiary, are determined by the board to be in excess of the actual cost of providing services during the beneficiary's lifetime, including the beneficiary's share of administrative costs, and of any amounts provided to a remainderman.

§ 3B:11-23. Nonprofit corporations

This act shall apply to every community trust established in this State after the effective date of this act. In addition to meeting the other requirements of the act, every board which administers a community trust shall incorporate as a nonprofit corporation in accordance with the provisions of Title 15A of the New Jersey Statutes. Except as otherwise provided herein, the provisions of Title 15A of the New Jersey Statutes shall apply to the community trust.

§ 3B:11-24. Board

Every community trust shall be administered by a board. The board shall be comprised of no less than nine and no more than 21 members, at least one-third of whom shall be parents or relatives of persons with severe chronic disabilities. Board members shall be selected, to the maximum extent possible, from geographic areas throughout the area served by the trust.
The certificate of incorporation filed with the Secretary of State pursuant to Title 15A of the New Jersey Statutes shall, in addition to the requirements set forth in that Title, demonstrate that the requirements of this section have been met.

§ 3B:11-25. No compensation

Notwithstanding any other provision of law to the contrary, no trustee may be compensated for services provided as a member of the board of a community trust. No fees or commissions shall be paid to these trustees; however, a trustee may be paid for necessary expenses incurred by the trustee and may receive indemnification as permitted under Title 15A of the New Jersey Statutes.

§ 3B:11-26. Bylaws

The board shall adopt bylaws which shall include a declaration delineating the primary geographic area serviced by the trust and the principal services to be provided and shall file the bylaws with the Secretary of State.

§ 3B:11-27. Services; guardianship

The board may retain paid staff as it may deem necessary to provide follow-along services to the extent required by each beneficiary. The board may authorize the expenditure of funds for any goods or services which, in its sole discretion, it determines will promote the well-being of any beneficiary, including recreational services. The board may pay for the burial of any beneficiary. The board, however, may not expend funds for any goods or services of comparable quality to those available to any particular beneficiary through any governmental or charitable program, insurance, or other sources. The board may expend funds to meet the reasonable costs of administering the community trust.

The board is not required to provide services to a beneficiary who is a competent adult and who has refused to accept the services. Further, the board shall not provide services of a nature or in a manner that would be contrary to the public policy of this State at the time the services are to be provided. In either case, the board may offer alternative services that are consistent with the purposes of this act and in keeping with the best interests of the beneficiary.

The board may accept appointment as guardian of the person, guardian of the estate or guardian of both on behalf of any beneficiary. If the board accepts appointment as guardian of the person of an individual, it shall assign a staff member to carry out its responsibilities as the guardian. The board may, on request, offer consultative and professional assistance to an individual, private or public guardian of any of its beneficiaries.

§ 3B:11-28. Contributions; written statement of services

The board may accept contributions, bequests, and designations under life insurance policies to the community trust on behalf of individuals with severe chronic disabilities for the purpose of qualifying them as beneficiaries.

At the time a contribution, bequest, or assignment of insurance proceeds is made, the trustor shall receive a written statement of the services to be provided to the beneficiary. The statement shall include a starting date for the delivery of services or the condition precedent, such as the death of the trustor, which shall determine the starting date. The statement shall describe the frequency with which services shall be provided and their duration, and the criteria or procedures for modifying the program of services from time to time in the best interests of the beneficiary.

§ 3B:11-29. Itemized annual statement

Along with the annual report filed with the Secretary of State pursuant to Title 15A of the New Jersey Statutes, the board shall file an itemized statement which shows the funds collected for the year, income earned, salaries, other expenses incurred, and the opening and final trust balances. A copy of this statement shall be made available, upon request, to any beneficiary, trustor, or designee of the trustor. In addition, once annually, each trustor or the trustor's designee shall receive a detailed individual statement of the services provided to the trustor's beneficiary during the previous 12 months and the services to be provided during the following 12 months. The board shall make a copy of the individual statement available to any beneficiary, upon request.

§ 3B:11-30. Qualification of indigent persons

The board may accept gifts and use surplus trust funds for the purpose of qualifying as beneficiaries any indigent person whose family members lack the resources to make a full contribution on that person's behalf. The extent and character of the services and selection of beneficiaries are at the discretion of the board. The board may not use surplus trust funds to make any charitable contribution on behalf of any beneficiary or any group or class of beneficiaries. The board may accept gifts to meet start-up costs, reduce the charges to the trust for the cost of administration, and for any other purpose that is consistent with this act. Gifts made to the trust for an unspecified purpose shall be used by the board either to qualify indigent persons whose families lack the means to qualify them as beneficiaries of the trust or to meet any start-up costs that the trust incurs.

§ 3B:11-31. Special requests; individual trusts

The board may agree to fulfill any special requests made on behalf of a beneficiary as long as the requests are consistent with this act and provided an adequate contribution has been made for this purpose on behalf of a beneficiary. The board may agree to serve as trustee for any individual trust created on behalf of a beneficiary, regardless of whether the trust is revocable or irrevocable, has one or more remaindermen or contingent beneficiaries, or any other condition, so long as the individual trust is consistent with the purposes of this act.

§ 3B:11-32. Community trust irrevocable

A community trust for persons with severe chronic disabilities is irrevocable, but the trustees in their sole discretion may provide compensation for any contribution to the trust to any trustor who, upon good cause, withdraws a beneficiary designated by the trustor from the trust, or if it becomes impossible to fulfill the conditions of the trust with regard to an individual beneficiary for reasons other than the death of the beneficiary. The trustor may also designate one or more remaindermen at the time the contribution is made to the trust.

§ 3B:11-33. Not deemed asset

Notwithstanding any other provision of law to the contrary, the beneficiary's interest in any community trust shall not be deemed to be an asset for the purpose of determining income eligibility for any publicly operated program, nor shall that interest be reached in satisfaction of a claim for support and maintenance of the beneficiary. No agency shall reduce the benefits or services available to any individual because that person is the beneficiary of a community trust.

§ 3B:11-34. Not subject to rule against perpetuities

A community trust shall not be subject to or held to be in violation of any principle of law against perpetuities or restraints on alienation or perpetual accumulations of trusts.

§ 3B:11-35. Settlement, dissolution, merger

The board shall settle a community trust by filing a final accounting in the Superior Court. In addition, at any time prior to the settlement of the final account, the board, the Secretary of State, or the Attorney General may bring an action for the dissolution of a nonprofit corporation in the Superior Court for the purpose of terminating the trust or merging it with another charitable trust. No trustee or any private individual shall be entitled to share in the distribution of any of the trust assets upon dissolution, merger, or settlement of the community trust. Upon dissolution, merger, or settlement, the Superior Court shall distribute all of the remaining net assets of the community trust in a manner that is consistent with the purposes of this act.

§ 3B:11-36. Findings, declarations regarding special needs trusts

The Legislature finds and declares that:

a. It is in the public interest to encourage persons to set aside amounts to supplement and augment assistance provided by government entities to persons with severe chronic disabilities;

b. By enacting section 13611 of the federal Omnibus Budget Reconciliation Act of 1993, 42 U.S.C. § 1396p(d)(4), the United States Congress affirmed this view by permitting the establishment of a trust to supplement and augment assistance for a person who is disabled without disqualifying that person from benefits under the Medicaid program;

c. In some instances, trusts must be established by a court in order to comply with the provisions of 42 U.S.C. § 1396p(d)(4);

d. However, the current law in New Jersey does not specifically authorize the establishment of these trusts and subsection f. of section 6 of P.L. 1968, c. 413 (C. 30:4D-6) may be construed as impeding their establishment; and

e. Therefore, legislation is appropriate to facilitate the establishment of trusts to supplement and augment assistance provided by government entities to persons with severe chronic disabilities and persons who are disabled under the federal Social Security Act.

§ 3B:11-37. Establishing an OBRA '93 trust

a. As used in this section "OBRA '93 trust" means a trust established pursuant to 42 U.S.C. § 1396p(d)(4)(A) or an account within a pooled trust pursuant to 42 U.S.C. § 1396p(d)(4)(C).

b. Upon the request of an interested party, a court may establish an OBRA '93 trust for a person who is disabled as defined in section 1614(a)(3) of the federal Social Security Act (42 U.S.C. § 1382c (a)(3)), whether or not the person is an incapacitated person as defined in N.J.S. 3B:1-2, and may direct that the assets of the person with a disability be placed in the OBRA '93 trust.

c. Prior to establishing an OBRA '93 trust for a person with a disability who is incapacitated, the court shall consider the factors listed in N.J.S. 3B:12-3.

d. Prior to establishing an OBRA '93 trust for a person who is a minor, the court shall consider the applicable Rules of Court and State law relating to the handling of funds for a minor, including, but not limited to, the provisions of N.J.S. 3B:15-16 and N.J.S. 3B:15-17.

e. Nothing in this section shall be construed to preclude an OBRA '93 trust from being created by any person in addition to a court as would be consistent with 42 U.S.C. § 1396p(d)(4).

f. Notwithstanding any provision or principle of law to the contrary, a beneficiary, grantor, trustee or other person shall not have authority to revoke an OBRA '93 trust. This provision shall apply whether or not an OBRA '93 trust instrument designates the trust as irrevocable or whether the OBRA '93 trust was created by a court or otherwise.

§ 3B:11-38. Trust funds for pets recognized as valid [Repealed]

Chapter 12. Minors and Incapacitated Persons

§ 3B:12-1. Power of the court to order a protective arrangement

If it is established that a minor, an incapacitated person or an alleged incapacitated person or a person not yet in being has property or an interest therein which may be wasted or dissipated or that a basis exists for affecting the property or interest and affairs of a minor, an incapacitated person or an alleged incapacitated person or person not yet in being, or that funds are needed for the support, care and welfare of the minor, incapacitated person or alleged incapacitated person or those entitled to be supported by him, the court may, subject to the appointment of a guardian ad litem and upon notice to the guardian ad litem, without appointing a guardian of the estate, authorize, direct or ratify any single or more than one transaction necessary or desirable to achieve any security, service, care or protective arrangement meeting the foreseeable needs of the minor, incapacitated person or alleged incapacitated person or those dependent upon him.

§ 3B:12-2. Matters within a protective arrangement

Protective arrangements include, but are not limited to, payment, delivery, deposit or retention of funds or property, sale, mortgage, lease or other transfer of property, entry into an annuity contract, a contract for life care, a deposit contract, a contract for training and education, addition to, or establishment of, a suitable trust. The court may authorize, direct or ratify any contract, trust or other transaction relating to the minor's, incapacitated person's, alleged incapacitated person's or person's not yet in being financial affairs or involving the estate if the court determines that the transaction is in the best interests of the minor, incapacitated person, alleged incapacitated person or person not yet in being or those dependent upon him.

§ 3B:12-3. Factors to be considered before approving a protective arrangement

Before approving a protective arrangement or other transaction the court shall consider the interests of creditors and dependents of the minor, incapacitated person or alleged incapacitated person and, in view of his disability, whether the minor, incapacitated person or alleged incapacitated person needs the continuing protection of a guardian.

§ 3B:12-4. Appointment of special guardian

The court may appoint a special guardian to assist in the accomplishment of any protective arrangement or other transaction authorized under this article who shall have authority conferred by the order and shall serve until discharged by the order after reporting to the court of all matters done pursuant to the order of appointment.

If the court has appointed a special guardian to assist in the accomplishment of a protective arrangement pursuant to this section, the special guardian shall be entitled to receive reasonable fees for his services, as well as reimbursement of his reasonable expenses, upon application to the court, payable by the estate of the minor, incapacitated person or alleged incapacitated person.

§ 3B:12-5. Right of alleged incapacitated person to trial on issue of incapacity

Where application is made to the court for proceedings to affect the property and affairs of an alleged incapacitated person, and the alleged incapacitated person has not been adjudicated as such, the alleged incapacitated person or someone acting in his behalf may apply for a trial of the issue of incapacity in accordance with N.J.S.3B:12-24 and the Rules Governing the Courts of the State of New Jersey.

§ 3B:12-6. Circumstances under which money may be paid or personal property delivered

Any person under a duty to pay or deliver money or personal property to a minor may perform this duty, in amounts not exceeding $5,000.00 per annum, by paying or delivering the money or property to:

a. The minor, if married;
b. A parent or parents of the minor;
c. Any person having the care and custody of the minor with whom the minor resides;
d. A guardian of the person of the minor; or
e. A financial institution incident to a deposit in a federally insured savings account in the sole name of the minor and giving written notice of the deposit to the minor.

§ 3B:12-7. When payment of money or delivery of property prohibited

The payment of money or delivery of personal property under N.J.S. 3B:12 6 shall not be made if the person making payment or delivery has actual knowledge that a guardian of the estate of the minor has been appointed or that an action for the appointment of a guardian of the estate of the minor is pending.

§ 3B:12-8. Application of money and property; reimbursement for out-of-pocket expenses

The persons, other than the minor or any financial institution under subsection e. of N.J.S. 3B:12-6, receiving money or property for a minor, are obligated to apply so much or all of the money or the income or proceeds of the property for the support, maintenance, education, general use and benefit of the minor in the manner, at the time or times and to the extent that those persons, in an exercise of reasonable discretion, deem suitable and proper, with or without court order, with due regard to the duty and ability of themselves or of any other person to support the minor, and with or without regard to any other funds, income or property which may be available for that purpose. But those persons may not pay themselves except by way of reimbursement for out-of-pocket expenses for goods and services necessary for the minor's support.

§ 3B:12-9. Preservation of excess sums; payment and delivery to minor upon attaining 18 years of age

Any excess sums shall be preserved for future support of the minor and any balance not so used and any property received for the minor must be turned over to the minor when he attains 18 years of age.

§ 3B:12-10. Persons paying money or delivering property not liable for application

Persons who pay or deliver in accordance with provisions of this article are not responsible for the proper application thereof.

§ 3B:12-11. Affidavit of receipt; contents; filing

The persons making payment of money or delivery of personal property as provided in this article shall obtain from the recipient thereof, if other than a financial institution or a married minor, an affidavit signed by the recipient acknowledging receipt of the money or personal property which shall set forth the recipient's status in relation to the minor and the purpose for which the money or personal property will be used. The affidavit shall be filed in the office of the Surrogate of the county in which the minor resides or if the minor resides outside the State, the county which has jurisdiction of the property.

Article 3. Guardians for Minors; Appointment

§ 3B:12-12. Jurisdiction of surrogate to appoint guardians for minors

In the appointment of guardians for minors, the surrogate's court of the county in which the minor may reside or if he is nonresident, then the county in which he may have real or personal estate, shall have and exercise the same powers as the Superior Court.

§ 3B:12-13. Power to designate testamentary guardian

Subject to the provisions of N.J.S.3B:12-14, either parent may, by his will, appoint a guardian of the person and a guardian of the estate, or a guardian of the person and estate, of any of the parent's children, including children en ventre sa mere, who are under the age of 18 years and unmarried at the death of the parent.

§ 3B:12-14. Consent of surviving parent; formal requisites

Where an appointment is made under N.J.S. 3B:12-13 and the other parent survives the appointing parent, the appointment shall be effective only when the surviving parent, at or before the issuance of the letters, consents thereto in writing and signs and acknowledges the consent in the presence of two witnesses present at the same time who subscribe their names as witnesses thereto in his presence.

§ 3B:12-15. Appointment of testamentary guardian by surviving parent

If no guardian has been appointed pursuant to N.J.S.3B:12-13 and N.J.S.3B:12-14, or if the surviving parent was so appointed, the surviving parent may, by his will, appoint a guardian of the person and a guardian of the estate, or a guardian of the person and estate, of any of the parent's children, including children en ventre sa mere, who are under the age of 18 years and unmarried at the death of the surviving parent.

§ 3B:12-16. Bond of testamentary guardian

Before receiving his letters, a testamentary guardian of a minor shall give bond in accordance with N.J.S.3B:15-1 et seq., unless the guardian is relieved from doing so by direction of the will of the parent appointing the guardian or by order of the court. However, regardless of the direction, the guardian shall, with respect to property to which the ward is or shall be entitled from any source, other than the parent or other than any policy of life insurance upon the life of the parent, give bond in accordance with that section before exercising any authority or control over the property.

The provisions of this section relieving a testamentary guardian of a minor from giving bond by direction of the will of the parent shall not apply to a testamentary guardian of a minor with a developmental disability. Such guardian shall be bonded pursuant to paragraph (1) of subsection i. of N.J.S.3B:15-1, unless the guardian is relieved from doing so pursuant to paragraph (2) of subsection i. of N.J.S.3B:15-1.

§ 3B:12-17. Determination into fitness of a testamentary guardian of a minor's person

If a will appointing a testamentary guardian of the person of a minor has been or is to be probated in the surrogate's court of any county or the Superior Court, the Superior Court may, in an action brought upon notice to the guardian named in the will, inquire into the present custody of the minor, and make an order touching the testamentary guardianship as may be for the best interest and welfare of the minor.

§ 3B:12-18. Effect of a testamentary appointment

The appointment of a testamentary guardian of the person or estate of a minor or his estate shall be good and effectual against any other person claiming the guardianship over or custody of the minor or his estate, as the case may be.

§ 3B:12-19. Guardian for property of nonresident minor

Where a nonresident minor has property within this State, the Superior Court may appoint a guardian of the minor to administer his property. The surrogate's court shall have concurrent authority to appoint a guardian for the property within the county.

The Superior Court has, with respect to the property, the same authority and control over him which it would have over a guardian of the estate of a resident minor. In any case not provided for by statute, it shall take any action in the matter as it shall deem most for the advantage of the minor.

§ 3B:12-20. Special guardian for consent to enlist; bond; fees

When any minor, who is of an age that the consent of his parent or guardian is necessary to enable him to enlist in the armed forces of the United States, desires to enlist in the armed forces of the United States and has no parent or guardian entitled to his custody and control available to sign the written consent required for the enlistment, letters of special guardianship may be granted by the surrogate's court of the county in which the minor resides, or the Superior Court, empowering the special guardian to give his written consent to the enlistment but limiting his authority and duty to that purpose. The guardian shall give consent only if he deems the enlistment advisable. A bond shall not be required from the guardian, and neither the clerk of the Superior Court nor the surrogate shall collect any fee or charge in connection with the action for the appointment of the guardian.

§ 3B:12-21. Persons entitled to appointment

In an action for the appointment of a guardian of the person, guardian of the estate, or a guardian of the person and estate of a minor, the surrogate's court of the county wherein he resides or, if he is a nonresident, where his real or personal estate may be, or the Superior Court, upon inquiry into the circumstances, may appoint the parents or either of them or the survivor of them as the guardian of the person, guardian of the estate or guardian of the person and estate of the minor. If neither parent or the survivor of them will accept the guardianship, then the heirs, or some of them, may be appointed as guardian. If none of the heirs will accept the guardianship, then some other person shall be appointed as the guardian of the person, guardian of the estate or as guardian of the person and estate of the minor. This section shall not be construed to restrict the power of the court to appoint a substitute guardian on the application of the minor or otherwise.

§ 3B:12-22. Appointment when heirs are nonresidents

When it shall appear to the Superior Court, or surrogate's court that the heirs of a minor residing in this State do not reside within this State, the court may take any action in respect to the appointment of a guardian of the person, guardian of the estate or as guardian of the person and estate for the minor as shall be to his advantage.

§ 3B:12-23. Guardian for child of absconding or absent parent

If a resident of this State has or shall abscond or absent himself from the State, leaving a child under the age of 18 without sufficient provision for his maintenance and education, the surrogate of the county wherein the child resides, or the Superior Court, may appoint a guardian for his person or estate or both. The Superior Court may revoke the appointment when it shall appear proper.

§ 3B:12-24. Issue of incapacity triable without jury unless jury is demanded

In civil actions or proceedings for the determination of incapacity or for the appointment of a guardian for an alleged incapacitated person, the trial of the issue of incapacity may be had without a jury pursuant to Rules Governing the Courts of the State of New Jersey, unless a trial by jury is demanded by the alleged incapacitated person or someone on his behalf.

§ 3B:12-24.1. Determination by the court of need for guardianship services, specific services

a. General Guardian. If the court finds that an individual is incapacitated as defined in N.J.S.3B:1-2 and is without capacity to govern himself or manage his affairs, the court may appoint a general guardian who shall exercise all rights and powers of the incapacitated person. The general guardian of the estate shall furnish a bond conditioned as required by the provisions of N.J.S.3B:15-1 et seq., unless the guardian is relieved from doing so by the court.

b. Limited Guardian. If the court finds that an individual is incapacitated and lacks the capacity to do some, but not all, of the tasks necessary to care for himself, the court may appoint a limited guardian of the person, limited guardian of the estate, or limited guardian of both the person and estate. A court, when establishing a limited guardianship shall make specific findings regarding the individual's capacity, including, but not limited to which areas, such as residential, educational, medical, legal, vocational and financial decision making, the incapacitated person retains sufficient capacity to manage. A judgment of limited guardianship may specify the limitations upon the authority of the guardian or alternatively the areas of decision making retained by the person. The limited guardian of the estate shall furnish a bond in accordance with the provisions of N.J.S.3B:15-1 et seq., unless the guardian is relieved from doing so by the court.

c. Pendente lite; Temporary Guardian.

(1) Whenever a complaint is filed in the Superior Court to declare a person incapacitated and appoint a guardian, the complaint may also request the appointment of a temporary guardian of the person or estate, or both, pendente lite. Notice of a pendente lite temporary guardian application shall be given to the alleged incapacitated person or alleged incapacitated person's attorney or the attorney appointed by the court to represent the alleged incapacitated person.

(2) Pending a hearing for the appointment of a guardian, the court may for good cause shown and upon a finding that there is a critical need or risk of substantial harm, including, but not limited to:

(a) the physical or mental health, safety and well-being of the person may be harmed or jeopardized;

(b) the property or business affairs of the person may be repossessed, wasted, misappropriated, dissipated, lost, damaged or diminished or not appropriately managed;

(c) it is in the best interest of the alleged incapacitated person to have a temporary guardian appointed and such may be dealt with before the hearing to determine incapacity can be held, after any notice as the court shall direct, appoint a temporary guardian pendente lite of the person or estate, or both, of the alleged incapacitated person.

(3) A pendente lite temporary guardian appointed pursuant to this section may be granted authority to arrange interim financial, social, medical or mental health services or temporary accommodations for the alleged incapacitated person determined to be necessary to deal with critical needs of or risk of substantial harm to the alleged incapacitated person or the alleged incapacitated person's property or assets. The pendente lite temporary guardian may be authorized to make arrangements for payment for such services from the estate of the alleged incapacitated person.

(4) A pendente lite temporary guardian appointed hereunder shall be limited to act for the alleged incapacitated person only for those services determined by the court to be necessary to deal with critical needs or risk of substantial harm to the alleged incapacitated person.

(5) The alleged incapacitated person's attorney or attorney appointed by the court to represent the alleged incapacitated person shall be given notice of the appointment of the pendente lite temporary guardian. The pendente lite temporary guardian shall communicate all actions taken on behalf of the alleged incapacitated individual to the alleged incapacitated person's attorney or attorney appointed by the court to represent the alleged incapacitated person who shall have the right to object to such actions.

(6) A pendente lite temporary guardian appointment shall not have the effect of an adjudication of incapacity or effect of limitation on the legal rights of the individual other than those specified in the court order.

(7) If the court enters an order appointing a pendente lite temporary guardian without notice, the alleged incapacitated person may appear and move for its dissolution or modification on two days' notice to the plaintiff and to the temporary guardian or on such shorter notice as the court prescribes.

(8) Every order appointing a pendente lite temporary guardian granted without notice expires as prescribed by the court, but within a period of not more than 45 days, unless within that time the court extends it for good cause shown for the same period.
(9) The pendente lite temporary guardian, upon application to the court, shall be entitled to receive reasonable fees for his services, as well as reimbursement of his reasonable expenses, which shall be payable by the estate of the alleged incapacitated person or minor.
(10) The pendente lite temporary guardian shall furnish a bond in accordance with the provisions of N.J.S.3B:15-1 et seq., unless the guardian is relieved from doing so by the court.
d. Disclosure of information. Physicians and psychologists licensed by the State are authorized to disclose medical information, including but not limited to medical, mental health and substance abuse information as permitted by State and federal law, regarding the alleged incapacitated person in affidavits filed pursuant to the Rules Governing the Courts of the State of New Jersey.
e. Court appearance. The alleged incapacitated person shall appear in court unless the plaintiff and the court-appointed attorney certify that the alleged incapacitated person is unable to appear because of physical or mental incapacity.
f. Communication. When a person who is allegedly in need of guardianship services appears to have a receptive or expressive communication deficit, all reasonable means of communication with the person shall be attempted for the purposes of this section, including written, spoken, sign or non-formal language, which includes translation of the person's spoken or written word when the person is unable to communicate in English, and the use of adaptive equipment.
g. Additional subject areas. At the request of the limited guardian, and if the incapacitated person is not represented, after appointment of an attorney for the incapacitated person and with notice to all interested parties, the court may determine that a person is in need of guardian services regarding additional subject areas and may enlarge the powers of the guardian to protect the person from significant harm.
h. Limitations of guardian powers. At the request of the guardian, the incapacitated person or another interested person, and if the incapacitated person is not represented, after appointment of an attorney for the incapacitated person and with notice to all interested parties, the court may limit the powers conferred upon a guardian.

§ 3B:12-25. Appointment of guardian

The Superior Court may determine the incapacity of an alleged incapacitated person and appoint a guardian for the person, guardian for the estate or a guardian for the person and estate. Letters of guardianship shall be granted to the spouse or domestic partner as defined in section 3 of P.L.2003, c.246 (C.26:8A-3), if the spouse is living with the incapacitated person as man and wife or as a domestic partner as defined in section 3 of P.L.2003, c.246 (C.26:8A-3) at the time the incapacitation arose, or to the incapacitated person's heirs, or friends, or thereafter first consideration shall be given to the Office of the Public Guardian for Elderly Adults in the case of adults within the statutory mandate of the office, or if none of them will accept the letters or it is proven to the court that no appointment from among them will be to the best interest of the incapacitated person or the estate, then to any other proper person as will accept the same, and if applicable, in accordance with the professional guardianship requirements of P.L.2005, c.370 (C.52:27G-32 et al.). Consideration may be given to surrogate decision-makers, if any, chosen by the incapacitated person before the person became incapacitated by way of a durable power of attorney pursuant to section 4 of P.L.2000, c.109 (C.46:2B-8.4), health care proxy or advance directive.

The Office of the Public Guardian for Elderly Adults shall have the authority to not accept guardianship in cases determined by the public guardian to be inappropriate or in conflict with the office.

§ 3B:12-26. Action against incapacitated person when guardian newly appointed; leave of court required

No action shall be brought or maintained against an incapacitated person within one month after appointment of a guardian except by leave of the court wherein the action is to be brought or maintained.

§ 3B:12-27. Distribution of property of an incapacitated person as intestate property

If an incapacitated person dies intestate or without any will except one which was executed after commencement of proceedings which ultimately resulted in adjudicating a person incapacitated and before a judgment has been entered adjudicating a return to competency, the person's property shall descend and be distributed as in the case of intestacy.

§ 3B:12-28. Return to competency; restoration of estate

The Superior Court may, on summary action filed by the person adjudicated incapacitated or the guardian, adjudicate that the incapacitated person has returned to full or partial competency and restore to that person his civil rights and estate as it exists at the time of the return to competency if the court is satisfied that the person has recovered his sound reason and is fit to govern himself and manage his affairs, or, in the case of an incapacitated person determined to be incapacitated by reason of chronic alcoholism, that the person has reformed and become habitually sober and has continued so for one year next preceding the commencement of the action, and in the case of an incapacitated person determined to be incapacitated by reason of chronic use of drugs that the person has reformed and has not been a chronic user of drugs for one year next preceding the commencement of the action.

§ 3B:12-29. Appointment of guardian of the property for nonresident incapacitated person [Repealed]

§ 3B:12-30. Appointment of guardian of adult by parents or spouse or domestic partner; judgment confirming appointment

The parents who have been appointed the guardian of an unmarried incapacitated person or the spouse or domestic partner as defined in section 3 of P.L. 2003, c. 246 (C.26:8A-3) who has been appointed the guardian of an incapacitated person may, by will, appoint a testamentary guardian of the person, or a guardian of the estate, or of both the person and estate of the incapacitated person. Before the appointment of a testamentary guardian becomes effective, the person designated as the testamentary guardian shall apply to the court in a summary manner, upon notice to the incapacitated person, to any guardian who may have been appointed for the incapacitated person, to the person or institution having the care of the incapacitated person and to such heirs as the court may direct, for a judgment confirming that appointment under the will.

§ 3B:12-31. Consent by surviving parent to guardian's appointment

Where an appointment of a testamentary guardian is made by a parent under N.J.S.3B:12-30 and the other parent survives the appointing parent, the appointment shall be effective only when the surviving parent, at or before the issuance of letters, consents to the appointment in writing and signs and acknowledges the consent in the presence of two witnesses present at the same time who subscribe their names as witnesses thereto in the presence of the surviving parent, unless the surviving parent has been adjudged an incapacitated person.

§ 3B:12-32. Temporary appointment of guardian if person not adjudicated an incapacitated person

If the person for whom a testamentary guardian has been appointed under the will of a parent, spouse or domestic partner as defined in section 3 of P.L. 2003, c. 246 (C.26:8A-3)has not been adjudicated as an incapacitated person in accordance with N.J.S.3B:12-24 and the Rules Governing the Courts of New Jersey, the person named as the testamentary guardian may apply to the court in the manner provided in N.J.S.3B:12-30 for a judgment designating that person as the temporary guardian of the person or of the estate, or of both the person and estate of the alleged incapacitated person until the issue of incapacity has been determined. Upon the determination of the issue of incapacity, the court shall either enter a judgment confirming the appointment of the testamentary guardian or vacating the appointment of the temporary guardian.

§ 3B:12-33. Bond of testamentary guardian

Before receiving his letters, a testamentary guardian of an incapacitated person shall give bond in accordance with N.J.S.3B:15-1 unless the guardian is relieved from doing so by direction of the will of the parent, spouse or domestic partner as defined in section 3 of P.L.2003, c.246 (C.26:8A-3) appointing the guardian. However, regardless of any direction, the guardian shall, with respect to property to which the ward is or shall be entitled from any source, other than the parent, spouse or domestic partner as defined in section 3 of P.L.2003, c.246 (C.26:8A-3) or other than any policy of life insurance upon the life of the parent, spouse or domestic partner as defined in section 3 of P.L.2003, c.246 (C.26:8A-3), give bond in accordance with that section before exercising any authority or control over that property.

The provisions of this section relieving a testamentary guardian of an incapacitated person from giving bond by direction of the will of the parent, spouse or domestic partner shall not apply to a testamentary guardian of a minor with a developmental disability. Such guardian shall be bonded pursuant to paragraph (1) of subsection i. of N.J.S.3B:15-1, unless the guardian is relieved from doing so pursuant to paragraph (2) of subsection i. of N.J.S.3B:15-1.

§ 3B:12-34. Determination into fitness of a testamentary guardian of the person of an incapacitated person

If a will appointing a testamentary guardian of the person of an incapacitated person has been or is to be probated in the Surrogate's Court of any county or the Superior Court, the Superior Court may, in an action brought upon notice to the ward and guardian named in the will, inquire into the present custody of the incapacitated person, and make any order touching the testamentary guardianship as may be for the best interest and welfare of the incapacitated person.

§ 3B:12-35. Effect of a testamentary appointment

The appointment of a testamentary guardian of the person of an incapacitated person or his estate shall be good and effectual against any other person claiming the guardianship over or custody of the incapacitated person or his estate, as the case may be.

§ 3B:12-36. Authority of court with respect to ward's person and estate

If a guardian has been appointed as to the person of a minor or an incapacitated person, the court shall have authority over the ward's person and all matters relating thereto; and if a guardian has been appointed to the estate of a minor or an incapacitated person, the court shall have authority over the ward's estate, and all matters relating thereto.

§ 3B:12-37. Letters of guardianship to state any limitations at the time of appointment or later

If the court limits any power conferred on the guardian, the limitation shall be so stated in certificates of letters of guardianship thereafter issued.

§ 3B:12-38. Title to ward's property vested in guardian as trustee

The appointment of a guardian of the estate of a minor or an incapacitated person vests in him title as trustee to all property of his ward, presently held or thereafter acquired, including title to any property theretofore held for the ward by attorneys in fact. The appointment of a guardian is not a transfer or alienation within the meaning of general provisions of any Federal or State statute or regulation, insurance policy, pension plan, contract, will or trust instrument, imposing restrictions upon or penalties for transfer or alienation by the ward of his rights or interest, but this section does not restrict the ability of persons to make specific provision by contract or dispositive instrument relating to a guardian.

§ 3B:12-39. Delegation of parent's or guardian's powers regarding ward's care, custody or property; limitations

A parent, other than where custody of a minor has been awarded by a court of competent jurisdiction, with the consent of the other parent, if the latter is living and not an incapacitated person or a guardian of the person of a minor or an incapacitated person, by a properly executed power of attorney, may delegate to another person, for a period not exceeding six months, any of his powers regarding care, custody, or property of the minor child or ward, except his power to consent to marriage or adoption of a minor ward.

§ 3B:12-40. Duty of guardian of ward's person to account to guardian of his estate

If another person has been appointed guardian of the estate, all of the ward's estate received by the guardian of the person in excess of those funds expended to meet current expenses for support, care and education of the ward must be paid to the guardian of the estate, and the guardian of the person must account to the guardian of the estate for funds expended.

§ 3B:12-41. Guardian of ward's person entitled to reimbursement for expenses; payments to third persons

If another person has been appointed guardian of the ward's estate, the guardian of the ward's person is entitled to receive reasonable reimbursement and fees for his services and for room and board furnished to the ward, provided the same has been agreed upon between the guardian of the person and the guardian of the estate; and provided, further, that the amounts agreed upon are reasonable under the circumstances. The guardian of the person may request the guardian of the estate to expend the ward's estate by payment to third persons or institutions for the ward's care and maintenance.

§ 3B:12-42. Reporting condition of ward's person and property to court

A guardian shall report at time intervals as ordered by the court, unless otherwise waived by the court, the condition of the ward and the condition of the ward's estate which has been subject to the guardian's possession or control as ordered by the court.

a. A report by the guardian of the person shall state or contain:
(1) the current mental, physical and social condition of the ward;
(2) the living arrangements for all addresses of the ward during the reporting period;
(3) the medical, educational, vocational and other services provided to the ward and the guardian's opinions as to the adequacy of the ward's care;
(4) a summary of the guardian's visits with the ward and activities on the ward's behalf and the extent to which the ward has participated in decision-making;
(5) if the ward is institutionalized, whether or not the guardian considers the current plan for care, treatment or habilitation to be in the ward's best interest;
(6) plans for future care; and
(7) a recommendation as to the need for continued guardianship and any recommended changes in the scope of the guardianship.
b. The court may appoint an individual to review a report, interview the ward or guardian and make any other investigation the court directs.
c. Agencies authorized to act pursuant to P.L.1985, c. 298 (C.52:27G-20 et seq.), P.L.1985, c. 145 (C.30:6D-23 et seq.), P.L.1965, c. 59 (C.30:4-165.1 et seq.) and P.L.1970, c. 289 (C.30:4-165.7 et seq.) and public officials appointed as limited guardians of the person for medical purposes for individuals in psychiatric facilities listed in R.S.30:1-7 shall be exempt from this section.

§ 3B:12-43. Expenditures to be made by guardian out of ward's estate

A guardian of the estate of a minor or incapacitated person may expend or distribute so much or all of the income or principal of his ward for the support, maintenance, education, general use and benefit of the ward and his dependents, in the manner, at the time or times and to the extent that the guardian, in an exercise of a reasonable discretion, deems suitable and proper, taking into account the requirements of the "Prudent Investor Act," P.L.1997, c.36 (C.3B:20-11.1 et seq.), with or without court order, with due regard to the duty and ability of any person to support or provide for the ward if the ward is a minor, and without due regard to the duty and ability of any person to support or provide for the ward if the ward is an incapacitated person, and with or without regard to any other funds, income or property which may be available for that purpose.

§ 3B:12-44. Recommendations to be considered by guardian of ward's estate in making expenditures

In making expenditures under N.J.S.3B:12-43, the guardian of the estate of a minor or incapacitated person shall consider recommendations relating to the appropriate standard of support, education and benefit for the ward made by a parent or guardian of the person, if any. The guardian of the estate may not be surcharged for sums paid to persons or organizations actually furnishing support, education or care to the ward pursuant to the recommendations of a parent or guardian of the person unless the guardian knows that the parent or the guardian is deriving personal financial benefit therefrom, or unless the recommendations are clearly not in the best interests of the ward.

§ 3B:12-45. Other factors to be considered by guardian of ward's estate in making expenditures

In making expenditures under N.J.S.3B:12-43, the guardian of the estate of a minor or incapacitated person shall expend or distribute sums reasonably necessary for the support, education, care or benefit of the ward with due regard to:
a. The size of the ward's estate;
b. The probable duration of the guardianship and the likelihood that the ward, at some future time, may be fully able to manage his affairs and the estate which has been conserved for him; and
c. The accustomed standard of living of the ward and members of the ward's household.

§ 3B:12-46. Persons for whose benefit expenditures may be made by guardian of ward's estate

The guardian of the estate of a minor or incapacitated person may expend funds of the ward's estate under N.J.S.3B:12-43 for the support of persons legally dependent on the ward and others who are members of the ward's household who are unable to support themselves, and who are in need of support.

§ 3B:12-47. Persons to whom funds may be paid

Funds expended by the guardian of the estate of a minor or an incapacitated person under N.J.S.3B:12-43 may be paid by the guardian to any person, including the ward, to reimburse for expenditures which the guardian might have made, or in advance for services to be rendered to the ward when it is reasonable to expect that they will be performed and where advance payments are customary or reasonably necessary under the circumstances.

§ 3B:12-48. Powers conferred upon a guardian

A guardian of the estate of a minor or an incapacitated person has all of the powers conferred upon the guardian by law and the provisions of this chapter except as limited by the judgment. These powers shall specifically include the right to file or defend any litigation on behalf of the ward, including but not limited to, the right to bring an action for divorce or annulment on any grounds authorized by law.

§ 3B:12-49. Powers conferred upon the court

The court has, for the benefit of the ward, the ward's dependents and members of his household, all the powers over the ward's estate and affairs which he could exercise, if present and not under a disability, except the power to make a will, and may confer those powers upon a guardian of the estate. These powers include, but are not limited to, the power to convey or release the ward's present and contingent and expectant interests in real and personal property, including dower and curtesy and any right of survivorship incident to joint tenancy or tenancy by the entirety, to exercise or release the ward's powers as trustee, personal representative, custodian for minor, guardian, or donee of a power of appointment, to enter into contracts, to create revocable or irrevocable trusts of property of the estate which may extend beyond the ward's disability or life, to exercise the ward's options to purchase securities or other property, to exercise the ward's rights to elect options and change beneficiaries under insurance annuity policies and to surrender the policies for their cash value, to exercise the ward's right to an elective share in the estate of the ward's deceased spouse or domestic partner as defined in section 3 of P.L.2003, c. 246 (C.26:8A-3) to the extent permitted by law and to renounce any interest by testate or intestate succession or by inter vivos transfer and to engage in planning utilizing public assistance programs consistent with current law.

§ 3B:12-50. Additional powers which may be exercised by the court

The court may exercise, or direct the exercise of, or release the powers of appointment of which the ward is donee, to renounce interests, to make gifts in trust or otherwise, or to change beneficiaries under insurance and annuity policies, only if satisfied, after notice and hearing, that it is in the best interests of the ward.

§ 3B:12-51. Powers and responsibilities of a guardian of the person of a minor generally

A guardian of the person of a minor has the powers and responsibilities of a parent who has not been deprived of custody of his minor and unemancipated child, except that a guardian is not legally obligated to provide for the ward from his own funds.

§ 3B:12-52. Powers and duties of a guardian of the person of a minor

In particular, and without qualifying the provisions of N.J.S. 3B:12-51, a guardian of the person of a minor has the following powers and duties, except as modified by order of the court:

a. He must take reasonable care of his ward's personal effects and institute an action for the appointment of a guardian of his ward's estate if necessary to protect it;

b. He may receive periodically money payable for the support of the ward to the ward's parent, guardian or custodian under the terms of any statutory benefit or insurance system, or any private contract, devise, trust, conservatorship or custodianship. Any sums so received shall be applied to the ward's current needs for support, care and education in the exercise of a reasonable discretion, with or without court order, with due regard to the duty or ability of any person to support or provide for the ward and with or without regard to any other funds, income or property which may be available for that purpose. He must exercise due care to conserve any excess funds for the ward's future needs unless a guardian has been appointed for the estate of the ward, in which case the excess shall be paid over at least annually to that guardian. He may institute an action to compel the performance by any person of a duty to support the ward or to pay sums for the welfare of the ward;

c. He is empowered to facilitate the ward's education, social, or other activities and to authorize medical or other professional care, treatment, or advice. He is not liable by reason of this consent for injury to the ward resulting from the negligence or acts of third persons unless it would have been illegal for a parent to have consented. He may consent to the marriage or adoption of his ward or to his ward's military service.

§ 3B:12-53. Powers and duties of a guardian of the estate of an unmarried minor as guardian of the minor's person

A guardian of the estate of an unmarried minor, as to whom no one has parental rights, has the duties and powers of a guardian of the person of a minor described in this article until the minor attains the age of 18 or marries, but the parental rights so conferred on a guardian of an estate do not preclude appointment of a guardian of the person.

§ 3B:12-54. Duty of guardian to deliver property when minor attains 18 years of age

Except as provided in section 2 of P.L.2003, c.258 (C.3B:12-54.1), when a minor who has not been adjudged an incapacitated person attains 18 years of age, his guardian, after meeting all prior claims and expenses of administration, shall pay over and distribute all funds and properties to the former ward as soon as possible.

§ 3B:12-54.1. Trusts for certain beneficiaries providing deferred distribution of funds

In the event that any part of an intestate estate passes to the decedent's issue pursuant to N.J.S.3B:5-4, and if any such issue shall not have attained the age of 18 at the time such part of the intestate estate would pass to such issue, such part may pass as follows:

a. The parent or guardian of such issue or any other individual with standing may apply to the Superior Court, Chancery Division, Probate Part in the county in which the decedent was domiciled for permission to place all, or any part, of the funds passing to such issue in a separate trust for the exclusive benefit of such issue.

b. The terms of the trust may provide as follows:

(1) The trust assets and the income therefrom shall be used for the exclusive benefit of the beneficiary, including but not limited to the beneficiary's health, support, maintenance and education, including college and post-graduate work, in the discretion of the trustees;

(2) The beneficiary shall have the right to request distributions of trust principal as follows: one-third of the principal after attaining the age of 25 years, one-half of the then balance after attaining the age of 30 years, and all of the then balance after attaining the age of 35 years; or at such other ages as the court, in its discretion, shall determine;

(3) Should the beneficiary die prior to the termination of the trust, the remaining trust principal and accrued income shall be distributed to the beneficiary's estate;

(4) Two individual trustees, or one corporate trustee, or a combination thereof, shall serve at all times, with or without bond, as the court shall determine in its discretion; and

(5) Such other terms and conditions of the trust as the court shall determine in its discretion.

c. In ruling on such an application, the court:

(1) may allow any award from the federal "September 11th Victim Compensation Fund of 2001" to be the subject of a trust created pursuant to this section or be included in such a trust, regardless of whether such an award is found to pass to a minor issue of the decedent pursuant to N.J.S.3B:5-4 or otherwise; and

(2) shall consider all relevant factors, including but not limited to the amount of money involved, the availability of other resources for current maintenance and support, the stability of the entity offering an investment covered by the application, income tax consequences, any special needs or vulnerabilities of the minor and the financial and psychological consequences of putting all or a substantial part of the minor's estate out of reach for a long period of time.

d. The court shall retain jurisdiction of the trust until its termination. The beneficiary's parent, guardian, trustee or other individual with standing, including the beneficiary if he or she has attained the age of 18 years, may apply to the court at any time for modifications to the terms of the trust. Modifications may be made in the court's discretion.

§ 3B:12-55. When authority and responsibility of guardian terminate

The authority and responsibility of a guardian of the person or estate of a minor terminate upon the death, resignation or removal of the guardian or upon the minor's death, adoption, marriage or attainment of 18 years of age, but termination does not affect the guardian's liability for prior acts, nor his obligation to account for funds and assets of his ward. Resignation of a guardian does not terminate the guardianship unless it has been approved by a judgment of the court.

§ 3B:12-56. Powers, rights and duties of a guardian of the person of a ward generally

a. A guardian of the person of a ward is not legally obligated to provide for the ward from his own funds.

b. A guardian of the person of a ward is not liable to a third person for acts of the ward solely by reason of the relationship and is not liable for injury to the ward resulting from the wrongful conduct of a third person providing medical or other care, treatment or service for the ward except to the extent that the guardian of the ward failed to exercise reasonable care in choosing the provider.

c. If a ward has previously executed a valid power of attorney for health care or advance directive under P.L.1991, c.201 (C.26:2H-53 et seq.), or revocation pursuant to section 5 of P.L.1991, c.201 (C.26:2H-57), a guardian of the ward shall act consistent with the terms of such document unless revoked or altered by the court.

d. To the extent specifically ordered by the court for good cause shown, the guardian of the person of the ward may initiate the voluntary admission, as defined in section 2 of P.L.1987, c.116 (C.30:4-27.2), of a ward to a State psychiatric facility, as defined in section 2 of P.L.1987, c.116 (C.30:4-27.2), or a private psychiatric facility. A ward so admitted shall be entitled to all of the rights of a voluntarily admitted patient, which rights shall be exercised on behalf of the ward by the guardian. The guardian of the ward shall exercise the ward's rights in a manner consistent with the wishes of the ward except to the extent that compliance with those wishes would create a significant risk to the health or safety of the ward. If the wishes of the ward are not ascertainable with reasonable efforts, the guardian of the ward shall exercise the ward's rights in a manner consistent with the best interests of the ward. Notwithstanding the provisions of this section to the contrary, if the ward objects to the initiation of voluntary admission for psychiatric treatment or to the continuation of that voluntary admission, the State's procedures for involuntary commitment pursuant to P.L.1987, c.116 (C.30:4-27.1 et seq.) shall apply. If the ward objects to any other decision of the guardian of the ward pursuant to this section, this objection shall be brought to the attention of the Superior Court, Chancery Division, Probate Part, which may, in its discretion, appoint an attorney or guardian ad litem for the ward, hold a hearing or enter such orders as may be appropriate in the circumstances.

§ 3B:12-57. Powers and duties of a guardian of the person of a ward

a. (Deleted by amendment, P.L.2005, c.304.)

b. (Deleted by amendment, P.L.2005, c.304.)

c. (Deleted by amendment, P.L.2005, c.304.)

d. (Deleted by amendment, P.L.2005, c.304.)

e. (Deleted by amendment, P.L.2005, c.304.)

f. In accordance with Section 12 of P.L.2005, c.304 (C.3B:12-24.1), a guardian of the person of a ward shall exercise authority over matters relating to the rights and best interest of the ward's personal needs, only to the extent adjudicated by a court of competent jurisdiction. In taking or forbearing from any action affecting the personal needs of a ward, a guardian shall give due regard to the preferences of the ward, if known to the guardian or otherwise ascertainable upon reasonable inquiry. To the extent that it is consistent with the terms of any order by a court of competent jurisdiction, the guardian shall:

(1) take custody of the ward and establish the ward's place of abode in or outside of this State;

(2) personally visit the ward or if a public agency which is authorized to act pursuant to P.L.1965, c.59 (C.30:4-165.1 et seq.) and P.L.1970, c.289 (C.30:4-165.7 et seq.) or the Office of the Public Guardian pursuant to P.L. 1985, c.298 (C.52:27G-20 et seq.) or their representatives which may include a private or public agency, visits the ward not less than once every three months, or as deemed appropriate by the court, and otherwise maintain sufficient contact with the ward to know his capacities, limitations, needs, opportunities and physical and mental health;

(3) provide for the care, comfort and maintenance and, whenever appropriate, the education and training of the ward;

(4) subject to the provisions of subsection c. of N.J.S.3B:12-56, give or withhold any consents or approvals that may be necessary to enable the ward to receive medical or other professional care, counsel, treatment or service;

(5) take reasonable care of the ward's clothing, furniture, vehicles and other personal effects and, where appropriate, sell or dispose of such effects to meet the current needs of the ward;

(6) institute an action for the appointment of a guardian of the property of the ward, if necessary for the protection of the property;

(7) develop a plan of supportive services for the needs of the ward and a plan to obtain the supportive services;

(8) if necessary, institute an action against a person having a duty to support the ward or to pay any sum for the ward's welfare in order to compel the performance of the duties;

(9) receive money, payable from any source for the current support of the ward, and tangible personal property deliverable to the ward. Any sums so received shall be applied to the ward's current needs for support, health care, education and training in the exercise of the guardian's reasonable discretion, with or without court order, with or without regard to the duty or ability of any person to support or provide for the ward and with or without regard to any other funds, income or property that may be available for that purpose, unless an application is made to the court to establish a supplemental needs trust or other trust arrangement. However, the guardian may not use funds from the ward's estate for room and board, which the guardian, the guardian's spouse or domestic partner as defined in section 3 of P.L.2003, c. 246 (C.26:8A-3), parent or child have furnished the ward, unless agreed to by a guardian of the ward's estate pursuant to N.J.S.3B:12-41, or unless a charge for the service is approved by order of the court made upon notice to at least one of the heirs of the ward, if possible. The guardian shall exercise care to conserve any excess funds for the ward's needs; and

(10) If necessary, institute an action that could be maintained by the ward including but not limited to, actions alleging fraud, abuse, undue influence and exploitation.

g. In the exercise of the foregoing powers, the guardian shall encourage the ward to participate with the guardian in the decision-making process to the maximum extent of the ward's ability in order to encourage the ward to act on his own behalf whenever he is able to do so, and to develop or regain higher capacity to make decisions in those areas in which he is in need of guardianship services, to the maximum extent possible.

§ 3B:12-58. Gifts to charities and other objects

If the estate is ample to provide for the purposes implicit in the distributions authorized by this article, a guardian for the estate of an incapacitated person may apply to the court for authority to make gifts to charity and other objects as the ward might have been expected to make.

§ 3B:12-59. Purchase of real property for use of an incapacitated person and his dependents

When it shall appear to the court that it would be advantageous to the incapacitated person and to those legally dependent upon him for their support or are members of the incapacitated person's household, or any of them, if a dwelling house and a lot of land were purchased or a lot of land were purchased and a dwelling house built thereon, for the use of the incapacitated person and to those legally dependent upon him for their support or who are members of the incapacitated person's household, or any of them, the court may direct the guardian of his estate to purchase a house and lot or to purchase a lot and build a dwelling house thereon and to enter into contracts therefor as the court shall deem advisable, and to expend all necessary funds from the ward's estate for that purpose.

§ 3B:12-60. Guardian's duty with respect to will of deceased incapacitated person

Upon the death of an incapacitated person, the guardian shall deliver to the Surrogate of the county where the incapacitated person resided prior to death for safekeeping any will of the deceased person which may have come into the guardian's possession, inform the executor or a beneficiary named therein that he has done so, and retain the estate for delivery to a duly appointed personal representative of the decedent or other persons entitled thereto.

§ 3B:12-61. Power of guardian to act as personal representative of the estate of a deceased incapacitated person

If within 40 days after the death of an incapacitated person, no other person has been appointed personal representative and no action for an appointment is pending in the Superior Court or Surrogate's court of the county where the incapacitated person resided at his death, the guardian may apply to the Superior Court for authority to exercise the powers and duties of a personal representative so that he may proceed to administer and distribute the decedent's estate without additional or further appointment. Upon application for an order granting the powers of a personal representative to a guardian, after notice to all persons interested in the incapacitated person's estate either as heirs or devisees and including any person nominated executor in any will of which the applicant is aware, the court may order the conferral of those powers, upon determining that there is no objection, and may enter judgment that the guardian has all of the powers and duties of a personal representative. The making and entry of a judgment under this section shall have the effect of an order of appointment of a personal representative, except that the estate in the name of the guardian, after administration, may be distributed to persons entitled to the decedent's estate under his will or the laws of intestacy without prior retransfer to the guardian as personal representative.

§ 3B:12-62. Factors to be considered by the court or guardian in exercising certain powers

In investing the estate, and in selecting assets of the estate for distribution under this article, in utilizing powers of revocation or withdrawal available for the support of the ward, and other powers exercisable by the guardian or a court, the guardian or the court should take into account any known estate plan of the ward, including his will, any revocable trust of which he is settlor, and any contract, transfer or joint ownership arrangement with provisions for payment or transfer of benefits or interests at his death to another or others which he may have originated. The guardian may examine the will of the ward.

§ 3B:12-63. Guardian's final account and delivery of property upon termination of guardianship

Upon termination of the guardianship, pursuant to N.J.S.3B:12-64 the guardian, after the allowance of his final account, shall pay over and distribute all funds and properties of the former ward or to the estate of the former ward in accordance with the order of the court.

§ 3B:12-64. When authority and responsibility of guardian terminate

a. The authority and responsibility of a guardian of the person or estate of an incapacitated person terminate upon:
(1) the death, resignation or removal of the guardian;
(2) upon the death of the incapacitated person; or
(3) upon the entry of a judgment adjudicating the restoration of competency or termination of guardianship for other reasons.
b. However, termination does not affect the guardian's liability for prior acts, nor the guardian's obligation to account for funds and assets of the ward.
c. Notwithstanding the termination of the guardianship, the guardian may make final burial and funeral arrangements if the body remains unclaimed for five days and may pay for burial and funeral costs, Surrogate fees of administration, probate and bond from the guardianship account. Resignation of a guardian does not terminate the guardianship unless it has been approved by a judgment of the court.
d. Upon the death of an incapacitated person the guardian shall provide written notification to the Surrogate and shall provide the Surrogate with a copy of the death certificate within seven days of the guardian's receipt of the death certificate.

Article 6. Substituted Guardian

§ 3B:12-65. Vacancy in guardianship

A vacancy in a guardianship shall be deemed to arise when a sole or sole surviving or remaining guardian dies, resigns or is removed or discharged after entering upon but before completing the duties of his office. The resignation of a guardian shall not be effective unless approved by a judgment of the court.

§ 3B:12-66. Filling vacancy in guardianship

The Superior Court, or the Surrogate's court in the case of a minor, shall have jurisdiction to fill the vacancy by the appointment of a substituted guardian. The Superior Court may fill the vacancy in case of a guardian of a minor or where letters of guardianship were granted by the Superior Court or when removing or discharging the guardian. The Surrogate's court may fill the vacancy in the case of a guardian of a minor where letters were granted by the Surrogate's Court.

§ 3B:12-66.1. Removal from New Jersey after appointment of guardian

a. A guardian appointed in this State desiring to move to another state with his ward who is a minor shall obtain an order from the Superior Court of this State consenting to the minor's removal and if applicable, the guardian's discharge. The Superior Court may transfer the guardianship to another state if the court is satisfied that a transfer will serve the best interest of the minor.
b. The minor's removal and discharge of the guardian shall be on such terms as the Superior Court deems necessary, including requiring filing and settlement of the guardian's account and filing of an exemplified copy of the order evidencing the other state court's acceptance of jurisdiction over the guardianship and the guardian.

§ 3B:12-66.2. Transfer into New Jersey of guardianship established in another state

a. A guardian or like fiduciary of a minor appointed in another state may file a summary action in the Superior Court for the transfer of the guardianship and the appointment as a guardian in this State if domicile in this State is or will be established.
b. Notice of hearing shall be given to the minor and to the persons who would be entitled to notice if the regular procedures for appointment of a guardian under the New Jersey Rules of Court were applicable.
c. The Superior Court shall grant an application for the transfer of a guardianship established in another state unless the court determines that the proposed guardianship is a collateral attack on an existing or proposed guardianship or the transfer and appointment would not be in the best interest of the minor.

d. An exemplified record of a court of competent jurisdiction evidencing the original proceeding adjudicating the minor's incapacity and any amendment or modification orders entered subsequent to the original judgment shall be filed with the Superior Court. Subject to due process principles, full faith and credit may be accorded to a court of another state's determination of the minor's incapacity. The Superior Court may fix the rights, powers, and duties of the guardian that the court determines are necessary to administer the minor's person or estate, or both person and estate, in this State.

e. The guardian shall give notice of the application to transfer guardianship to the court of the other state.

Article 7. Standby Guardianship Act

§ 3B:12-67. Short title

This act shall be known and may be cited as the "New Jersey Standby Guardianship Act."

§ 3B:12-68. Findings, declarations

The Legislature finds and declares that there is an imperative need to create an expeditious manner of establishing a guardianship known as a standby guardianship, in order to enable a custodial parent or legal custodian suffering from a progressive chronic condition or a fatal illness to make plans for the permanent future care or the interim care of a child without terminating parental or legal rights. The Legislature further finds that current law does not adequately address the needs of custodial parents or legal custodians who are suffering from a progressive chronic condition or a fatal illness and who desire to make plans for the future care of their children without terminating parental or legal rights.

§ 3B:12-69. Definitions

As used in P.L.1995, c.76 (C.3B:12-67 et seq.):

"Appointed standby guardian" means a person appointed pursuant to section 6 of P.L.1995, c.76 (C.3B:12-72) to assume the duties of guardian over the person and, when applicable, the property of a minor child upon the death or a determination of incapacity or debilitation, and with the consent, of the parent or legal custodian.

"Attending physician" means the physician who has primary responsibility for the treatment and care for the petitioning parent or legal custodian. When more than one physician shares this responsibility, or when a physician is acting on the primary physician's behalf, any such physician may act as the attending physician pursuant to this act. When no physician has this responsibility, a physician who is familiar with the petitioner's medical condition may act as the attending physician pursuant to P.L.1995, c.76 (C.3B:12-67 et seq.).

"Consent" means written consent signed by the parent or legal custodian in the presence of two witnesses who shall also sign the document. The written consent shall constitute the terms for the commencement of the duties of the standby guardian.

"Debilitation" means a chronic and substantial inability, as a result of a physically debilitating illness, disease, or injury, to care for one's minor child.

"Designated standby guardian" means a person designated pursuant to section 8 of P.L.1995, c.76 (C.3B:12-74) to assume temporarily the duties of guardianship over the person and, when applicable, the property of a minor child upon the death or a determination of incapacity or debilitation, and with the consent, of the parent or legal custodian.

"Designation" means a written document voluntarily executed by the designator pursuant to P.L.1995, c.76.

"Designator" means a competent parent or legal custodian of a minor child who makes a designation pursuant to P.L.1995, c.76.

"Determination of debilitation" means a written determination made by the attending physician which contains the physician's opinion to a reasonable degree of medical certainty regarding the nature, cause, extent, and probable duration of the parent's or legal custodian's debilitation.

"Determination of incapacity" means a written determination made by the attending physician which contains the physician's opinion to a reasonable degree of medical certainty regarding the nature, cause, extent, and probable duration of the parent's or legal custodian's incapacity.

"Incapacity" means a chronic and substantial inability, as a result of mental or organic impairment, to understand the nature and consequences of decisions concerning the care of one's minor child, and a consequent inability to make these decisions.

"Minor child" means a child under the age of eighteen years but excludes a child residing in a placement funded or approved by the Division of Child Protection and Permanency in the Department of Children and Families pursuant to either a voluntary placement agreement or court order.

"Triggering event" means an event stated in the designation, petition or decree which empowers the standby guardian to assume the duties of the office, which event may be the death, incapacity or debilitation, with the consent, of the custodial parent or legal custodian, whichever occurs first.

§ 3B:12-70. Jurisdiction

The surrogate's court of the county in which a minor child resides or has real or personal property shall have jurisdiction under this act pursuant to N.J.S. 3B:12-12.

§ 3B:12-71. Applicability

The provisions of N.J.S. 3B:12-1 et seq. shall apply to a standby guardian except as otherwise provided in this act.

§ 3B:12-72. Appointment of standby guardian by court

a. Upon petition of the parent, legal custodian or designated standby guardian, the court may appoint a standby guardian of a minor child. The court may also appoint an alternate standby guardian, if identified by the petitioner, to act if the appointed standby

guardian dies, becomes incapacitated, or otherwise refuses or is unable to assume the duties of the standby guardian after the death, incapacity or debilitation of the parent or legal custodian of the minor child.
b. A petition for the judicial appointment of a standby guardian of a minor child shall state:
(1) which triggering event or events shall cause the authority of the appointed standby guardian to become effective;
(2) that there is a significant risk that the parent or legal custodian will die, become incapacitated, or become debilitated as a result of a progressive chronic condition or a fatal illness; however, a petitioner shall not be required to submit medical documentation of the parent's or legal custodian's terminal status by his attending physician; and
(3) the name, address, and qualifications of the proposed standby guardian.
c. A parent or legal custodian petitioning the court pursuant to this section shall not be required to appear in court if unable to appear, except upon motion of the court or by any party and for good cause shown.
d. The court shall appoint the standby guardian if the court finds that there is a significant risk that the parent or legal custodian will die, become incapacitated, or become debilitated as a result of a progressive chronic condition or a fatal illness, and that the interests of the minor child would be promoted by the appointment of the standby guardian.
e. The decree appointing the standby guardian shall specify the triggering event which shall activate the authority of the standby guardian.
f. Upon petition for the appointment of a standby guardian by a person as specified in subsection a. of this section, notice shall be served on the minor child's parent or legal custodian, or the designated standby guardian, as appropriate, within 30 days of the filing. The court shall give preference to maintaining custody with either the parent or legal custodian, or the designated standby guardian, during the time that the petition is pending. Nothing in this section shall be construed to deprive any parent of parental rights. If the petition alleges that after diligent search, the parent or legal custodian cannot be found, the parent or legal custodian shall be served by notice delivered pursuant to New Jersey court rules. No notice is necessary to a parent who is deceased or whose parental rights have been previously terminated by court order or consent.

§ 3B:12-73. Immediate assumption of duties of appointed standby guardian; revocation in writing

a. Upon the occurrence of a triggering event set forth in a decree appointing a standby guardian, the standby guardian shall be empowered to assume the duties of his office immediately.
b. If the triggering event is the incapacity or debilitation of the parent or legal custodian, the attending physician shall provide a copy of his determination to the appointed standby guardian if the guardian's identity is known to the attending physician.
c. Within 60 days following the assumption of guardianship duties, the appointed standby guardian shall petition the court for confirmation. The confirmation petition shall include a determination of incapacity or debilitation or a death certificate, as appropriate.
d. The court shall confirm an appointed standby guardian named in accordance with this act and otherwise qualified to serve as guardian pursuant to N.J.S. 3B:12-1 et seq. unless there is a judicial determination of unfitness with regard to the appointed standby guardian.
e. A standby guardian appointed pursuant to section 6 of this act may decline appointment at any time before the assumption of his duties by filing a written statement to that effect with the court, with notice to be provided to the petitioner and to the minor child if the latter is 14 years of age or older.
f. Commencement of the duties of the standby guardian shall confer upon the appointed standby guardian shared authority with the custodial parent or legal custodian of the minor child, unless the petition states otherwise.
g. A parent or legal custodian may revoke a standby guardianship by executing a written revocation, filing it with the court where the petition was filed, and promptly notifying the appointed standby guardian of the revocation. An unwritten revocation may be considered by the court if the revocation can be proved by clear and convincing evidence submitted to the court.

§ 3B:12-74. Designation of standby guardian by parent

a. When the consent of a parent or legal custodian for the execution of a power of attorney delegating another person to exercise the parent's or legal custodian's powers is not appropriate or is unavailable pursuant to N.J.S. 3B:12-39, the other parent or legal custodian may execute a written statement to designate a standby guardian, as follows:
(1) The parent or legal custodian may choose a standby guardian by means of a written designation that names the standby guardian in the event of the designator's death, incapacity or debilitation. The written designation shall reasonably identify the designator, the minor child and the standby guardian.
(2) A written designation pursuant to this section shall be signed by the designator in the presence of two witnesses who shall also sign the designation. Another person may sign the written designation on the parent's or legal custodian's behalf if the parent or legal custodian is physically unable to do so, provided the designation is signed at the express request of the parent or legal custodian and in the presence of the parent or legal custodian and two witnesses.
(3) The designation shall state the triggering event by which the parent or legal custodian intends the designated standby guardianship of the minor child to be activated.
(4) A parent or legal custodian may designate an alternate standby guardian in the same document, and by the same manner, as the designation of a standby guardian.
b. A designation may, but need not, be in the following form:
DESIGNATION OF STANDBY GUARDIAN
I, (name of parent or legal custodian) hereby name (name, home address and telephone number of standby guardian) as designated standby guardian of (name of child(ren)), my child(ren).

By this consent and designation, I am providing that the designated standby guardian's authority shall take effect if and when the following event or events occur: (choose as follows):
(1) my attending physician concludes that I am mentally incapacitated, and thus unable to care for my child(ren); or
(2) my attending physician concludes that I am physically debilitated, and thus unable to care for my child(ren), and I consent in writing before two witnesses to the designated standby guardian's authority taking effect; or
(3) upon my death.
In the event that the person designated above is unable or unwilling to act as guardian to my child(ren), I hereby name (name, address and telephone number of alternate designated standby guardian), as alternate designated standby guardian of my child(ren). I understand that this designation will expire six months from the date of this designation, and that the authority of the designated standby guardian, if any, will cease, unless by that date either I or the designated standby guardian petitions the court for appointment as standby guardian pursuant to section 6 of P.L. 1995, c. 76 (C. 3B:12-72).
I hereby authorize that the person designated standby guardian as set forth above shall be provided with a copy of the attending physician's statement.
In the event that I am incapacitated or debilitated and a designated standby guardianship is activated pursuant to this statement, I declare that it is my intention to retain full parental rights to the extent consistent with my condition and, further, that I retain the authority to revoke the designated standby guardianship consistent with my rights herein at any time.
Designator's Signature:
Witness' Signature:
Address:
Date:
Witness' Signature:
Address:
Date:
c. Nothing in this section shall be construed to involuntarily deprive any parent of parental rights.

§ 3B:12-75. Immediate assumption of duties of designated standby guardian; revocation

a. Upon the occurrence of the triggering event stated in the written designation executed pursuant to section 8 of this act, the designated standby guardian shall be empowered to assume the duties of his office immediately.
b. If the triggering event is the designator's incapacity or debilitation, a copy of the attending physician's determination shall be provided to the designated standby guardian if the guardian's identity is known to the attending physician.
c. A designated standby guardian may decline the designation at any time before the assumption of his duties by notifying the designator of this refusal in writing.
d. Commencement of the designated standby guardian's duties shall confer upon the designated standby guardian shared authority with the custodial parent or legal custodian of the minor child, unless the designation of the parent or legal custodian states otherwise.
e. A designator may revoke a designation of standby guardianship by notifying the designated standby guardian orally or in writing or by any other act evidencing a specific intent to revoke the designation.

§ 3B:12-76. Petition for judicial appointment of designated standby guardian

a. Unless a petition for judicial appointment of a standby guardian is made by the designator or the designated standby guardian, the designation made under section 8 of this act shall expire six months from the date of the written designation.
b. In a proceeding for judicial appointment of a designated standby guardian, a designation shall constitute a rebuttable presumption that the designated standby guardian is capable of serving as guardian. In the event of the designator's death, a designation shall be deemed to confer a preference upon the designated standby guardian for the choice of a permanent guardian, notwithstanding any law to the contrary, subject to the rights of the other parent.
c. Except as set forth in this section, the petition for the judicial appointment of a designated standby guardian shall comply with the procedure set forth in section 6 of this act.

§ 3B:12-77. Notice of petition to child

Notice of a petition or designation filed with the court pursuant to this act shall be served upon the minor child for whom the standby guardianship is sought if the minor is 14 years of age or older. Notice to a minor child less than 14 years of age shall be served at the discretion of the court. The court may appoint a guardian ad litem or counsel to represent the child. The court shall consider the preferences of the minor child in the appointment of a standby guardian pursuant to this act.

§ 3B:12-78. Filing, delivery of appointment, designation

a. The county clerk, upon being paid the fees allowed by law, shall receive for filing any instrument appointing or designating a standby guardian pursuant to this act made by a domiciliary of the county, and shall give a written receipt therefor to the person delivering it. The filing of an appointment or designation of standby guardian shall be for the sole purpose of safekeeping and shall not affect the validity of the appointment or designation.
b. The appointment or designation shall be delivered only to: the parent or legal custodian who appointed or designated the standby guardian; or the person appointed or designated as standby guardian or alternate standby guardian; or the minor child, upon his request or the request of his legal representative, if applicable; or any other person directed by the court.

Chapter 12A. Kinship Legal Guardianship

§ 3B:12A-1. Findings, declarations relative to kinship legal guardianship

The Legislature finds and declares that:

a. There is an increase in the number of children who cannot reside with their parents due to the parents' incapacity or inability to perform the regular and expected functions of care and support of the child;

b. An increasing number of relatives, including grandparents, find themselves providing care on a long-term basis to these children without court approved legal guardianship status because the caregivers either are unable or unwilling to seek termination of the legal relationships between the birth parent and the child, particularly when it is the caregiver's own child or sibling who is the parent. In these cases, adoption of the child is neither feasible nor likely, and it is imperative that the State create an alternative, permanent legal arrangement for children and their caregivers. One such alternative arrangement, which does not require the termination of parental rights, is a court awarded kinship legal guardianship that is intended to be permanent and self-sustaining, as evidenced by the transfer to the caregiver of certain parental rights, but retains the birth parents' rights to consent to adoption, the obligation to pay child support, and the parents' right to have some ongoing contact with the child;

c. In considering kinship legal guardianship, the State is seeking to add another alternative, permanent placement option, beyond custody, without rising to the level of termination of parental rights, for caregivers in relationships where adoption is neither feasible nor likely; and

d. Therefore, it is in the public interest to create a new type of legal guardianship that addresses the needs of children and caregivers in long-term kinship relationships.

§ 3B:12A-2. Definitions relative to kinship legal guardianship

As used in sections 1 through 6 of P.L.2001, c.250 (C.3B:12A-1 et seq.):

"Caregiver" means a person over 18 years of age, other than a child's parent, who has a kinship relationship with the child and has been providing care and support for the child, while the child has been residing in the caregiver's home, for either the last 12 consecutive months or 15 of the last 22 months. "Caregiver" includes a resource family parent as defined in section 1 of P.L.1962, c.136 (C.30:4C-26.4).

"Child" means a person under 18 years of age, except as otherwise provided in P.L.2001, c.250 (C.3B:12A-1 et al.).

"Commissioner" means the Commissioner of Children and Families.

"Court" means the Superior Court, Chancery Division, Family Part.

"Department" means the Department of Children and Families.

"Division" means the Division of Child Protection and Permanency in the Department of Children and Families.

"Family friend" means a person who is connected to a child or the child's parent by an established positive psychological or emotional relationship that is not a biological or legal relationship.

"Home review" means the basic review of the information provided by the petitioner and a visit to the petitioner's home where the child will continue to reside, in accordance with the provisions of P.L.2001, c.250 (C.3B:12A-1 et al.) and pursuant to regulations adopted by the commissioner.

"Kinship caregiver assessment" means a written report prepared in accordance with the provisions of P.L.2001, c.250 (C.3B:12A-1 et al.) and pursuant to regulations adopted by the commissioner.

"Kinship legal guardian" means a caregiver who is willing to assume care of a child due to parental incapacity, with the intent to raise the child to adulthood, and who is appointed the kinship legal guardian of the child by the court pursuant to P.L.2001, c.250 (C.3B:12A-1 et al.). A kinship legal guardian shall be responsible for the care and protection of the child and for providing for the child's health, education and maintenance.

"Kinship relationship" means a family friend or a person with a biological or legal relationship with the child.

"Parental incapacity" means incapacity of such a serious nature as to demonstrate that the parent is unable, unavailable, or unwilling to perform the regular and expected functions of care and support of the child.

§ 3B:12A-3. Jurisdiction, venue

The Superior Court, Chancery Division, Family Part shall have jurisdiction under sections 1 through 6 of P.L. 2001, c. 250 (C. 3B:12A-1 et seq.). Venue of a kinship legal guardianship action shall be determined in accordance with the applicable Rules of Court.

§ 3B:12A-4. Rights, responsibilities, authority of kinship legal guardian

a.

(1) Except as provided in paragraph (2) of this subsection, a kinship legal guardian shall have the same rights, responsibilities and authority relating to the child as a birth parent, including, but not limited to: making decisions concerning the child's care and well-being; consenting to routine and emergency medical and mental health needs; arranging and consenting to educational plans for the child; applying for financial assistance and social services for which the child is eligible; applying for a motor vehicle operator's license; applying for admission to college; responsibility for activities necessary to ensure the child's safety, permanency and well-being; and ensuring the maintenance and protection of the child.

(2) A kinship legal guardian may not consent to the adoption of the child or a name change for the child. The birth parent of the child shall retain the authority to consent to the adoption of the child or a name change for the child.

(3) The birth parent of the child shall retain the obligation to pay child support.

(4) The birth parent of the child shall retain the right to visitation or parenting time with the child, as determined by the court.
(5) The appointment of a kinship legal guardian does not limit or terminate any rights or benefits derived from the child's parents, including, but not limited to, those relating to inheritance or eligibility for benefits or insurance.
(6) Kinship legal guardianship terminates when the child reaches 18 years of age or when the child is no longer continuously enrolled in a secondary education program, whichever event occurs later, or when kinship legal guardianship is otherwise terminated.
b. There shall be no filing fee charged for kinship legal guardianship complaints or motions in the court.
c. For the purposes of P.L. 2001, c. 250 (C. 3B:12A-1 et al.), a kinship legal guardian shall have the same meaning as the term "legal guardian" as defined in 42 U.S.C. § 675, except that the process, procedure and ruling for kinship legal guardianship shall be apart from, and shall not amend, supplant or contravene, the provisions of Chapter 12 of Title 3B of the New Jersey Statutes.
d.
(1) The provisions of P.L. 2001, c. 250 (C. 3B:12A-1 et al.) shall not be construed to grant or confer upon any person appointed kinship legal guardian of a child any of the additional rights or privileges accorded to persons appointed guardian of a minor's person or estate by a Surrogate or the Superior Court, Chancery Division, Probate Part pursuant to the provisions of Chapter 12 of Title 3B of the New Jersey Statutes.
(2) The provisions of P.L. 2001, c. 250 (C. 3B:12A-1 et al.) shall not be construed to preclude an application to the court for guardianship of the person or estate of a minor by any person appointed kinship legal guardian of a child.

§ 3B:12A-5. Appointment as kinship legal guardian; contents of petition

a. Upon petition of a caregiver, the court may appoint the caregiver as kinship legal guardian of a child residing in the caregiver's home pursuant to the provisions of P.L. 2001, c. 250 (C. 3B:12A-1 et al.).
b. A petition for the appointment of a kinship legal guardian shall include a kinship caregiver assessment, which shall contain:
(1) the full name and address of the person seeking to become the kinship legal guardian;
(2) the circumstances of the kinship relationship;
(3) the whereabouts of the child's parents, if known;
(4) the nature of the parents' incapacitation, if known;
(5) the wishes of the parents, if known;
(6) the ability of the kinship caregiver family to assume permanent care of the child;
(7) the child's property and assets, if known;
(8) the wishes of the child, if appropriate;
(9) any current involvement of a child with the division if the child has an open division case and is actively receiving services;
(10) certification from the caregiver that the caregiver has been providing care and support for the child, while the child has been residing in the caregiver's home, for at least the last 12 consecutive months;
(11) the results from a criminal history record background check and a domestic violence central registry check of the caregiver and any adult residing in the caregiver's household conducted pursuant to section 9 of P.L. 2001, c. 250 (C. 30:4C-86);
(12) the results from a child abuse record check arranged for and coordinated by the division pursuant to section 9 of P.L. 2001, c. 250 (C. 30:4C-86); and
(13) the results of the caregiver's home review.

§ 3B:12A-6. Considerations for appointment as kinship legal guardian

a. In making its determination about whether to appoint the caregiver as kinship legal guardian, the court shall consider:
(1) if proper notice was provided to the child's parents;
(2) the best interests of the child;
(3) the kinship caregiver assessment;
(4) in cases in which the division is involved with the child as provided in subsection a. of section 8 of P.L.2001, c.250 (C.30:4C-85), the recommendation of the division, including any parenting time or visitation restrictions;
(5) the potential kinship legal guardian's ability to provide a safe and permanent home for the child;
(6) the wishes of the child's parents, if known to the court;
(7) the wishes of the child if the child is 12 years of age or older, unless unique circumstances exist that make the child's age irrelevant;
(8) the suitability of the kinship caregiver and the caregiver's family to raise the child;
(9) the ability of the kinship caregiver to assume full legal responsibility for the child;
(10) the commitment of the kinship caregiver and the caregiver's family to raise the child to adulthood;
(11) the results from the child abuse record check conducted pursuant to section 9 of P.L.2001, c.250 (C.30:4C-86); and
(12) the results from the criminal history record background check and domestic violence check conducted pursuant to section 9 of P.L.2001, c.250 (C.30:4C-86). In any case in which the caregiver petitioning for kinship legal guardianship, or any adult residing in the prospective caregiver's home, has a record of criminal history or a record of being subjected to a final domestic violence restraining order under P.L.1991, c.261 (C.2C:25-17 et seq.), the court shall review the record with respect to the type and date of the criminal offense or the provisions and date of the final domestic violence restraining order and make a determination as to the suitability of the person to become a kinship legal guardian. For the purposes of this paragraph, with respect to criminal history, the court shall consider convictions for offenses specified in subsections c., d. and e. of section 1 of P.L.1985, c.396 (C.30:4C-26.8).

b. The court shall not award kinship legal guardianship of the child unless proper notice was served upon the parents of the child and any other party to whom the court has awarded custody or parenting time for that child, in accordance with the Rules of Court.

c. The court shall not award kinship legal guardianship of the child solely because of parental incapacity.

d. The court shall appoint the caregiver as a kinship legal guardian if, based upon clear and convincing evidence, the court finds that:

(1) each parent's incapacity is of such a serious nature as to demonstrate that the parents are unable, unavailable or unwilling to perform the regular and expected functions of care and support of the child;

(2) the parents' inability to perform those functions is unlikely to change in the foreseeable future;

(3) in cases in which the division is involved with the child as provided in subsection a. of section 8 of P.L.2001, c.250 (C.30:4C-85), (a) the division exercised reasonable efforts to reunify the child with the birth parents and these reunification efforts have proven unsuccessful or unnecessary; and (b) adoption of the child is neither feasible nor likely; and

(4) awarding kinship legal guardianship is in the child's best interests.

e. The court order appointing the kinship legal guardian shall specify, as appropriate, that:

(1) a kinship legal guardian shall have the same rights, responsibilities and authority relating to the child as a birth parent, including, but not limited to: making decisions concerning the child's care and well-being; consenting to routine and emergency medical and mental health needs; arranging and consenting to educational plans for the child; applying for financial assistance and social services for which the child is eligible; applying for a motor vehicle operator's license; applying for admission to college; responsibility for activities necessary to ensure the child's safety, permanency and well-being; and ensuring the maintenance and protection of the child; except that a kinship legal guardian may not consent to the adoption of the child or a name change for the child;

(2) the birth parent of the child retains the authority to consent to the adoption of the child or a name change for the child;

(3) the birth parent of the child retains the obligation to pay child support;

(4) the birth parent of the child retains the right to visitation or parenting time with the child, as determined by the court;

(5) the appointment of a kinship legal guardian does not limit or terminate any rights or benefits derived from the child's parents, including, but not limited to, those relating to inheritance or eligibility for benefits or insurance; and

(6) kinship legal guardianship terminates when the child reaches 18 years of age or when the child is no longer continuously enrolled in a secondary education program, whichever event occurs later, or when kinship legal guardianship is otherwise terminated.

f. An order or judgment awarding kinship legal guardianship may be vacated by the court prior to the child's 18th birthday if the court finds that the kinship legal guardianship is no longer in the best interests of the child or, in cases where there is an application to return the child to the parent, based upon clear and convincing evidence, the court finds that the parental incapacity or inability to care for the child that led to the original award of kinship legal guardianship is no longer the case and termination of kinship legal guardianship is in the child's best interests.

In cases in which the division was involved, when determining whether a child should be returned to a parent, the court may refer a parent for an assessment prepared by the division, in accordance with regulations adopted by the commissioner.

g. An order or judgment awarding kinship legal guardianship may be vacated by the court if, based upon clear and convincing evidence, the court finds that the guardian failed or is unable, unavailable or unwilling to provide proper care and custody of the child, or that the guardianship is no longer in the child's best interests.

§ 3B:12A-7. Court rules

The Supreme Court of New Jersey may adopt court rules to effectuate the purposes of this act.

§ 3B:12B-1. Short title

This act shall be known and may be cited as the "New Jersey Adult Guardianship and Protective Proceedings Jurisdiction Act."

§ 3B:12B-2. Scope of act

a. P.L.2012, c.36(C.3B:12B-1 et al.) governs the exercise of jurisdiction over guardianship or protective orders, as those terms are defined in P.L.2012, c.36 (C.3B:12B-1 et al.), when there are interstate conflicts or uncertainty regarding whether a court of this State or a court of another state should act. The act establishes uniform procedures that are intended to be used to facilitate proceedings between courts in different states and to resolve uncertainty about appropriate jurisdiction.

b. P.L.2012, c.36(C.3B:12B-1 et al.) is not intended to and does not alter substantive law pertaining to guardianship, conservatorship and protective proceedings, or arrangements and protective orders as defined elsewhere in Title 3B of the New Jersey Statutes or the original general jurisdiction of the Superior Court throughout the State in all causes.

§ 3B:12B-3. Definitions

As used in P.L.2012, c.36 (C.3B:12B-1 et al.), unless otherwise defined:

a. "Adult" means a person at least 18 years of age.

b. "Conservatee" means, as used in this State, a person who has not been adjudicated incapacitated but who by reason of advanced age, illness, or physical infirmity, is unable to care for or manage his property or has become unable to provide for himself or others dependent upon him for support.

c. "Conservator" means a person appointed by the court to administer the property of an adult who has not been adjudicated incapacitated, including a person appointed, as appropriate, under N.J.S.3B:13A-1 et seq.

d. "Court of this State" means the Superior Court of New Jersey.

e. "Guardian" means a person appointed by the court to make decisions regarding the person or estate of an incapacitated adult, including a person who has qualified as a guardian of the person or estate, or both, of an incapacitated person pursuant to court appointment in accordance with N.J.S.3B:12-1 et seq. or its equivalent in a state other than New Jersey.

f. "Guardianship order" means an order declaring a person incapacitated and appointing a guardian.

g. "Guardianship proceeding" means a judicial proceeding in which an order for the appointment of a guardian is sought or has been issued to declare a person incapacitated and to appoint a guardian.

h. "Home state" means the state in which the respondent was physically present, including any period of temporary absence, for at least six consecutive months immediately before the filing of a petition for the appointment of a guardian or a protective order; or if none, the state in which the respondent was physically present, including any period of temporary absence, for at least six consecutive months ending within the six months prior to the filing of the petition.

i. "Incapacitated person" means an adult declared incapacitated and for whom a guardian has been appointed.

j. "Party" means the respondent, petitioner or plaintiff, as applicable, guardian, conservator or conservatee, or any other person authorized by the court to participate in a guardianship or protective proceeding.

k. "Petition" means an initiating court document for proceedings under P.L.2012, c.36 (C.3B:12B-1 et al.). In New Jersey, a petition shall mean a verified complaint filed with the Superior Court pursuant to the Rules of Court of the State of New Jersey.

l. "Protected person" means an adult for whom a protective order has been issued.

m. "Protective order" means:

(1) An order related to an adult who has been declared incapacitated by a court or for whom such a declaration is sought, including, but not limited to, an arrangement or order related to management of the incapacitated person's property, which is issued pursuant to N.J.S.3B:12-1 and N.J.S.3B:12-2; or

(2) An order appointing a conservator, including, but not limited to, an order which is issued pursuant to N.J.S.3B:13A-1 et seq.; or

(3) An order to protect a "vulnerable adult" as that term is defined in section 2 of P.L.1993, c.249 (C.52:27D-407), including, but not limited to, an order which is issued pursuant to the "Adult Protective Services Act," P.L.1993, c.249 (C.52:27D-406 et seq.); or

(4) An order or arrangement, pursuant to N.J.S.3B:12-1, for a person for whom a declaration of incapacity is not sought.

The term "protective order," as used in P.L.2012, c.36 (C.3B:12B-1 et al.), shall not be construed to conflict with the provisions of N.J.S.3B:12-1 through N.J.S.3B:12-4.

n. "Protective proceeding" means a judicial proceeding in which a protective order is sought or has been issued.

o. "Record" means information that is inscribed on a tangible medium or that is stored in an electronic or other medium and is retrievable in perceivable form.

p. "Registration" means a filing in this State of a guardianship or conservatorship order of another state, pursuant to the Rules of Court of the State of New Jersey and in accordance with the provisions of section 19 of P.L.2012, c.36 (C.3B:12B-19).

q. "Respondent" means an adult for whom the appointment of a guardian or the issuance of a protective order is sought.

r. "Significant-connection state" means a state, other than the home state, with which a respondent has a significant connection other than mere physical presence and in which substantial evidence concerning the respondent is available.

s. "State" means a state of the United States, the District of Columbia, Puerto Rico, the United States Virgin Islands, a federally recognized Indian tribe, or any territory or insular possession subject to the jurisdiction of the United States.

§ 3B:12B-4. International application of the act

A court of this State may treat a foreign country as if it were a state for the purpose of applying all sections of P.L.2012, c.36 (C.3B:12B-1 et al.) except for sections 19 and 20 of P.L.2012, c.36 (C.3B:12B-19 and C.3B:12B-20) pertaining to registration.

§ 3B:12B-5. Which act governs; exclusive jurisdictional basis; applicability

P.L.2012, c.36(C.3B:12B-1 et al.) governs jurisdiction of guardianship proceedings and provides the exclusive jurisdictional basis for a court of this State to appoint a guardian or issue a protective order. The appointment of a guardian shall continue to be governed by N.J.S.3B:12-1 et seq. and the appointment of a conservator shall continue to be governed by N.J.S.3B:13A-1 et seq. P.L.2012, c.36(C.3B:12B-1 et al.) shall be construed and applied in conjunction with N.J.S.3B:12-1 et seq. and N.J.S.3B:13A-1 et seq.

§ 3B:12B-6. Communication between courts

a. A court of this State may communicate with a court of another state concerning a proceeding arising pursuant to P.L.2012, c.36 (C.3B:12B-1 et al.). The court may allow the parties to participate in the communication in accordance with the Rules Governing the Courts of the State of New Jersey.

b. Except as otherwise provided in subsection c., the court shall make a record of the communication. The record may be limited to the fact that the communication occurred.

c. Courts may communicate concerning schedules, calendars, court records, and other administrative matters without making a record.

§ 3B:12B-7. Cooperation between courts

a. In a guardianship or protective proceeding, a court of this State may request the appropriate court of another state to do any of the following:

(1) hold an evidentiary hearing;

(2) order a person in that state to produce evidence or give testimony pursuant to procedures of that state;

(3) order that an evaluation or assessment be made of the respondent;

(4) order any appropriate investigation of a person involved in a proceeding;
(5) forward to the court of this State a certified copy of the transcript or other record of a hearing under paragraph (1) or any other proceeding, any evidence otherwise produced under paragraph (2), and any evaluation or assessment prepared in compliance with an order under paragraph (3) or (4);
(6) issue any order necessary to assure the appearance in the proceeding of a person whose presence is necessary for the court to make a determination, including the respondent or the incapacitated or protected person; and
(7) issue an order authorizing the release of medical, financial, criminal, or other relevant information in that state, including protected health information which meets federal and state laws.
b. If a court of another state in which a guardianship or protective proceeding is pending requests assistance of the kind provided in subsection a., a court of this State has jurisdiction for the limited purpose of granting the request or making reasonable efforts to comply with the request.

§ 3B:12B-8. Taking testimony in another state; documentary evidence

a. A court of this State may permit a witness located in another state to be deposed or to testify by any means permitted by the Rules Governing the Courts of the State of New Jersey. A court of this State shall cooperate with the court of another state in designating an appropriate location for the deposition or testimony.
b. Documentary evidence transmitted from another state to a court of this State may be admitted into evidence consistent with the New Jersey Rules of Evidence.

§ 3B:12B-9. Jurisdiction; determination

a. A court of this State has jurisdiction to declare a person incapacitated and appoint a guardian or issue a protective order for a respondent if:
(1) This State is the respondent's home state as defined in section 3 of P.L.2012, c.36 (C.3B:12B-3); or
(2) On the date the petition is filed, this State is a significant-connection state, as defined in section 3 of P.L.2012, c.36 (C.3B:12B-3) and determined in accordance with section 10 of P.L.2012, c.36 (C.3B:12B-10), and:
(a) the respondent either does not have a home state or a court of the respondent's home state has declined to exercise jurisdiction because this State is a more appropriate forum; or
(b) the respondent has a home state, a petition for an appointment or order is not pending in a court of another state or another significant-connection state, and, before this State's court acts:
(i) a petition for an appointment or order is not filed in the respondent's home state;
(ii) an objection to the court's jurisdiction is not filed by a person required to be notified of the proceeding; and
(iii) the court concludes that it is an appropriate forum under the factors set forth in section 13 of P.L.2012, c.36 (C.3B:12B-13);
(3) Although this State does not have jurisdiction under either subsection a. or b. of this section, the home state and all significant-connection states have declined to exercise jurisdiction because this State is the more appropriate forum, and jurisdiction in this State is consistent with the New Jersey and United States Constitutions; or
b. A court of this State may assume emergency jurisdiction under section 11 of P.L.2012, c.36 (C.3B:12B-11).

§ 3B:12B-10. Significant-connection state; determination

In determining whether a respondent has a significant connection with a particular state, the court shall consider:
a. the location of the respondent's family and other persons required to be notified of the guardianship or protective proceeding;
b. the length of time the respondent at any time was physically present in the state and the duration of any absence;
c. the location of the respondent's property; and
d. the extent to which the respondent has ties to the state such as voting registration, state or local tax return filing, vehicle registration, driver's license, social relationship, and receipt of services.

§ 3B:12B-11. Emergency jurisdiction

a. A court of this State lacking jurisdiction under section 9 of P.L.2012, c.36 (C.3B:12B-9) has emergency jurisdiction to do any of the following:
(1) appoint a guardian or issue a protective order in an emergency, in accordance with subsection c. of section 12 of P.L.2005, c.304 (C.3B:12-24.1) and this section, for a respondent who is physically present in this State;
(2) appoint a guardian of real or tangible personal property located in this State for which the respondent has an ownership interest;
(3) issue a protective order with respect to real or tangible personal property in this State; or
(4) appoint, under procedures similar to section 17 of P.L.2012, c.36 (C.3B:12B-17), a guardian or conservator for an incapacitated or protected person for whom a provisional order to transfer the proceeding from another state has been issued.
b. If a petition for the appointment of a guardian or issuance of a protective order in an emergency in accordance with subsection c. of section 12 of P.L.2005, c.304 (C.3B:12-24.1) and this section is brought in this State and this State was not the respondent's home state on the date the petition was filed, the court shall dismiss the proceeding at the request of the court of the home state, if any, whether dismissal is requested before or after the emergency appointment.

§ 3B:12B-12. Exclusive and continuing jurisdiction

Except as otherwise provided in section 11 of P.L.2012, c.36 (C.3B:12B-11), a court that has appointed a guardian or issued a protective order consistent with P.L.2012, c.36 (C.3B:12B-1 et al.) has exclusive and continuing jurisdiction over the proceeding until the proceeding is terminated by the court, or the appointment or order expires by its own terms.

§ 3B:12B-13. Appropriate forum

a. A court of this State having jurisdiction under section 9 of P.L.2012, c.36 (C.3B:12B-9) to declare a person incapacitated, appoint a guardian, or issue a protective order, may decline to exercise jurisdiction if it determines at any time that a court of another state is a more appropriate forum.

b. If a court of this State declines to exercise jurisdiction under subsection a. of this section, it shall either dismiss or stay the proceeding. The court may impose any condition it deems just and proper, including the condition that a petition for the appointment of a guardian or issuance of a protective order be filed promptly in another state.

c. In determining whether it is an appropriate forum, the court shall consider all relevant factors, including:

(1) any expressed preference of the respondent;

(2) whether abuse, neglect, or exploitation of the respondent has occurred or is likely to occur and which state could best protect the respondent from the abuse, neglect, or exploitation;

(3) the length of time the respondent was physically present in or was a legal resident of this or another state;

(4) the distance of the respondent from the court of each state;

(5) the financial circumstances of the respondent's estate;

(6) the nature and location of the evidence;

(7) the ability of the court of each state to decide the issue expeditiously and the procedures necessary to present evidence;

(8) the familiarity of the court of each state with the facts and issues in the proceeding; and

(9) if an appointment were to be made, the court's ability to monitor the conduct of the guardian or the conservator.

§ 3B:12B-14. Jurisdiction declined by reason of conduct

a. If, at any time, a court of this State determines that it acquired jurisdiction to declare a person incapacitated, appoint a guardian, or issue a protective order because of unjustifiable conduct, the court may:

(1) decline to exercise jurisdiction;

(2) exercise jurisdiction for the limited purpose of fashioning an appropriate remedy to ensure the health, safety, and welfare of the respondent or the protection of the respondent's property or prevent a repetition of the unjustifiable conduct, including staying the proceeding until a petition for the appointment of a guardian or issuance of a protective order is filed in a court of another state having jurisdiction; or

(3) continue to exercise jurisdiction after considering:

(a) the extent to which the respondent and all persons required to be notified of the proceedings have acquiesced in the exercise of the court's jurisdiction;

(b) whether it is a more appropriate forum than the court of any other state under the factors set forth in subsection c. of section 13 of P.L.2012, c.36 (C.3B:12B-13); and

(c) whether the court of any other state would have jurisdiction under factual circumstances in substantial conformity with the jurisdictional standards of section 9 of P.L.2012, c.36 (C.3B:12B-9).

b. If a court of this State determines that it acquired jurisdiction to appoint a guardian or issue a protective order because a party seeking to invoke its jurisdiction engaged in unjustifiable conduct, it may assess against that party necessary and reasonable expenses, including attorneys' fees, investigative fees, court costs, communication expenses, witness fees and expenses, and travel expenses. The court may not assess fees, costs, or expenses of any kind against this State or a governmental subdivision, agency, or instrumentality of this State unless authorized by law other than P.L.2012, c.36 (C.3B:12B-1 et al.).

§ 3B:12B-15. Notice of proceeding

If this State was not the respondent's home state on the date a petition to declare a person incapacitated for the appointment of a guardian or issuance of a protective order is filed in this State, notice of the petition shall be given, in the same manner as notice is required to be given in this State, to the respondent and to the persons who would be entitled to notice if the regular procedures for appointment of a guardian or a conservator under the Rules Governing the Courts of the State of New Jersey were applicable.

§ 3B:12B-16. Proceedings in more than one state

Except for a petition for the appointment of a guardian or issuance of a protective order in an emergency under paragraph (1) of subsection a. of section 11 of P.L.2012, c.36 (C.3B:12B-11), or appointment of a guardian of estate or issuance of a protective order limited to property located in this State under paragraph (2) or (3) of subsection a. of section 11 of P.L.2012, c.36 (C.3B:12B-11), if a petition for the appointment of a guardian or issuance of a protective order is filed in this State and in another state and neither petition has been dismissed or withdrawn, the following shall apply:

a. A court of this State with jurisdiction under section 9 of P.L.2012, c.36 (C.3B:12B-9) may proceed unless a court of another state acquires jurisdiction under similar provisions before the appointment or issuance of the order.

b. A court of this State without jurisdiction under section 9 of P.L.2012, c.36 (C.3B:12B-9), whether at the time the petition is filed or at any time before the appointment or issuance of a judgment or order, shall stay the proceeding and communicate with the court of another state. If the court in the other state has jurisdiction, the court of this State shall dismiss the petition unless the court in the other state determines that the court of this State is a more appropriate forum.

§ 3B:12B-17. Transfer of guardianship or conservatorship to another state

a. A guardian or conservator appointed, or a conservatee, in this State may petition the court to transfer the guardianship or conservatorship to another state.

b. Notice of a petition for transfer shall be given to the persons that would be entitled to notice of a petition in this State for the appointment of a guardian or conservator.

c. On the court's own motion or upon request of the guardian or conservator or conservatee, or other person required to be notified of the petition, the court shall hold a hearing on a petition to transfer.

d. The court shall issue an order provisionally granting a petition to transfer a guardianship and direct the guardian to petition for guardianship in the other state if the court is satisfied that the guardianship will be accepted by the court of the other state and the court finds that:

(1) in the case of a guardianship of the person, the incapacitated person is physically present in or is reasonably expected to move permanently to the other state, or in the case of a guardianship of estate, the incapacitated person is physically present in or is reasonably expected to move permanently to, or has a significant connection to, the other state; and

(2) an objection to the transfer has not been made or, that the transfer would not be contrary to the interests of the incapacitated person; and

(3) in the case of a guardianship of the person, plans for care and services for the incapacitated person in the other state are reasonable and sufficient, or in the case of a guardianship of the estate, adequate arrangements are made for management of the incapacitated person's property.

e. The court shall issue a provisional order granting a transfer of a conservatorship and shall direct the conservator to petition for conservatorship in the other state if the court is satisfied that the conservatorship will be accepted by the court of the other state and the court finds that:

(1) the protected person is physically present in or is reasonably expected to move permanently to the other state, or the protected person has a significant connection to the other state considering the factors in section 10 of P.L.2012, c.36 (C.3B:12B-10);

(2) an objection to the transfer has not been made or, that the transfer would not be contrary to the interests of the incapacitated person; and

(3) adequate arrangements will be made for management of the protected person's property.

f. The court shall issue a final order confirming the transfer and terminating the guardianship or conservatorship upon receipt of:

(1) a provisional order accepting the guardianship or conservatorship from the court to which the guardianship or conservatorship is to be transferred under provisions similar to section 18 of P.L.2012, c.36 (C.3B:12B-18); and

(2) the documents required to terminate a guardianship or conservatorship in this State.

§ 3B:12B-18. Accepting guardianship or conservatorship transferred from another state

a. To confirm transfer of a guardianship or conservatorship to this State under provisions similar to section 17 of P.L.2012, c.36 (C.3B:12B-17), the guardian or conservator in the other state shall file a petition in the court of this State to accept the guardianship of the person or the person's estate, or both, or the conservatorship. The petition shall include a certified copy of the other state's provisional order of transfer.

b. Notice of a petition under this section shall be given, in the same manner as notice is required to be given in this State, to those persons that would be entitled to notice if the petition were for the appointment of a guardian or issuance of a protective order in both the transferring state and this State.

c. On the court's own motion or upon request of the guardian or of the conservator or conservatee, or other person required to be notified of the proceeding, the court shall hold a hearing on a petition filed pursuant to this section.

d. The court shall issue an order provisionally granting relief under this section unless:

(1) an objection is made and the court determines that transfer of the proceeding would be contrary to the interests of the incapacitated or protected person or conservatee; or

(2) the guardian or conservator is ineligible for appointment in this State.

e. The final order accepting the proceeding and appointing the guardian or conservator from the other state as guardian of the person or estate, or both, or conservator in this State shall be issued upon the receipt by this State's court of a final order issued under provisions similar to section 17 of P.L.2012, c.36 (C.3B:12B-17) transferring the proceeding to this State.

f. Upon application of a party or upon the court's own motion, the court shall determine whether the guardianship of the person or estate, or both, or the conservatorship needs to be modified to conform to the law of this State.

g. In granting an application under this section, the court shall recognize a guardianship or conservatorship order from the other state, including the determination of the incapacitated person's incapacity and the appointment of the guardian of the person or estate, or both, or of the conservator.

h. The denial by a court of this State of an application to accept a guardianship or conservatorship transferred from another state does not affect the ability of the guardian or conservator to seek appointment as guardian of the person or estate, or both, in this State under N.J.S.3B:12-25 or as conservator under N.J.S.3B:13A-1 et seq., if the court has jurisdiction to make an appointment other than by reason of the provisional order of transfer.

§ 3B:12B-19. Registration of guardianship or conservatorship orders

If a guardian has been appointed in another state and an application for the appointment of a guardian of the person or estate, or both, is not pending in this State, or if a conservator has been appointed in another state and an application for the appointment of a conservator is not pending in this State, the guardian or conservator appointed in the other state, after giving notice to the appointing court of an intent to register, may register the guardianship or conservatorship order in this State with the Surrogate, as Deputy Clerk of the Superior Court, Chancery Division, Probate Part, in an appropriate county of this State, pursuant to the Rules of Court of the State of New Jersey, by filing certified copies of the order and letters of office, and of any bond, as appropriate. For purposes of a guardian of the person, an appropriate county is any county where the guardian seeks to maintain an action or proceeding on behalf of the incapacitated person; for purposes of a guardian of the property or of a conservatorship, an appropriate county is the county where the property belonging to the incapacitated person or conservatee is located.

§ 3B:12B-20. Effect of registration

a. Upon registration of a guardianship or protective order from another state, the guardian or conservator may exercise in this State all powers authorized in the order of appointment except as prohibited under the laws of this State, including maintaining actions and proceedings in this State and, if the guardian or conservator is not a resident of this State, subject to any conditions imposed upon nonresident parties.

b. A court of this State may grant any relief available under P.L.2012, c.36 (C.3B:12B-1 et al.) and other law of this State to enforce a registered order.

c. A court of this State shall recognize and enforce, but may not modify, except in accordance with P.L.2012, c.36 (C.3B:12B-1 et al.), a registered order.

§ 3B:12B-21. Uniformity of application and construction

In applying and construing this uniform act, consideration shall be given to the need to promote uniformity of the law with respect to its subject matter among states that enact it.

§ 3B:12B-22. Transitional provision

a. P.L.2012, c.36(C.3B:12B-1 et al.) applies to guardianship and protective proceedings filed on or after the effective date.

b. Sections 1 through 4 of P.L.2012, c.36 (C.3B:12B-1 through C.3B:12B-4); sections 6 through 8 of P.L.2012, c.36 (C.3B:12B-6 through C.3B:12B-8); sections 17 through 21 of P.L.2012, c.36 (C.3B:12B-17 through C.3B:12B-21); apply to proceedings begun before the effective date of P.L.2012, c.36 (C.3B:12B-1 et al.), regardless of whether a guardianship or protective order has been issued.

Chapter 13. Guardianship of Veterans

Article 1. In General

§ 3B:13-1. Short title

This chapter shall be known and may be cited as the "Uniform Veterans' Guardianship Law."

§ 3B:13-2. Definitions

As used in this chapter:

a. "Federal agency" means any bureau, office, board, or officer of the United States by whatever name known, now or hereafter charged by Congress:
(1) With payment of pensions, bounties, and allowances to veterans of the military service of the United States, their widows, widowers, children, mothers, and fathers; or
(2) With the administration of the affairs of any of the aforesaid persons who may be minors or persons who are incapacitated or with the management of pensions, bounties, and allowances payable to them.

b. "Military" has reference to the army, navy, marine, air, and coast guard services.

c. "Estate" and "income" include only moneys received by the guardian from a Federal agency and earnings, interest, and profits derived therefrom.

d. "Benefits" means moneys payable by the United States to the aforesaid persons or their guardians through a Federal agency.

e. "Chief officer" means an officer of a Federal agency, charged by the laws of the United States with the particular duty in connection with which the term is used.

f. "Ward" means a beneficiary of a Federal agency.

g. "Guardian" means a person acting as fiduciary for a ward.

§ 3B:13-3. General rules of construction

This chapter shall be liberally construed to secure the beneficial intent and purpose thereof and shall apply only to beneficiaries enumerated in N.J.S. 3B:13-2. This chapter shall also be so interpreted and construed as to effectuate its general purpose to make uniform the law of those states which enact the "Uniform Veterans' Guardianship Act."

§ 3B:13-4. Fees and costs

Except as otherwise provided in this chapter, no costs or fees shall be charged or taxed by the surrogates of the respective counties or by the Superior Court for accounts rendered or other proceedings had under this chapter.

§ 3B:13-5. No charges to be made for copies of certain records

When a copy of a public record is required by a Federal agency for use in determining the eligibility of a person to participate in benefits made available by the agency, the official charged with the custody of the public record shall furnish a certified copy of the record without charge.

Article 2. Appointment of Guardians

§ 3B:13-6. Determination of incapacity by Superior Court

For the purpose of appointing a guardian pursuant to this chapter, the incapacity of a beneficiary of a Federal agency shall be determined by the Superior Court.

§ 3B:13-7. Guardians; when and how appointed

When, pursuant to any law of the United States or regulation of a Federal agency, the chief officer of the agency requires, prior to payment of benefits, that a guardian be appointed for a ward, the appointment for a person who is incapacitated shall be made in the Superior Court, and the appointment for a minor shall be made in the Superior Court or in the surrogate's court.

§ 3B:13-8. Guardian to have no more than five wards; exceptions

Except as provided in this section, no person shall accept appointment as guardian of a ward if acting as guardian for five wards.

In an action brought by an attorney of a Federal agency, establishing that a guardian is acting in a fiduciary capacity for more than five wards, the Superior Court shall require a final accounting forthwith from the guardian and shall discharge the guardian.

The limitation of this section shall not apply where the guardian is a bank or trust company or a public guardian of veterans who are incapacitated, and an individual may be guardian of more than five wards if they are all members of the same family.

Article 3. Guardians' Accounts

§ 3B:13-9. Filing account with the court

Every guardian appointed by the surrogate of any county or by the Superior Court, who receives any moneys from a Federal agency for the benefit of his ward, shall, at intervals as the court may require, render to the Superior Court a true account of all moneys received by him, as guardian, by way of pension, bounty or other allowance from the United States. The account shall be submitted in duplicate.

§ 3B:13-10. Filing account with Federal agency

Each year when not required to render an account to the court, the guardian shall render an account to the regional office of the Veterans' Administration on forms to be supplied by the Federal agency.

§ 3B:13-11. Times for accounting

The times for rendering accounts shall be as follows:

a. In the counties of Hudson, Somerset or Sussex, on or before January 5;
b. In the counties of Warren or Essex, on or before February 5;
c. In the counties of Bergen, Morris or Passaic, on or before March 5;
d. In the counties of Union, Hunterdon or Middlesex, on or before April 5;
e. In the counties of Mercer, Burlington, Monmouth or Gloucester, on or before May 5;
f. In the counties of Camden, Atlantic or Salem, on or before June 5;
g. In the counties of Cape May, Cumberland or Ocean, on or before July 5.

§ 3B:13-12. Notice to Federal agency

The clerk of the court shall, within 5 days of the date of filing of the account, mail a copy of the account to the office of the Veterans' Administration having jurisdiction over the area in which the county lies.

§ 3B:13-13. Accounting without filing vouchers

The Superior Court may allow the account without proof or the submission of vouchers if the written approval of the attorney in this State for the Veterans' Administration shall be filed with the account. The approval shall set forth the facts upon which the approval is based.

§ 3B:13-14. Removal of guardian for failure to account; costs

If the Federal agency, the sureties on the guardian's bond, any person interested in the benefits in the hands of the guardian or any person as next friend of the ward serves notice upon the guardian that his account has not been filed in accordance with this article, and if the guardian fails to render his account within 30 days from the date of mailing of the notice or from the time of service or within the time as the court may otherwise provide, the court shall remove him. The notice may be mailed to the guardian's last known address.

The cost of the proceedings, as well as the cost incident to an order to show cause when it is necessary to obtain an accounting, shall be paid by the guardian out of his own estate, unless the court shall otherwise order.

Article 4. Management of Estates; Property Received from Sources Other than the United States Government

§ 3B:13-15. Investments

A guardian shall invest the funds of the estate in a manner and in securities, in which the guardian has no interest, as allowed by law or approved by the court.

§ 3B:13-16. Support of dependents

When directed in writing by the proper Federal agency, the guardian shall apply that portion of the estate to the ward's spouse, child, father or mother as may be set forth in the direction. The direction shall be submitted to the Superior Court when an account is filed as proof of the guardian's authority for those payments.

Except as permitted by this section, a guardian shall not apply any of the estate of his ward to the support of any person other than his ward.

§ 3B:13-17. Compensation of guardian

Compensation payable to a guardian shall not exceed 5% of the income of the ward during any year.

For extraordinary services rendered by the guardian, the Superior Court may, after hearing upon the settlement of his account, authorize additional compensation payable from the estate of the ward, but no compensation shall be allowed on the corpus of an estate received from a preceding guardian.

The guardian may be allowed from the estate of his ward reasonable premiums paid by him to a corporate surety upon his bond.

§ 3B:13-18. Authorization for guardian of incapacitated ward to receive additional personal property not exceeding $10,000

When a ward for whom a guardian has been appointed is incapacitated and becomes entitled to personal property amounting to not more than $10,000.00 from any source other than the United States Government, the court may authorize the guardian to receive the personal property for conservation and administrative care. On payment of any money or delivery of property to the guardian, a release executed by the guardian to the person or persons paying the money or delivering the property shall be valid and effective.

§ 3B:13-19. Direction of court for expenditure required; investment

The guardian shall not expend any portion of the personal property received from any source other than the United States Government, except as directed by the court to which he is accountable; but he may invest the personal property as provided by N.J.S. 3B:13-15.

§ 3B:13-20. Fees

The fees allowed by law shall be applicable to proceedings with respect to personal property received from sources other than the United States Government, and may be taxed by the clerk of the court.

Article 5. Public Guardian of Incompetent Veterans

§ 3B:13-21. "Public guardian of veterans who are incapacitated."

There may be appointed in each county a person to be known as "public guardian of veterans who are incapacitated for the county of (naming county)", who shall be appointed by the Assignment Judge of the Superior Court in the county. The person appointed shall hold office for the term of five years from the date of appointment and until a successor is appointed and qualified.

§ 3B:13-22. Guardian's bond

Before entering upon the duties of office, a public guardian of veterans who are incapacitated shall execute a bond to the Superior Court in an amount and with sureties as shall be approved by the Superior Court, conditioned for the faithful discharge of all duties imposed by law upon the person appointed public guardian.

The bond shall be renewed annually and shall, from time to time, be increased or reduced as the court may direct.

The expense of procuring the bond shall be paid by the county treasurer upon presentation of a proper voucher approved by the Assignment Judge of the Superior Court in the county.

§ 3B:13-23. Salary of public guardian

A public guardian of veterans who are incapacitated shall receive an annual salary to be fixed by the Assignment Judge of the Superior Court of the county for which the guardian is appointed, with the approval of the board of freeholders or governing body of the county.

The salary shall be paid by the county treasurer in semimonthly payments and shall be in lieu of all other charges, compensation, and commissions. A guardian shall not accept any other money whatsoever by way of fee, compensation, gratuity, or present for any services provided by the guardian.

§ 3B:13-24. Duties of public guardian as adviser of other guardians

The public guardian of veterans who are incapacitated shall, in each county, assist, supervise, advise, and otherwise aid the duly appointed guardians of these veterans and give help as may be necessary in preparing and drawing papers and documents, and also help them to work in conjunction with the United States Department of Veterans Affairs, so that their wards may be fully protected.

§ 3B:13-25. Discharge and removal of public guardian

The public guardian of veterans who are incapacitated shall be subject to discharge or removal, by the court, on the grounds and in the manner in which other guardians of persons who are incapacitated are discharged or removed.

§ 3B:13-26. Public guardian may be appointed general guardian for veteran

Where an action is brought in the Superior Court for the appointment of a guardian for a person who, while in the military, naval, marine, air, or coast guard service of the United States, or after discharge therefrom, is determined to be incapacitated, whether or not committed or confined to an institution for the care of persons who are incapacitated, and the heirs of the person are unwilling, unable, or unqualified for the appointment, or if the best interests of the person require it, the Superior Court may appoint the public guardian of the county in which the person resides as guardian of the person.

§ 3B:13-27. Powers of public guardian as guardian of veterans' estates

The public guardian of veterans who are incapacitated shall have, in respect of any veteran and the estate of any veteran for whom the public guardian is appointed, the same power and authority as any other duly appointed guardian of a person who is incapacitated.

§ 3B:13-28. Settlement of accounts

The public guardian shall settle accounts in each estate in which the guardian is appointed at the times and in the same manner as other guardians of persons who are incapacitated.

§ 3B:13-29. Termination of guardianship; settlement of account

Upon the termination of a guardianship, by death of the ward or otherwise, the public guardian shall settle the account in the same manner as other guardians of persons who are incapacitated.

§ 3B:13-30. Settlement of accounts upon expiration of public guardian's term

The public guardian shall proceed to settle the accounts of all estates of which he is duly appointed guardian upon the expiration of his term of office.

§ 3B:13-31. Counsel to represent public guardian; compensation

The public guardian of veterans who are incapacitated may, when authorized by the Superior Court, employ counsel to represent the public guardian.

The compensation of counsel shall be fixed by the court and paid from moneys in the guardian's control belonging to the estate involved in litigation.

Chapter 13A. Conservators

§ 3B:13A-1. Definitions

a. "Conservatee" means a person who has not been adjudicated incapacitated but who by reason of advanced age, illness, or physical infirmity, is unable to care for or manage property or has become unable to provide self-support or support for others who depend upon that support.

b. "Conservator" means a person appointed by the court to manage the estate of a conservatee.

§ 3B:13A-2. Civil action to appoint conservator

The Superior Court may, in a civil action brought by the conservatee or some other person in his behalf, appoint a conservator to manage the estate of a conservatee, except that if the conservatee objects to the imposition of a conservatorship, a conservator shall not be appointed.

§ 3B:13A-3. Appointment of counsel to represent conservatee

The court shall have the right to appoint counsel for the proposed conservatee if it believes that counsel is necessary to adequately protect the interests of the conservatee.

§ 3B:13A-4. Conservatee to be present at hearing; court ordered investigation if conservatee unable to attend

The conservatee shall be present at the hearing unless he is unable to attend by reason of physical or other inability, and that inability is established to the satisfaction of the court. If the conservatee is found to be unable to attend, the court shall, subject to rules of court, order an investigation to be conducted to assure the conservatee does not object to the conservatorship unless the court believes, in its discretion, that the interests of the conservatee are adequately protected by counsel representing the conservatee.

§ 3B:13A-5. By whom action for appointment of conservator in behalf of conservatee may be brought

An action for the appointment of a conservator may be brought by the conservatee as provided in section 3B:13A-2 or in the conservatee's behalf by:

a. His spouse;

b. His adult children or, where there are none, the person or persons closest in degree of kinship to the conservatee;

c. Any person having concern for the financial or personal well-being of the conservatee;

d. A public agency or a social services official of the State or of the county in which the conservatee resides regardless of whether or not the conservatee is a recipient of public assistance; or

e. The chief administrator of a State licensed hospital, school or institution in which the conservatee is a patient or from which he receives services.

f. The chief administrator of a non-profit charitable institution in which the conservatee is a patient or from which he receives services.

§ 3B:13A-6. Service of notice to appoint conservator

Notice of the action to appoint a conservator shall be served upon the following persons:

a. The conservatee unless he is the plaintiff;

b. The spouse and adult children of the conservatee or, where there are none, upon the person or persons closest in degree of kinship to the conservatee;

c. The person with whom the conservatee resides, or if the conservatee resides in an institution, upon the chief administrator of that institution.

§ 3B:13A-7. Right of persons to be heard

The persons receiving notice pursuant to N.J.S. 3B:13A-6 may, upon approval of the court and in the interest of the conservatee, appear and be heard concerning all matters relating to the conservatorship.

§ 3B:13A-8. Designation of conservator

The court may appoint a person or a financial institution, qualified under the laws of this State to act as a fiduciary, as the conservator of the conservatee's estate. If the court appoints a conservator, it shall do so in the following order of priority:

a. A person or financial institution nominated or designated by the conservatee;
b. The conservatee's spouse;
c. One or more of the conservatee's adult children, or where there are none, the person or persons closest in degree of kinship to the conservatee; or
d. Some other proper person or financial institution as the court shall determine.

The court may, in its discretion, deviate from this order of priority if a potential conservator is unable or unwilling to serve or for some other good cause.

§ 3B:13A-9. Acceptance of appointment

Before letters of conservatorship are issued, the conservator shall accept the appointment in accordance with the Rules Governing the Courts of the State of New Jersey.

§ 3B:13A-10. Power of attorney; filing; contents

Every conservator, whether or not a resident of this State, who is granted letters of conservatorship within this State shall, at the time of the grant of letters of conservatorship to him, file a power of attorney with the clerk of the court. The power of attorney shall be duly executed in writing, shall set forth the post office address, street and number of the conservator and, by sufficient language, constitute the clerk with whom the power of attorney is filed and his successors in office, his true and lawful attorney to receive process affecting the estate in his charge, or any interest therein, with the same force and effect as if the process were duly served on the conservator within this State.

§ 3B:13A-11. Service of process

Service of process under N.J.S. 3B:13A-10 shall be made by leaving a copy of the process with the clerk of the court together with a fee of $2.00 to be taxed in the costs.

The clerk shall forthwith notify the conservator of the service by mailing a letter, with a copy of the process served enclosed, with full postage prepaid, directed to the conservator at the post office address given in the power of attorney.

§ 3B:13A-12. "Process" defined

The word "process" as used in N.J.S. 3B:13A-10 and N.J.S. 3B:13A-11 shall have the same meaning as set forth in N.J.S. 3B:14-46.

§ 3B:13A-13. Bond

The court may, upon appointing a conservator in order to secure the faithful performance of the duties of his office, require him to furnish bond to the Superior Court in a sum and with proper conditions and sureties having due regard to the value of the estate in his charge and the extent of his authority, as the court shall approve.

§ 3B:13A-14. Conditions of bond

If a bond is required of a conservator, it shall be conditioned substantially as follows:

a. To well and truly take care of the estate of the conservatee and all writings and evidences concerning his real estate and to deliver them to the person or persons who by law are or may be entitled to receive them;
b. To improve the real estate to the best advantage and to commit no waste or destruction thereof or thereon;
c. To make a just and true account of the rents, issues and profits of the real estate and of the proceeds of the sale of any real estate that may be ordered to be sold;
d. To make a just and true account of the expenditures and disbursements of the goods, chattels and personal estate of the conservatee that shall come into his hands; and
e. If required by court, to settle those accounts therein within the time so required.

§ 3B:13A-15. Bond premium

A conservator may include as a part of the lawful expense of executing his trust a reasonable sum, not exceeding 1% per annum on the amount of any bond, paid a company authorized under the laws of this State to become a surety on his bonds, as may be allowed by the court in which he is required to account.

§ 3B:13A-16. Limitations on appointment of conservator

The appointment of a conservator shall not:

a. Be evidence of the capacity or incapacity of a conservatee; or
b. Transfer title of the conservatee's real and personal property to the conservator; or
c. Deprive or modify any civil right of the conservatee, including but not limited to civil service status and appointment or rights relating to the granting, forfeiture, or denial of a license, permit, privilege, or benefit pursuant to any law.

§ 3B:13A-17. Inventory

A conservator may, and if required by the court shall, file with the clerk of the court an inventory, under oath, of all the real and personal property which has come into his hands or control or into the hands of any other person for him. The court shall not require an inventory and appraisement to be filed until 3 months have elapsed after the grant of letters.

§ 3B:13A-18. Expenditures to be made by conservator out of conservatee's estate

A conservator may expend or distribute so much or all of the income or principal of the conservatee for his support, maintenance, education, general use and benefit and for the support, maintenance, education, general use and benefit of his dependents, in the manner, at the time or times and to the extent that the conservator, in an exercise of a reasonable discretion, deems suitable and proper, with or without court order, with or without regard to the duty or ability of any person to support or provide for the conservatee, and with or without regard to any other funds, income or property which may be available for any of those purposes.

§ 3B:13A-19. Recommendations to be considered by conservator in making expenditures

In making expenditures under N.J.S. 3B:13A-18, a conservator shall consider recommendations relating to the appropriate standard of support, education and benefit for the conservatee made by any party set forth in N.J.S. 3B:13A-6. He may not be surcharged for sums paid to persons or organizations actually furnishing support, education or care to the conservatee pursuant to the recommendations of a parent, spouse or heir of the conservatee unless he knows that the parent, spouse or heir of the conservatee is deriving personal financial benefit therefrom, or unless the recommendations are clearly not in the best interests of the conservatee.

§ 3B:13A-20. Other factors to be considered by conservator in making expenditures

In making expenditures under N.J.S. 3B:13A-19, the conservator shall expend or distribute sums reasonably necessary for the support, education, care or benefit of the conservatee with due regard to:

a. The size of the conservatee's estate;
b. The probable duration of the conservatorship and the likelihood that the conservatee, at some future time, may be fully able to manage his affairs and the estate which has been conserved for him; and
c. The accustomed standard of living of the conservatee and members of his household.

§ 3B:13A-21. Persons for whose benefit expenditures may be made

The conservator may expend funds of the conservatee's estate for the support of persons legally dependent on the conservatee and others who are members of the conservatee's household who are unable to support themselves, and who are in need of support.

§ 3B:13A-22. Persons to whom funds may be paid

Funds expended under N.J.S. 3B:13A-18 may be paid by the conservator to any person, including the conservatee, to reimburse the conservator for expenditures which he has made, or in advance for services to be rendered to the conservatee when it is reasonable to expect that they will be performed and where advance payments are customary or reasonably necessary under the circumstances.

§ 3B:13A-23. Powers conferred upon conservator

A conservator has all of the powers conferred upon him by law and the terms of this chapter, except that a conservator's powers over the property of the conservatee are limited to the investment of income or the expenditure and distribution of income and principal as set forth in N.J.S. 3B:13A-18 and N.J.S. 3B:13A-21, unless other powers are specifically conferred upon the conservator by the court or by the conservatee in an acknowledged writing.

§ 3B:13A-24. Expansion or limitation of conservator's powers

The court may, at the time of appointment or later, expand or limit the powers of a conservator otherwise conferred by this chapter, or previously conferred by the court, and may at any time relieve him of any expansion or limitation. If the court expands or limits any power conferred on the conservator, the expansion or limitation shall be stated in certificates of letters of conservatorship thereafter issued. The court shall confer powers to the conservator authorizing only that intervention which it finds to be least restrictive of the conservatee's rights while consistent with the conservatee's welfare and safety. The basis for the finding shall be in the record of the court.

§ 3B:13A-25. Formal accounting

A conservator shall settle his account in the Superior Court at intervals as the court may require, except that a conservator may settle his first account within 1 year after his appointment, or as soon thereafter as may be practicable.

§ 3B:13A-26. Effect of judgment allowing intermediate account

A judgment, made upon notice and hearing, allowing an intermediate account of a conservator, shall have the same effect as a judgment allowing an intermediate account of any other fiduciary.

§ 3B:13A-27. Annual informal report or accounting

The conservator shall present to the conservatee an annual informal report or accounting setting forth the collection and disposition of income and other assets within the conservator's control. The annual informal report or accounting shall be filed with the court and available for inspection by any party set forth in N.J.S. 3B:13A-6. In addition, the court may order, upon a showing of good cause by the conservatee, a full accounting by the conservator of all the conservatee's assets within the conservator's control.

§ 3B:13A-28. Personal liability of conservator on contracts

Unless otherwise provided in the contract, a conservator is not individually liable on a contract properly entered into in his fiduciary capacity in the course of administration of the estate unless he fails to reveal his representative capacity and identify the estate in the contract.

§ 3B:13A-29. Personal liability of conservator for obligations arising from control of estate

A conservator is individually liable for obligations arising from control of property of the estate or for any act or omission committed in the course of administration of the estate only if he is personally at fault.

§ 3B:13A-30. Asserting claims against estate

Claims based on contracts entered into by a conservator in his fiduciary capacity, on obligations arising from control of the estate, or on any act or omission committed in the course of administration of the estate may be asserted against the estate by proceeding against the conservator in his fiduciary capacity, whether or not the conservator is individually liable therefor.

§ 3B:13A-31. Determining issues of liability between estate and conservator

Any question of liability between the estate and the conservator individually may be determined in a proceeding for accounting, surcharge, or indemnification, or other appropriate proceeding or action.

§ 3B:13A-32. Liability of conservator for improper exercise of power concerning estate

If the exercise of power concerning the estate is improper, the conservator is liable to the conservatee or interested persons for damage or loss resulting from breach of his fiduciary duty to the same extent as a trustee of an express trust.

§ 3B:13A-33. Termination of conservatorship by conservatee

Upon application of the conservatee, the court shall terminate the conservatorship, and the conservator, after the allowance of his final account, shall pay over and distribute all funds and property in his hands and under his control to the former conservatee.

§ 3B:13A-34. Termination of conservatorship

A conservatorship shall terminate upon the death of the conservatee or upon adjudication of the conservatee to be incapacitated as provided by law, but the termination shall not affect the conservator's liability for prior acts nor obligation to account funds and property of the conservatee.

§ 3B:13A-35. Substituted conservator

Upon the death of the conservator or his removal by the court for good cause or if he resigns with court approval and after filing his account, the court may appoint another conservator in the manner provided for by this chapter.

§ 3B:13A-36. Conservator's compensation

A conservator shall be compensated for services in the same manner as a guardian for a minor or for a person who is incapacitated.

Chapter 14. Fiduciaries

Article 1. In General

§ 3B:14-1. Survivorship and succession among cofiduciaries; duties and powers

There shall be survivorship and succession between and among cofiduciaries. If only one fiduciary survives or remains qualified to act, no substituted fiduciary need be appointed to act in the place of any cofiduciary who may have died or may have been removed, discharged or otherwise disabled to act.

The surviving fiduciary or cofiduciaries shall proceed with the duties of the office and shall be entitled to the property and assets, and to sue for and recover them, and to sell and convey them, as if the remaining fiduciary or cofiduciaries had been solely appointed to the office.

§ 3B:14-2. Appointment of substituted fiduciary in place of one deceased or removed

A substituted fiduciary may be discharged or removed in the same manner and for the same causes as an originally named or appointed fiduciary. Upon the death or removal of a substituted fiduciary, a substituted fiduciary may be appointed in his stead with the same powers, authority, duties and liabilities as his predecessor in office.

§ 3B:14-3. Powers and duties of substituted fiduciary

A substituted fiduciary may demand, receive and recover the property and assets of the estate, and maintain all proper actions for the recovery thereof, and do all acts necessary for the administration and settlement of the estate and execution of the powers and performance of the trusts contained in the will or other instrument, in the same manner and to the same effect as if he had been appointed or named in the first instance. The fiduciary shall in the same manner be liable for any neglect or failure to perform the duties of his appointment.

§ 3B:14-4. Actions of succeeding or substituted fiduciary to recover assets misapplied by predecessor

A fiduciary appointed in the place of a removed or discharged fiduciary, or the cofiduciary remaining in office after the discharge or removal of the fiduciary, may sue for assets as shall have come into the possession of the discharged or removed fiduciary for any breach of trust, waste, embezzlement or misapplication thereof and may sue for the recovery of the assets of the estate against the discharged or removed fiduciary or against any other person in possession of the assets.

§ 3B:14-5. Removed or discharged fiduciary to deliver assets to successor

A fiduciary when removed or discharged shall forthwith deliver to his cofiduciary or the substituted fiduciary succeeding him all the assets of the estate which he holds, and shall, within 60 days after the accounting and settlement as provided in N.J.S. 3B:14-7, pay over to the cofiduciary or substituted fiduciary, as the circumstances of the case may require or the court may order, any balance shown to be due.

§ 3B:14-6. Penalty for failure of removed or discharged fiduciary to account or deliver assets

A fiduciary who fails to account as provided by N.J.S. 3B:14-7 or who fails to comply with the provisions of N.J.S. 3B:14-5, or any order entered thereunder, shall be liable to a fine not exceeding the amount of the estate in the hands of the fiduciary and shall also be liable for contempt for disobeying or failing to perform any court order or for failing to pay the fine.

All fines hereunder shall be collected by execution against the real or personal property of the defaulting fiduciary and shall be collected in favor of the person to whom the defaulting fiduciary should have made the payment or delivery and shall be received as assets by the cofiduciary or substituted fiduciary succeeding to the management of the estate.

§ 3B:14-7. Account of removed or discharged fiduciary

A removed or discharged fiduciary shall, within 60 days after removal or discharge or within a shorter or longer period as the court may direct, state and settle his account before the Superior Court for all the assets of the estate in his charge.

Article 2. War Service; Substitute for Fiduciary

§ 3B:14-8. "Engaged in war service" defined

For the purposes of this article, a fiduciary or person named to act as fiduciary shall be deemed to be engaged in war service if in time of war:

a. He is a member of the armed forces of the United States or of any of its allies or has been accepted for service and is awaiting induction into the service; or

b. He is engaged in any work abroad in connection with a governmental agency of the United States or in connection with the American Red Cross Society or any other body with similar objects; or

c. He is interned in an enemy country or is in a foreign country or a possession or dependency of the United States and is unable to return to this State.

§ 3B:14-9. Appointment of substitute for fiduciary engaged in war service

If a person is named to act as a fiduciary in a will or in any instrument creating a trust, who has not accepted the appointment or has not qualified, or if a person acting as a fiduciary is engaged in war service, the court may suspend the right of that person to be appointed as the fiduciary or suspend the powers of the fiduciary while he is engaged in war service and until the further order of the court. The court may appoint a substituted fiduciary until the termination of the suspension and reinstatement of the fiduciary or the person named to act as fiduciary is appointed.

§ 3B:14-10. Cofiduciaries; terms of instrument

If the fiduciary or person named to act as fiduciary is one of several cofiduciaries or one of several named to act as cofiduciaries, the court may appoint a substituted cofiduciary or may appoint the fiduciary's cofiduciary or cofiduciaries or the person or persons named to act as cofiduciaries to act as the substituted fiduciary. If the will or other instrument under which the fiduciary is appointed or person is named to act as fiduciary provides for a substitute or alternate fiduciary in the event of his death or otherwise, the court shall appoint as substituted fiduciary the substitute or alternate fiduciary or person named to act as substitute or alternate fiduciary to act if he is willing to act and can qualify.

§ 3B:14-11. Substituted fiduciary; bond

The substituted fiduciary shall give bond in the same terms as to condition, security and amount as were required of the fiduciary or person named to act as fiduciary in whose stead he is appointed or as the court shall direct. If the fiduciary or person named to act as fiduciary was not required to give bond the court may, in its discretion, require the substituted fiduciary to give bond in such terms as to condition, security and amount as the court may determine.

§ 3B:14-12. Substituted fiduciary; powers and duties

The substituted fiduciary, upon qualifying in accordance with the order of the court, shall be entitled to the control and possession of all of the unadministered assets of the estate, trust or fund, and shall be vested with title to and powers over the estate, trust or fund as the fiduciary or person named to act as fiduciary, in whose place and stead the substituted fiduciary is appointed, had or would have had except for the suspension of rights or powers and shall have power to administer the estate, trust or fund and shall be required to administer the estate, trust or fund and to account for his administration according to law.

§ 3B:14-13. Reinstatement of original fiduciary

When the fiduciary or person named to act as fiduciary in whose place a substituted fiduciary is appointed ceases to be engaged in war service, he may apply to the court to be reinstated as fiduciary or may be appointed to act as fiduciary if any part of the estate, trust or fund remains unadministered and if any of the duties of the office of fiduciary remain unexecuted, except the duty to account.

§ 3B:14-14. Termination of substituted fiduciary's powers and duties; accounting and delivery of assets

Upon reinstatement of the original fiduciary or person named to act as fiduciary, any substituted fiduciary of the estate, trust or fund, appointed by the court shall be removed and all of his powers as substituted fiduciary shall cease, except the power and duty to account for his administration of the estate, trust or fund. The substituted fiduciary shall deliver to the reinstated fiduciary all of the unadministered assets of the estate, trust or fund remaining in his possession and control and shall promptly account to the court for his administration of the estate, trust or fund.

§ 3B:14-15. Powers and duties of reinstated fiduciary

Upon reinstatement, the fiduciary or person named to act as fiduciary shall be vested with all of the title to that portion of the estate, trust or fund as has not been administered by the substituted fiduciary, and shall have all of the powers and duties as to the estate, trust or fund which he had or would have had by virtue of his original appointment as fiduciary or his being named to act as fiduciary. He shall have no responsibility for the administration of the estate, trust or fund by the substituted fiduciary or person named to act as substituted fiduciary. He shall be responsible for and shall account for his own administration of the estate, trust or fund, which may have remained in his hands or for which he may be accountable by his own action or neglect.

§ 3B:14-16. Commissions; apportionment

Commissions on the administration of the estate, trust or fund shall be apportioned between the original fiduciary and the substituted fiduciary as the court shall direct.

§ 3B:14-17. More than one substituted fiduciary

The court may appoint more than one substituted fiduciary in place of any fiduciary or person named to act as fiduciary engaged in war service if, in its discretion, the court determines that it is for the best interests of the estate, trust or fund, or of the parties interested therein, that the appointment be made.

Article 3. Discharge and Removal

§ 3B:14-18. Discharge from office of fiduciary; account; allowances

A fiduciary may be discharged from the further duties of his office by the court.

The court shall examine into the matter and if sufficient cause appears, the court may grant the discharge unless it will be prejudicial to the estate or persons interested therein or for any other reason the discharge ought not to be granted.

A discharge so granted shall discharge the fiduciary of all the further duties of his office except accounting for and paying over the money and assets with which he is chargeable by virtue of his office.

If the fiduciary is discharged, the court shall make orders respecting his commissions as may be just and equitable.

§ 3B:14-19. Discharge from particular trust; effect

Where a fiduciary is appointed by a will to perform a particular trust thereunder, he may be discharged from the performance thereof by the court.

The court may grant the discharge and the fiduciary shall be relieved of all further duties and liabilities with respect to the trust, except accounting for and paying over to his successor all moneys or assets pertaining to the trust, for which he is accountable.

§ 3B:14-20. Discharge of one or more joint fiduciaries

When there is more than one fiduciary they may all, or any one or more of them, be discharged.

§ 3B:14-21. Removal for cause

The court may remove a fiduciary from office when the fiduciary:

a. After due notice of an order or judgment of the court so directing, neglects or refuses, within the time fixed by the court, to file an inventory, render an account, or give security or additional security;

b. After due notice of any other order or judgment of the court made under its proper authority, neglects or refuses to perform or obey the order or judgment within the time fixed by the court;

c. Embezzles, wastes, or misapplies any part of the estate for which the fiduciary is responsible, or abuses the trust and confidence reposed in the fiduciary;

d. No longer resides nor has an office in the State and neglects or refuses to proceed with the administration of the estate and perform the duties required;

e. Is incapacitated for the transaction of business; or

f. Neglects or refuses, as one of two or more fiduciaries, to perform the required duties or to join with the other fiduciary or fiduciaries in the administration of the estate for which they are responsible whereby the proper administration and settlement of the estate is or may be hindered or prevented.

§ 3B:14-22. Discharge or removal not to release fiduciary or sureties from certain liabilities

The discharge or removal of a fiduciary for any cause authorized by this article shall not release or discharge him or his surety or sureties, or any of them, from liability for the estate, or any part thereof, which has been received or ought to have been received by him or them, or for any neglect, default, miscarriage or breach of trust in the execution of his office.

§ 3B:14-23. Powers

In the absence of contrary or limiting provisions in the judgment or order appointing a fiduciary, in the will, deed, or other instrument or in a subsequent court judgment or order, every fiduciary shall, in the exercise of good faith and reasonable discretion, have the power:

a. To accept additions to any estate or trust from sources other than the estate of the decedent, the minor, the person who is incapacitated, or the settlor of a trust;

b. To acquire the remaining undivided interest in an estate or trust asset in which the fiduciary, in a fiduciary capacity, holds an undivided interest;

c. To invest and reinvest assets of the estate or trust under the provisions of the will, deed, or other instrument or as otherwise provided by law and to exchange assets for investments and other property upon terms as may seem advisable to the fiduciary;

d. To effect and keep in force fire, rent, title, liability, casualty, or other insurance to protect the property of the estate or trust and to protect the fiduciary;

e. With respect to any property or any interest therein owned by an estate or trust, including any real property belonging to the fiduciary's decedent at death, except where the property or any interest therein is specifically disposed of:

(1) To take possession of and manage the property and to collect the rents therefrom, and pay taxes, mortgage interest, and other charges against the property;
(2) To sell the property at public or private sale, and on terms as in the opinion of the fiduciary shall be most advantageous to those interested therein;
(3) With respect to fiduciaries other than a trustee, to lease the property for a term not exceeding three years, and in the case of a trustee to lease the property for a term not exceeding 10 years, even though the term extends beyond the duration of the trust, and in either case including the right to explore for and remove mineral or other natural resources, and in connection with mineral leases to enter into pooling and unitization agreements;
(4) To mortgage the property;
(5) To grant easements to adjoining owners and utilities;
(6) A fiduciary acting under a will may exercise any of the powers granted by this subsection e. notwithstanding the effects upon the will of the birth of a child after its execution;
f. To make repairs to the property of the estate or trust for the purpose of preserving the property or rendering it rentable or saleable;
g. To grant options for the sale of any property of the estate or trust for a period not exceeding six months;
h. With respect to any mortgage held by the estate or trust to continue it upon and after maturity, with or without renewal or extension, upon terms as may seem advisable to the fiduciary and to foreclose, as an incident to collection of any bond or note, any mortgage and purchase the mortgaged property or acquire the property by deed from the mortgagor in lieu of foreclosure;
i. In the case of the survivor or survivors of two or more fiduciaries to administer the estate or trust without the appointment of a successor to the fiduciary or fiduciaries who have ceased to act and to exercise or perform all of the powers given unless contrary to the express provision of the will, deed, or other instrument;
j. As a new, alternate, successor, substitute, or additional fiduciary or fiduciaries, to have or succeed to all of the powers, duties, and discretion of the original fiduciary or fiduciaries, with respect to the estate or trust, as were given to the original fiduciary or fiduciaries named in or appointed by a will, deed, or other instrument, unless the exercise of the powers, duties, or discretion of the original fiduciary or fiduciaries is expressly prohibited by the will, deed, or other instrument to any successor or substitute fiduciary or fiduciaries;
k. Where there are three or more fiduciaries qualified to act, to take any action with respect to the estate or trust which a majority of the fiduciaries shall determine; a fiduciary who fails to act through absence or disability, or a dissenting fiduciary who joins in carrying out the decision of a majority of the fiduciaries if the dissent is expressed promptly in writing to the cofiduciaries, shall not be liable for the consequences of any majority decision, provided that liability for failure to join in administering the trust or to prevent a breach of trust may not thus be avoided;
l. To employ and compensate attorneys for services rendered to the estate or trust or to a fiduciary in the performance of the fiduciary's duties;
m. To compromise, contest, or otherwise settle any claim in favor of the estate, trust, or fiduciary or in favor of third persons and against the estate, trust, or fiduciary, including transfer inheritance, estate, income, and other taxes;
n. To vote in person or by proxy, discretionary or otherwise, shares of stock or other securities held by the estate or trust;
o. To pay calls, assessments, and any other sums chargeable or accruing against or on account of shares of stock, bonds, debentures, or other corporate securities in the control of a fiduciary, whenever the payments may be legally enforceable against the fiduciary or any property of the estate or trust or the fiduciary deems payment expedient and for the best interests of the estate or trust;
p. To sell or exercise stock subscription or conversion rights, participate in foreclosures, reorganizations, consolidations, mergers, or liquidations, and to consent to corporate sales or leases and encumbrances, and, in the exercise of those powers, the fiduciary is authorized to deposit stocks, bonds, or other securities with any custodian, agent, protective or other similar committee, or trustee under a voting trust agreement, under terms and conditions respecting the deposit thereof as the fiduciary may approve;
q. To execute and deliver agreements, assignments, bills of sale, contracts, deeds, notes, receipts, and any other instrument necessary or appropriate for the administration of the estate or trust;
r. In the case of a trustee:
(1) To hold two or more trusts or parts of trusts created by the same instrument, as an undivided whole, without separation as between the trusts or parts of the trusts, provided that separate trusts or parts of trusts shall have undivided interests and provided further that no holding shall defer the vesting of any estate in possession or otherwise;
(2) To divide a trust, before or after its initial funding, into two or more separate trusts, provided that such division will not materially impair the accomplishment of the trust purposes or the interests of any beneficiary. Distributions provided for by the governing instrument may be made from one or more of the separate trusts;
s. To distribute in kind any property of the estate or trust as provided in article 1 of chapter 23 of this Title;
t. To join with the surviving spouse, partner in a civil union, or domestic partner, the executor of the decedent's will, or the administrator of the decedent's estate in the execution and filing of a joint income tax return for any period prior to the death of a decedent for which no return or gift tax return on gifts made by the decedent's surviving spouse, partner in a civil union, or domestic partner was filed, and to consent to treat the gifts as being made one-half by the decedent, for any period prior to a decedent's death, and to pay taxes thereon as are chargeable to the decedent;

u. To acquire or dispose of an asset, including real or personal property in this State or another state, for cash or on credit, at public or private sale, and to manage, develop, improve, exchange, partition, change the character of, or abandon an estate asset;

v. To continue any business constituting the whole or any part of the estate for so long a period of time as the fiduciary may deem advisable and advantageous for the estate and persons interested therein;

w. In the case of a qualified bank as defined in section 1 of P.L.1948, c.67 (C.17:9A-1), and an out-of-State bank as defined in section 1 of P.L.1948, c.67 (C.17:9A-1), which has established a trust office in this State to purchase, sell, and maintain for any fiduciary account, securities issued by an investment company which is operated and maintained in accordance with the "Investment Company Act of 1940," 15 U.S.C. § 80a-1 et seq., and for which the qualified bank or out-of-State bank is providing services as an investment advisor, investment manager, custodian, or otherwise, including those for which it receives compensation, if:

(1) The investment is otherwise in accordance with applicable fiduciary standards; and

(2) The investment is authorized by the agreement or instrument creating the fiduciary account that gives the qualified bank or out-of-State bank investment authority, or by court order; or

(3) The qualified bank or out-of-State bank provides written notice not less than annually by prospectus, account statement, or otherwise, disclosing to any current income beneficiaries of the trust the services provided by the qualified bank or its affiliate or out-of-State bank to the investment company, and the rate, formula, or other method by which compensation paid to the qualified bank or its affiliate or out-of-State bank is determined and the qualified bank or out-of-State bank does not receive a written objection from any current income beneficiary within 30 days after receipt of this notice. If a written objection is received from any current income beneficiary pursuant to this paragraph (3), no such investment of the trust assets of that fiduciary account shall be made or maintained.

Such investment shall not be deemed self-dealing or a fiduciary conflict; nor shall the fact that other beneficiaries of fiduciary accounts of the qualified bank or out-of-State bank have similar investments be deemed to be an improper commingling of assets by the qualified bank or out-of-State bank.

For purposes of this subsection, "fiduciary account" shall include a trust, estate, agency, or other account in which funds, property, or both, are held by a qualified bank pursuant to section 28 of P.L.1948, c.67 (C.17:9A-28), or an account for which a qualified bank or out-of-State bank acts as investment advisor or manager or an account held by an out-of-State bank as defined in section 1 of P.L.1948, c. 67 (C.17:9A-1);

x. To employ and compensate accountants from the fiduciary fund for services rendered to the estate or trust or to a fiduciary in the performance of the fiduciary's duties, including the duty of a corporate or other fiduciary with respect to the preparation of accountings, without reduction in commissions due to the fiduciary, so long as such accountings are not the usual, customary, or routine services provided by the fiduciary in light of the nature and skill of the fiduciary. In evaluating the actions of the fiduciary under this subsection, the court shall consider the size and complexity of the fiduciary fund, the length of time for which the accounting is rendered, and the increased risk and responsibilities imposed on fiduciaries as a result of revisions to laws affecting fiduciaries including, but not limited to, the "Uniform Principal and Income Act of 2001," P.L.2001, c.212 (C.3B:19B-1 et seq.) and the "Prudent Investor Act," P.L.1997, c.26 (C.3B:20-11.1 et seq.) provided that such revisions of the laws affecting fiduciaries were enacted after the fiduciary responsibilities under the corresponding will, deed, or other instrument, or court judgment or order, were imposed on, and assumed by, the fiduciary. For purposes of this subsection, "Accountant" means a person who is registered as a certified public accountant pursuant to the provisions of the "Accountancy Act of 1997," P.L.1997, c.259 (C.45:2B-42 et seq.), or an accounting firm which is organized for the practice of public accounting pursuant to the provisions of the "Accountancy Act of 1997," P.L.1997, c.259 (C.45:2B-42 et seq.) and "The Professional Service Corporation Act," P.L.1969, c.232 (C.14A:17-1 et seq.); and

y. The powers set forth in this section are in addition to any other powers granted by law, and by a will, deed, or other instrument.

§ 3B:14-24. Authorization to exercise other powers

The court having jurisdiction of the estate or trust may authorize the fiduciary to exercise any other power or to disclaim any power, if the court determines such exercise or disclaimer is necessary or advisable which in the judgment of the court is necessary for the proper administration of the estate or trust.

§ 3B:14-25. Payment of debt or delivery of certain personal property; requirements

After the expiration of 60 days from the appointment of a domiciliary foreign fiduciary, any person indebted to the estate or having possession or control of personal property, or of an instrument evidencing a debt, obligation, stock or chose in action belonging to the estate may pay the debt, deliver the personal property, or the instrument evidencing the debt, obligation, stock or chose in action, to the domiciliary foreign fiduciary upon being presented with a certificate of his letters or other proof of his authority and an affidavit made by or on his behalf stating:

a. The date of the letters of the domiciliary foreign fiduciary, or the date when he first received authority to act;

b. That no letters have issued in this State and no action therefor is pending in this State; and

c. That the domiciliary foreign fiduciary is entitled to payment or delivery.

§ 3B:14-26. Release upon payment or delivery in good faith

Payment or delivery made in good faith under N.J.S. 3B:14-25 on the basis of the proof of authority and affidavit releases the debtor or person having possession of the personal property to the same extent as if payment or delivery had been made to a local fiduciary.

§ 3B:14-27. When payment or delivery may not be made

Payment or delivery under N.J.S. 3B:14-25 may not be made if a resident creditor of the estate has notified the debtor or the person having possession of the personal property that the debt should not be paid nor the property delivered to the domiciliary foreign fiduciary.

§ 3B:14-28. Filing proof of domiciliary foreign fiduciary's authority

If letters have not issued in this State or an action therefor is not pending in this State, a domiciliary foreign fiduciary or any other person may file in the office of the Clerk of the Superior Court, or if the decedent, ward, or trust has an interest in real estate in any county of this State, then either in that office or in the office of the surrogate of that county, authenticated copies of the letters of appointment of the fiduciary and of any official bond he has given.

§ 3B:14-29. Exercise of powers by domiciliary foreign fiduciary; security for costs

Upon compliance with N.J.S. 3B:14-28, a domiciliary foreign fiduciary may exercise as to assets in this State all powers he would have had if he had received letters or been appointed in this State, including the power to release and discharge real or personal estate from a mortgage, judgment or other lien or encumbrance held by his decedent, ward or trust. Whether N.J.S. 3B:14-28 is complied with prior to, pending, or subsequent to the action, a domiciliary foreign fiduciary may maintain, or be made a party defendant or otherwise, to any action in any court of this State as if letters had been granted to him in this State, subject to any conditions generally imposed upon nonresident parties. Security for costs may be required of him.

§ 3B:14-30. Termination of domiciliary foreign fiduciary's powers; protection of third persons; exercise of powers binding on local fiduciary

The power of a domiciliary foreign fiduciary under N.J.S. 3B:14-28 or N.J.S. 3B:14-29 shall be exercised only if letters have not been issued or an action therefor is not pending in this State. The issuance of local letters or an action therefor terminates the power of the domiciliary foreign fiduciary to act under N.J.S. 3B:14-29, but a court in this State may allow the domiciliary foreign fiduciary to exercise limited powers to preserve the estate. No person who, before receiving actual notice of local letters or an action therefor, has changed his position in reliance upon the powers of the domiciliary foreign fiduciary, shall be prejudiced by reason of the action for, or issuance of, local letters. The local fiduciary is subject to all duties and obligations which have accrued by virtue of the exercise of the powers by the domiciliary foreign fiduciary and may be substituted for him in any action in this State.

Article 5. Liability; Protection of Persons Dealing or Assisting with Fiduciaries

§ 3B:14-31. Personal liability of fiduciary on contracts

Unless otherwise provided in the contract, a fiduciary is not individually liable on a contract properly entered into in his fiduciary capacity in the course of administration of the estate unless he fails to reveal his fiduciary capacity and identify the estate in the contract.

§ 3B:14-32. Personal liability for obligations arising from ownership or control of estate; torts

A fiduciary is individually liable for obligations arising from ownership or control of the estate or for torts committed in the course of administration of the estate only if he is personally at fault.

§ 3B:14-33. Asserting claims against estate

Claims based on contracts entered into by a fiduciary in his fiduciary capacity, on obligations arising from ownership or control of the estate or on torts committed in the course of estate administration may be asserted against the estate by proceeding against the fiduciary in his fiduciary capacity, whether or not the fiduciary is individually liable therefor.

§ 3B:14-34. Determining issues of liability between estate and fiduciary

Issues of liability as between the estate and the fiduciary individually may be determined in a proceeding for accounting, surcharge or indemnification or other appropriate proceeding.

§ 3B:14-35. Liability of fiduciary for improper exercise of power concerning estate

If the exercise of power concerning the estate is improper, the fiduciary is liable to interested persons for damage or loss resulting from breach of his fiduciary duty to the same extent as a trustee of an express trust. The rights of purchasers and others dealing with a fiduciary shall be determined as provided in N.J.S. 3B:14-28 and N.J.S. 3B:14-29.

§ 3B:14-36. Voidable sales, encumbrances or transactions; exceptions

Any sale or encumbrance to the fiduciary, his spouse, agent or attorney, or any corporation or trust in which he has a substantial beneficial interest, or any transaction which is affected by a substantial conflict of interest on the part of the fiduciary, is voidable by any person interested in the estate except one who has consented after fair disclosure, unless:
a. The will or a contract entered into by the decedent expressly authorized the transaction; or
b. The transaction is approved by the court after notice to interested persons.

§ 3B:14-37. Protection of persons assisting or dealing with fiduciary

a. A person other than a beneficiary who in good faith either assists a fiduciary or deals with him for value is protected as if the fiduciary properly exercised his power.
b. The fact that a person knowingly deals with a fiduciary does not alone require the person to inquire into the existence of a power or the propriety of its exercise.

c. Except as to real property specifically devised by will, no provision in any will, trust or order of court purporting to limit the power of a fiduciary is effective except as to persons with actual knowledge thereof.

d. A person who in good faith pays, transfers or delivers to a fiduciary money or other property is not responsible for the proper application thereof by the fiduciary; and any right or title acquired from the fiduciary in consideration of the payment, transfer or delivery is not invalid in consequence of a misapplication by the fiduciary.

e. A person other than a beneficiary who in good faith assists a former trustee, or who in good faith and for value deals with a former trustee, without knowledge that the trusteeship has terminated is protected from liability as if the former trustee were still a trustee.

f. The protection here expressed extends to instances in which some procedural irregularity or jurisdictional defect occurred in proceedings leading to the issuance of letters, including a case in which the alleged decedent is found to be alive.

g. The protection here expressed is in addition to that provided by comparable provisions of the laws relating to commercial transactions and laws simplifying transfers of securities by fiduciaries.

Article 6. Actions by or Against Fiduciaries

§ 3B:14-38. Actions by fiduciaries

The fiduciary or a majority of the fiduciaries who qualify may maintain an action in any court of this State without joining any fiduciary who has failed to qualify or join in the action. An action so brought and judgment recovered thereon in the name of the majority shall be as valid and effectual as if brought by and in the names of all the qualified fiduciaries.

§ 3B:14-39. Several fiduciaries sued; judgment and execution

In a civil action in any court of this State against two or more fiduciaries, those served shall defend the action on behalf of all of them.

If, in the action, judgment is recovered by the plaintiff payable out of the decedent's estate, he shall have judgment and execution against all the fiduciaries named in the process, to be satisfied out of the decedent's estate.

§ 3B:14-40. No actions against personal representatives within 6 months of grants of letters; exceptions; execution

To enable personal representatives to examine into the condition of the estate and to ascertain its amount and value and the debts to be paid, no actions, except for funeral expenses, shall be brought or maintained against personal representatives within 6 months after letters testamentary or of administration have been granted, as the case may be, unless by special leave of the court in which the action is brought; and, if leave is given, no execution shall issue within the period of 6 months.

§ 3B:14-41. Actions against fiduciaries; proof of proper administration

The failure of a fiduciary to plead in an action against him in a representative capacity that he has fully administered the estate or the extent to which he has administered the estate shall not preclude him from proving his due administration of the estate in an action against him personally on a judgment recovered against him in the original action in his representative capacity. Notice by the fiduciary of his intention to prove administration must be given 20 days before trial.

§ 3B:14-42. Recovery of damages for injury to property subsequently transferred

A person injuring, damaging or destroying property while in the hands of a fiduciary shall be liable to the fiduciary in an action for damages for the benefit of his cestui que trust or persons in interest. The fiduciary's right to substantial damages shall not be affected by the fact that he may have transferred or conveyed the property to his cestui que trust, or other person, after the time of the injury, damage or destruction and before action brought.

§ 3B:14-43. Adjudication binding on local fiduciary

An adjudication rendered in any jurisdiction in favor of or against any fiduciary of the estate is as binding on the local fiduciary upon notice to him as if he were a party to the adjudication.

§ 3B:14-44. Discovery of assets in action by fiduciary

Upon application by a fiduciary, the court may require any person to appear before and make discovery of his possession of, or knowledge of the existence or whereabouts of personal property of the fiduciary's decedent, ward or trust by the production of books, papers or securities relating to the estate, guardianship or trusteeship or by the examination of the person and other witnesses.

§ 3B:14-45. Discovery of assets in action against the fiduciary

The court may, if it shall appear that a fiduciary may have wasted, embezzled or misapplied the estate intrusted to him, compel discovery to be made of the condition of the estate by the production of books, papers, securities and documents relating to the estate, or the examination of the fiduciary and other witnesses.

§ 3B:14-46. "Process" defined

The word "process" as used in this subarticle shall include any summons, subpena, writ, attachment and levy thereunder, garnishment, rule, order, notice, decision, judgment or execution and levy thereunder, or any other process whatsoever, that may lawfully be issued out of any court of this State against a fiduciary in any proceeding affecting the estate which he may represent or affecting the property or interest of any beneficiary of, or interested in, the estate or against the property or interest of any beneficiary which is held or claimed to be held by the fiduciary for the account or benefit of the beneficiary.

§ 3B:14-47. Fiduciary to file power of attorney; requisites of power

Every fiduciary, whether or not a resident within this State, who is granted letters testamentary or of administration, trusteeship or guardianship within this State shall, at the time of the grant, or before he undertakes to perform his duties, file a power of attorney with the surrogate of the county or clerk of the court granting the letters. The power of attorney shall be duly executed in writing, shall set forth the post office address, street and number, of the fiduciary and, by sufficient language, constitute the surrogate or clerk with whom it is filed, and his successors in office, his true and lawful attorney to receive process affecting the estate in charge of the fiduciary, or any interest therein, with the same force and effect as if the process were duly served on the fiduciary within this State.

§ 3B:14-48. Service of process

Service of process, under the provisions of this subarticle, shall be made by leaving a copy of the process with the surrogate or clerk, or with a deputy or a clerk employed in his office, together with a fee of $2.00 to be taxed in the costs.

The surrogate, deputy or clerk shall forthwith notify the fiduciary of the service by mailing a letter, with a copy of the process served inclosed, with full postage prepaid, directed to the fiduciary at the post office address given in the power of attorney.

§ 3B:14-49. Submission to jurisdiction of courts

A domiciliary foreign fiduciary submits himself personally to the jurisdiction of the courts of this State in any proceeding relating to the estate by:

a. Filing authenticated copies of his letters as provided in N.J.S. 3B:14-28;

b. Receiving payment of money or taking delivery of personal property under N.J.S. 3B:14-25, but jurisdiction hereunder is limited to the money or value of personal property received;

c. Doing any act as a fiduciary in this State which would have given the State jurisdiction over him as an individual.

§ 3B:14-50. Jurisdiction by act of decedent

In addition to jurisdiction conferred by N.J.S. 3B:14-49, a domiciliary foreign fiduciary for a decedent is subject to the jurisdiction of the courts of this State to the same extent that his decedent was subject to their jurisdiction immediately prior to death.

§ 3B:14-51. Service of process

If a domiciliary foreign fiduciary has submitted himself to the jurisdiction of the courts of this State, service of process shall be made upon him as provided by the Rules of the Supreme Court of New Jersey.

Article 7. Uniform Fiduciaries Law

§ 3B:14-52. Short title

This article shall be known and may be cited as the "Uniform Fiduciaries Law."

§ 3B:14-53. Definitions

As used in this article:

a. "Bank" includes any person or association of persons, whether incorporated or not, carrying on the business of banking and any State chartered savings and loan association, or any Federal savings and loan association, having its principal office in this State; The inclusion of savings and loan associations within the provisions of this article shall not be construed as conferring upon those associations any powers not otherwise conferred by this article, nor as enlarging any powers so conferred;

b. "Fiduciary" includes a trustee under any trust, express, implied, resulting or constructive, executor, administrator, guardian, conservator, curator, receiver, trustee in bankruptcy, assignee for the benefit of creditors, partner, agent, officer of a corporation, public or private, public officer, or any other person acting in a fiduciary capacity for any person, trust or estate;

c. "Person" includes two or more persons having a joint or common interest;

d. "Principal" includes any person to whom a fiduciary as such owes an obligation;

e. A thing is done "in good faith" within the meaning of this article, when it is in fact done honestly, whether it be done negligently or not.

§ 3B:14-54. Application of payments of money or transfer of property made to fiduciaries

A person who in good faith pays or transfers to a fiduciary money or other property which the fiduciary is authorized to receive, is not responsible for the proper application thereof by the fiduciary. Any right or title acquired from the fiduciary in consideration of the payment or transfer is not invalid in consequence of a misapplication by the fiduciary.

§ 3B:14-55. Check drawn by and payable to fiduciary

If a check or other bill of exchange is drawn by a fiduciary as such or in the name of his principal by a fiduciary empowered to draw the instrument in the name of his principal, payable to the fiduciary personally, or payable to a third person and by him transferred to the fiduciary, and is thereafter transferred by the fiduciary, whether in payment of a personal debt of the fiduciary or otherwise, the transferee is not bound to inquire whether the fiduciary is committing a breach of his obligation as fiduciary in transferring the instrument, and is not chargeable with notice that the fiduciary is committing a breach of his obligation as fiduciary unless he takes the instrument with actual knowledge of the breach or with knowledge of facts that his action in taking the instrument amounts to bad faith.

§ 3B:14-56. Deposit in name of fiduciary; checks; when bank liable

If a deposit is made in a bank to the credit of a fiduciary as such, the bank is authorized to pay the amount of the deposit or any part thereof upon the check of the fiduciary, signed with the name in which the deposit is entered, without being liable to the principal, unless the bank pays the check with the actual knowledge that the fiduciary is committing a breach of his obligation as fiduciary in drawing the check or with knowledge of facts that its action in paying the check amounts to bad faith. If, however, a check is payable to the drawee bank and is delivered to it in payment of or as security for a personal debt of the fiduciary to it, the bank is liable to the principal if the fiduciary in fact commits a breach of his obligation as fiduciary in drawing or delivering the check.

§ 3B:14-57. Checks drawn by fiduciary upon principal's account

If a check is drawn upon the account of his principal in a bank by a fiduciary who is empowered to draw checks upon his principal's account, the bank is authorized to pay the check without being liable to the principal, unless the bank pays the check with actual knowledge that the fiduciary is committing a breach of his obligation as fiduciary in drawing the check, or with knowledge of facts that its action in paying the check amounts to bad faith. If, however, a check is payable to the drawee bank and is delivered to it in payment of or as security for a personal debt of the fiduciary to it, the bank is liable to the principal if the fiduciary in fact commits a breach of his obligation as fiduciary in drawing or delivering the check.

§ 3B:14-58. Deposit in fiduciary's personal account; liability of bank receiving deposit and paying checks

a. If a fiduciary makes a deposit in a bank to his personal credit of checks drawn by him upon an account in his own name as fiduciary, or of checks drawn by him upon an account in the name of his principal, if he is empowered to draw thereon, or, except as provided in subsection b. of this section, if he otherwise makes a deposit of funds held by him as fiduciary, the bank receiving the deposit is not bound to inquire whether the fiduciary is committing thereby a breach of his obligation as fiduciary. The bank is authorized to pay the amount of the deposit of any part thereof upon the personal check of the fiduciary without being liable to the principal, unless the bank receives the deposit or pays the check with actual knowledge that the fiduciary is committing a breach of his obligation as fiduciary in making the deposit or in drawing the check, or with knowledge of facts that its action in receiving the deposit of paying the check amounts to bad faith.

b. In the case of an instrument payable to the principal or the fiduciary as fiduciary, the bank has notice of the breach of fiduciary duty if the instrument is deposited to an account other than an account of the fiduciary, as fiduciary, or an account of the principal.

§ 3B:14-59. Deposit in names of two or more trustees; liability of payee, holder or bank

When a deposit is made in a bank in the names of two or more persons as trustees and a check is drawn upon the trust account by any trustee or trustees authorized by the other trustee or trustees to draw checks upon the trust account, neither the payee nor other holder nor the bank is bound to inquire whether it is a breach of trust to authorize the trustee or trustees to draw checks upon the trust account, and is not liable unless the circumstances be such that the action of the payee or other holder or the bank amounts to bad faith.

§ 3B:14-60. Cases not provided for in article

In any case not provided for in this article, the rules of law and equity, including the law merchant and those rules of law and equity relating to trusts, agency, commercial transactions and banking, shall continue to apply.

§ 3B:14-61. Uniformity of interpretation

The article shall be so interpreted and construed as to effectuate its general purpose to make uniform laws of those states which enact it.

§ 3B:14-61.1. Short title.

This act shall be known and may be cited as the "Uniform Fiduciary Access to Digital Assets Act."

§ 3B:14-61.2. Definitions.

As used in this act:

"Account" means an arrangement under a terms-of-service in which a custodian carries, maintains, processes, receives, or stores a digital asset of the user or provides goods or services to the user.

"Agent" means an attorney-in-fact granted authority under a durable or nondurable power of attorney.

"Carries" means engages in the transmission of an electronic communication.

"Catalogue of electronic communications" means information that identifies each person with which a user has had an electronic communication, the time and date of the communication, and the electronic address of the person.

"Content of an electronic communication" means information concerning the substance or meaning of the communication which:
(a) has been sent or received by a user;
(b) is in electronic storage by a custodian providing an electronic communication service to the public or is carried or maintained by a custodian providing a remote computing service to the public; and
(c) is not readily accessible to the public.

"Court" means the Probate Part of the Chancery Division of the Superior Court. For the purposes of this act, "court" includes the Surrogate's Court acting within the scope of its authority pursuant to statute or the Rules of Court.

"Custodian" means a person that carries, maintains, processes, receives, or stores a digital asset of a user.

"Designated recipient" means a person chosen by a user using an online tool to administer digital assets of the user.

"Digital asset" means an electronic record in which an individual has a right or interest. The term does not include an underlying asset or liability unless the asset or liability is itself an electronic record.

"Electronic" means relating to technology having electrical, digital, magnetic, wireless, optical, electromagnetic, or similar capabilities.

"Electronic communication" has the meaning set forth in 18 U.S.C. § 2510(12).

"Electronic-communication service" means a custodian that provides to a user the ability to send or receive an electronic communication.

"Fiduciary" means an original, additional, or successor personal representative, guardian, agent, or trustee.

"Guardian" means a person appointed by the court to make decisions regarding the property of an incapacitated adult, including a person appointed in accordance with N.J.S.3B:12-1 et seq. or its equivalent in a state other than New Jersey.

"Incapacitated person" means an incapacitated individual, as defined in N.J.S.3B:1-2, for whom a guardian has been appointed.

"Information" means data, text, images, videos, sounds, codes, computer programs, software, databases, or the like.

"Online tool" means an electronic service provided by a custodian that allows the user, in an agreement distinct from the terms-of-service agreement between the custodian and user, to provide directions for disclosure or nondisclosure of digital assets to a third person.

"Person" means an individual, estate, business or nonprofit entity, public corporation, government or governmental subdivision, agency, or instrumentality, or other legal entity.

"Personal representative" means an executor, administrator, special administrator, or person that performs substantially the same function under the law of this State other than this act.

"Power of attorney" means a written instrument by which an individual known as the principal authorizes another individual or individuals or a qualified bank within the meaning of section 28 of P.L.1948, c.67 (C.17:9A-28) known as the attorney-in-fact to perform specified acts on behalf of the principal as the principal's agent.

"Principal" means an individual, at least 18 years of age, who, in a power of attorney, authorizes an agent to act.

"Record" means information that is inscribed on a tangible medium or that is stored in an electronic or other medium and is retrievable in perceivable form.

"Remote-computing service" means a custodian that provides to a user computer processing services or the storage of digital assets by means of an electronic communications system, as defined in 18 U.S.C. § 2510(14).

"Terms-of-service agreement" means an agreement that controls the relationship between an account holder and a custodian.

"Trustee" means a fiduciary with legal title to property pursuant to an agreement or declaration that creates a beneficial interest in another. "Trustee" includes an original, additional, or successor trustee, whether or not appointed or confirmed by court.

"User" means a person that has an account with a custodian.

"Will" means the last will and testament of a testator or testatrix and includes any codicil and any testamentary instrument that merely appoints an executor, revokes or revises another will, nominates a guardian, or expressly excludes or limits the right of a person or class to succeed to property of the decedent passing by intestate succession.

§ 3B:14-61.3. User's residence in State, inapplicability of act to employers' digital assets.

a. This act applies to a custodian if the user resides in this State or resided in this State at the time of the user's death.

b. This act does not apply to a digital asset of an employer used by an employee in the ordinary course of the employer's business.

§ 3B:14-61.4. User direction for disclosure of digital assets.

a. A user may use an online tool to direct the custodian to disclose or not to disclose to a designated recipient some or all of the user's digital assets, including the content of electronic communications. If the online tool allows the user to modify or delete a direction at all times, a direction regarding disclosure using an online tool overrides a contrary direction by the user in a will, trust, power of attorney, or other record.

b. If a user has not used an online tool to give direction under subsection a. of this section or if the custodian has not provided an online tool, the user may allow or prohibit in a will, trust, power of attorney, or other record, disclosure to a fiduciary of some or all of the user's digital assets, including the content of electronic communications sent or received by the user.

c. A user's direction under subsection a. or b. of this section overrides a contrary provision in a terms-of-service agreement that does not require the user to act affirmatively and distinctly from the user's assent to the terms of service.

§ 3B:14-61.5. Terms-of-service agreement.

a. This act does not change or impair a right of a custodian or a user under a terms-of-service agreement to access and use digital assets of the user.

b. This act does not give a fiduciary or designated recipient any new or expanded rights other than those held by the user for whom, or for whose estate, the fiduciary or designated recipient acts or represents.

c. A fiduciary's or designated recipient's access to digital assets may be modified or eliminated by a user, by federal law, or by a terms-of-service agreement if the user has not provided direction under section 4 [C.3B:14-61.4] of this act.

§ 3B:14-61.6. Procedure for disclosing digital assets.

a. When disclosing digital assets of a user under this act, the custodian shall either:

(1) grant a fiduciary or designated recipient full access to the user's account;

(2) grant a fiduciary or designated recipient partial access to the user's account sufficient to perform the tasks with which the fiduciary or designated recipient is charged; or

(3) provide a fiduciary or designated recipient a copy in a record of any digital asset that, on the date the custodian received the request for disclosure, the user could have accessed if the user were alive and had full capacity and access to the account.

b. A custodian may assess a reasonable administrative charge for the cost of disclosing digital assets under this act.

c. A custodian need not disclose under this act a digital asset deleted by a user.

d. If a user directs or a fiduciary requests a custodian to disclose under this act some, but not all, of the user's digital assets, the custodian need not disclose the assets if segregation of the assets would impose an undue burden on the custodian. If the custodian believes the direction or request imposes an undue burden, the custodian or fiduciary may seek an order from the court to disclose:
(1) a subset limited by date of the user's digital assets;
(2) all of the user's digital assets to the fiduciary or designated recipient;
(3) none of the user's digital assets; or
(4) all of the user's digital assets to the court for review in camera.

§ 3B:14-61.7. Disclosure of content of electronic communications of deceased user.

If a deceased user consented or a court directs disclosure of the contents of electronic communications of the user, the custodian shall disclose to the personal representative of the estate of the user the content of an electronic communication sent or received by the user if the representative gives the custodian:

a. a written request for disclosure in physical or electronic form;
b. a copy of the death certificate of the user;
c. a certificate evidencing the appointment of the representative or a small-estate affidavit;
d. unless the user provided direction using an online tool, a copy of the user's will, trust, power of attorney, or other record evidencing the user's consent to disclosure of the content of electronic communications; and
e. if requested by the custodian, any of the following:
(1) a number, username, address, or other unique subscriber or account identifier assigned by the custodian to identify the user's account;
(2) evidence linking the account to the user; or
(3) a finding by the court of any of the following:
(a) the user had a specific account with the custodian, identifiable by the information specified in paragraph (1) of this subsection;
(b) disclosure of the content of electronic communications of the user would not violate 18 U.S.C. § 2701 et seq., Unlawful Access to Stored Communications; 47 U.S.C. § 222, Privacy of Customer Information; or other applicable law;
(c) unless the user provided direction using an online tool, the user consented to disclosure of the content of electronic communications; or
(d) disclosure of the content of electronic communications of the user is reasonably necessary for administration of the estate.

§ 3B:14-61.8. Disclosure of other digital assets of deceased user.

Unless the user prohibited disclosure of digital assets or the court directs otherwise, a custodian shall disclose to the personal representative of the estate of a deceased user a catalogue of electronic communications sent or received by the user and digital assets, other than the content of electronic communications, of the user, if the representative gives the custodian:

a. a written request for disclosure in physical or electronic form;
b. a copy of the death certificate of the user;
c. a certificate evidencing the appointment of the representative or a small-estate affidavit; and
d. if requested by the custodian, any of the following:
(1) a number, username, address, or other unique subscriber or account identifier assigned by the custodian to identify the user's account;
(2) evidence linking the account to the user;
(3) an affidavit stating that disclosure of the user's digital assets is reasonably necessary for administration of the estate; or
(4) a finding by the court of either of the following:
(a) the user had a specific account with the custodian, identifiable by the information specified in paragraph (1) of this subsection; or
(b) disclosure of the user's digital assets is reasonably necessary for administration of the estate.

§ 3B:14-61.9. Disclosure of content of electronic communications of principal.

To the extent a power of attorney expressly grants an agent authority over the content of electronic communications sent or received by the principal and unless directed otherwise by the principal or the court, a custodian shall disclose to the agent the content if the agent gives the custodian:

a. a written request for disclosure in physical or electronic form;
b. an original or copy of the power of attorney expressly granting the agent authority over the content of electronic communications of the principal;
c. a certification by the agent, under penalty of perjury, that the power of attorney is in effect; and
d. if requested by the custodian:
(1) a number, username, address, or other unique subscriber or account identifier assigned by the custodian to identify the principal's account; or
(2) evidence linking the account to the principal.

§ 3B:14-61.10. Disclosure of other digital assets of principal.

Unless otherwise ordered by the court, directed by the principal, or provided by a power of attorney, a custodian shall disclose to an agent with specific authority over digital assets or general authority to act on behalf of a principal a catalogue of electronic communications sent or received by the principal and digital assets, other than the content of electronic communications, of the principal if the agent gives the custodian:

a. a written request for disclosure in physical or electronic form;

b. an original or a copy of the power of attorney that gives the agent specific authority over digital assets or general authority to act on behalf of the principal;

c. a certification by the agent, under penalty of perjury, that the power of attorney is in effect; and

d. if requested by the custodian:

(1) a number, username, address, or other unique subscriber or account identifier assigned by the custodian to identify the principal's account; or

(2) evidence linking the account to the principal.

§ 3B:14-61.11. Disclosure of digital assets held in trust when trustee is original user.

Unless otherwise ordered by the court or provided in a trust, a custodian shall disclose to a trustee that is an original user of an account any digital asset of the account held in trust, including a catalogue of electronic communications of the trustee and the content of electronic communications.

§ 3B:14-61.12. Disclosure of contents of electronic communications held in trust when trustee not original user.

Unless otherwise ordered by the court, directed by the user, or provided in a trust, a custodian shall disclose to a trustee that is not an original user of an account the content of an electronic communication sent or received by an original or successor user and carried, maintained, processed, received, or stored by the custodian in the account of the trust if the trustee gives the custodian:

a. a written request for disclosure in physical or electronic form;

b. a certified copy of the trust instrument or a certification of the trust under N.J.S.3B:31-81 that includes consent to disclosure of the content of electronic communications to the trustee;

c. a certification by the trustee, under penalty of perjury, that the trust exists and the trustee is a currently acting trustee of the trust; and

d. if requested by the custodian:

(1) a number, username, address, or other unique subscriber or account identifier assigned by the custodian to identify the trust's account; or

(2) evidence linking the account to the trust.

§ 3B:14-61.13. Disclosure of other digital assets held in trust when trustee not original user.

Unless otherwise ordered by the court, directed by the user, or provided in a trust, a custodian shall disclose, to a trustee that is not an original user of an account, a catalogue of electronic communications sent or received by an original or successor user and stored, carried, or maintained by the custodian in an account of the trust and any digital assets, other than the content of electronic communications, in which the trust has a right or interest if the trustee gives the custodian:

a. a written request for disclosure in physical or electronic form;

b. a certified copy of the trust instrument or a certification of the trust under N.J.S.3B:31-81;

c. a certification by the trustee, under penalty of perjury, that the trust exists and the trustee is a currently acting trustee of the trust; and

d. if requested by the custodian:

(1) a number, username, address, or other unique subscriber or account identifier assigned by the custodian to identify the trust's account; or

(2) evidence linking the account to the trust.

§ 3B:14-61.14. Disclosure of digital assets to guardian of incapacitated person.

a. After an opportunity for a hearing under N.J.S.3B:12-1 et seq., the court may grant a guardian access to the digital assets of an incapacitated person.

b. Unless otherwise ordered by the court or directed by the user, a custodian shall disclose to a guardian the catalogue of electronic communications sent or received by the incapacitated person and any digital assets, other than the content of electronic communications, in which the incapacitated person has a right or interest if the guardian gives the custodian:

(1) a written request for disclosure in physical or electronic form;

(2) a copy of the court order that gives the guardian authority over the digital assets of the incapacitated person; and

(3) if requested by the custodian:

(a) a number, username, address, or other unique subscriber or account identifier assigned by the custodian to identify the account of the incapacitated person; or

(b) evidence linking the account to the incapacitated person.

c. A guardian with general authority to manage the assets of an incapacitated person may request a custodian of the digital assets of the incapacitated person to suspend or terminate an account of the incapacitated person for good cause. A request made under this section shall be accompanied by a copy of the court order giving the guardian authority over the incapacitated person's property.

§ 3B:14-61.15. Fiduciary and designated recipient duty and authority.

a. The legal duties imposed on a fiduciary charged with managing tangible property apply to the management of digital assets, including:
(1) the duty of care;
(2) the duty of loyalty; and
(3) the duty of confidentiality.
b. A fiduciary's or designated recipient's authority with respect to a digital asset of a user:
(1) except as otherwise provided in section 4 [C.3B:14-61.4] of this act, is subject to the applicable terms of service;
(2) is subject to other applicable law, including copyright law;
(3) in the case of a fiduciary, is limited by the scope of the fiduciary's duties; and
(4) may not be used to impersonate the user.
c. A fiduciary with authority over the property of a decedent, incapacitated person, principal, or settlor has the right to access any digital asset in which the decedent, incapacitated person, principal, or settlor had a right or interest and that is not held by a custodian or subject to a terms-of-service agreement.
d. A fiduciary acting within the scope of the fiduciary's duties is an authorized user of the property of the decedent, incapacitated person, principal, or settlor for the purpose of applicable computer-fraud and unauthorized-computer-access laws, including but not limited to the provisions of P.L.1984, c.184 (C.2C:20-23 et seq.) and N.J.S.2C:20-2.
e. A fiduciary with authority over the tangible, personal property of a decedent, incapacitated person, principal, or settlor:
(1) has the right to access the property and any digital asset stored in it; and
(2) is an authorized user for the purpose of computer-fraud and unauthorized-computer-access laws, including but not limited to the provisions of P.L.1984, c.184 (C.2C:20-23 et seq.) and N.J.S.2C:20-2.
f. A custodian may disclose information in an account to a fiduciary of the user when the information is required to terminate an account used to access digital assets licensed to the user.
g. A fiduciary of a user may request a custodian to terminate the user's account. A request for termination must be in writing, in either physical or electronic form, and accompanied by:
(1) if the user is deceased, a copy of the death certificate of the user;
(2) a copy of the letters testamentary or letters of administration, court order, power of attorney, or trust giving the fiduciary authority over the account; and
(3) if requested by the custodian:
(a) a number, username, address, or other unique subscriber or account identifier assigned by the custodian to identify the user's account;
(b) evidence linking the account to the user; or
(c) a finding by the court that the user had a specific account with the custodian, identifiable by the information specified in subparagraph (a) of this paragraph.

§ 3B:14-61.16. Custodian compliance and immunity.

a. Not later than 60 days after receipt of the information required under sections 7 through 15 [C.3B:14-61.7 through 3B:14-61.15] of this act, a custodian shall comply with a request under this act from a fiduciary or designated recipient to disclose digital assets or terminate an account. If the custodian fails to comply, the fiduciary or designated recipient may apply to the court for an order directing compliance.
b. An order under subsection a. of this section directing compliance must contain a finding that compliance is not in violation of 18 U.S.C. § 2702.
c. A custodian may notify the user that a request for disclosure or to terminate an account was made under this act.
d. A custodian may deny a request under this act from a fiduciary or designated recipient for disclosure of digital assets or to terminate an account if the custodian is aware of any lawful access to the account following the receipt of the fiduciary's request.
e. This act does not limit a custodian's ability to obtain or require a fiduciary or designated recipient requesting disclosure or termination under this act to obtain a court order which:
(1) specifies that an account belongs to the incapacitated person or principal;
(2) specifies that there is sufficient consent from the incapacitated person or principal to support the requested disclosure; and
(3) contains a finding required by law other than this act.
f. A custodian and its officers, employees, and agents are immune from liability for an act or omission done in good faith in compliance with this act.

§ 3B:14-61.17. Electronic Signatures in Global and National Commerce Act

In applying and construing this uniform act, consideration must be given to the need to promote uniformity of the law with respect to its subject matter among states that enact it.

§ 3B:14-61.18. Relation to electronic signatures in global and national commerce act.

This act modifies, limits, or supersedes the Electronic Signatures in Global and National Commerce Act, 15 U.S.C. § 7001 et seq., but does not modify, limit, or supersede section 101(c) of that act, 15 U.S.C. § 7001(c), or authorize electronic delivery of any of the notices described in s.103(b) of that act, 15 U.S.C. § 7003(b).

Article 8. Real Property; Abandonment

§ 3B:14-62. Abandonment of real property may be authorized

A fiduciary of or any person interested in an estate or a trust may apply to the court for a judgment or order directing the fiduciary to abandon any improved or unimproved real property that is an asset of the estate or trust and, which because of liens, encumbrances, the absence or lack of revenue, or for other reasons, does not have a value worth protecting, and that it is for the best interests of persons having an interest in the estate or trust that the real property be abandoned.

§ 3B:14-63. Directions of court when abandonment ordered

If the fiduciary is ordered to abandon real property:
a. The court may direct the fiduciary to refrain from
(1) Paying any arrearages of real property taxes and assessments and those thereafter assessed,
(2) Paying water rents or charges,
(3) Paying arrearages in mortgage principal and interest and those thereafter becoming due,
(4) Making repairs to or maintaining any improvements upon the real property,
(5) Keeping the real property or any improvements thereon insured against fire or other loss and liability or as the court may direct;
b. The court may direct that the fiduciary may, if a buyer can be found, convey the real property for a nominal consideration or no consideration so as to avoid liability arising to the fiduciary or to the estate or trust.

§ 3B:14-64. Order approving abandonment of real property by fiduciary and authorizing conveyance of title

Where it appears that a fiduciary in good faith and in the exercise of a reasonable discretion has abandoned real property by refraining from paying real property taxes, assessments, water rents or charges, mortgage principal and interest, making repairs or improvements to the property, and that because of the liens, encumbrances, the absence or lack of revenues or other reasons the real property did not have a value worth protecting and that it was advisable for the best interests of those interested in the estate or trust to abandon the real property, or that as a result of an abandonment, the fiduciary has been divested of title to or right of possession of the real property by foreclosure of a mortgage or the enforcement of any other lien or encumbrance, the court may ratify and approve the abandonment of the real property upon terms and conditions as it may deem proper. If the fiduciary still has title to the real property, the court may authorize the fiduciary to convey all right, title and interest therein for a nominal consideration or no consideration in order to avoid liability which might arise by reason of continued ownership of the property.

§ 3B:14-65. Public liability after abandonment but before being divested of title

Whenever a fiduciary, trust or estate abandons any real property pursuant to this article, the fiduciary, trust or estate shall remain liable for injury or damage to persons or property arising out of the ownership of the real property notwithstanding the abandonment, until the fiduciary, trust or estate has divested itself or has been divested of title thereto.

Chapter 15. Bonds and Sureties

Article 1. In General

§ 3B:15-1. Bonds of fiduciaries; exceptions

The court or surrogate appointing a fiduciary in any of the instances enumerated below shall secure faithful performance of the duties of the office by requiring the fiduciary thereby authorized to act to furnish bond to the Superior Court in a sum and with proper conditions and sureties, having due regard to the value of the estate and the extent of the fiduciary's authority, as the court shall approve:

a. When an appointment is made upon failure of the will, or other instrument creating or continuing a fiduciary relationship, to name a fiduciary;
b. When a person is appointed in the place of the person named as fiduciary in the will, or other instrument creating or continuing the fiduciary relationship;
c. When the office to which the person is appointed is any form of administration, except: (1) administration ad litem which may be granted with or without bond; or (2) administration granted to a surviving spouse where the decedent's entire estate is payable to the surviving spouse;
d. When the office to which the person is appointed is any form of guardianship of a minor or a person who is incapacitated, except as otherwise provided in N.J.S.3B:12-16 or N.J.S.3B:12-33 with respect to a guardian appointed by will;
e. When letters are granted to a nonresident executor, except in cases where the will provides that no security shall be required of the person named as executor therein;
f. When an additional or substituted fiduciary is appointed;
g. When an appointment is made under chapter 26 of this title, of a fiduciary for the estate or property, or any part thereof, of an absentee;
h. When a fiduciary moves from the State, in which case the court may require the fiduciary to give such security as the court determines; or

i.
(1) When an appointment is made, regardless of any direction in a last will and testament relieving a personal representative, testamentary guardian, or testamentary trustee or their successors from giving bond, that person shall, before receiving letters or exercising any authority or control over the property, provide bond to secure performance of the person's duties with respect to property to which a person with a developmental disability as defined in section 3 of P.L.1985, c.145 (C.30:6D-25) is, or shall be entitled, if:
(a) the testator has identified that a devisee or beneficiary of property of the decedent's estate is a person with a developmental disability; or
(b) the person seeking appointment has actual knowledge that a devisee or beneficiary of property of the decedent's estate is a person with a developmental disability.
(2) No bond shall be required pursuant to paragraph (1) of this subsection if:
(a) the court has appointed another person as guardian of the person or guardian of the estate for the person with a developmental disability;
(b) the person seeking the appointment is a family member within the third degree of consanguinity of the person with a developmental disability; or
(c) the total value of the real and personal assets of the estate or trust does not exceed $25,000.
(3) A personal representative, testamentary guardian, or testamentary trustee who is required to provide bond pursuant to paragraph (1) of this subsection shall file with the Superior Court an initial inventory and a final accounting of the estate in that person's charge containing a true account of all assets of the estate. That person shall file an interim accounting every five years, or a lesser period of time if so ordered by the Superior Court, in the case of an extended estate or trust administration.
(4) A personal representative, testamentary guardian, or testamentary trustee who is required to provide bond pursuant to paragraph (1) of this subsection may make application to the court to waive the bond or reduce the amount of bond for good cause shown, including the need to preserve assets of the estate.
This subsection shall not apply to qualified financial institutions pursuant to section 30 of P.L.1948, c.67 (C.17:9A-30) or to non-profit community trusts organized pursuant to P.L.1985, c.424 (C.3B:11-19 et seq.).
Nothing contained in this section shall be construed to require a bond in any case where it is specifically provided by law that a bond need not be required.

§ 3B:15-2. Bonds not to be approved unless prescribed conditions are included

When specific conditions as to a particular bond are prescribed by law, the bond shall not be approved unless the prescribed conditions are included therein, and where by law security is authorized to be given other than by sureties on the bond, compliance with the law shall be deemed compliance with this section.

§ 3B:15-3. Bond where will requires bond and fails to name obligee; prosecution

When a will nominating an executor or devising or bequeathing property to a trustee by its terms requires the executor or trustee to give bond but is silent as to who shall be the obligee in the bond, the Superior Court of this State may be made the obligee therein and the bond shall be approved as to amount and sureties by, and filed with, the surrogate of the county wherein the will was probated, unless the will was probated before the Superior Court, in which case the bond shall, after approval, be filed with the clerk thereof.
If forfeited, the bond may be prosecuted and the money recovered thereon be applied, all as in the case of other bonds of fiduciaries given to the Superior Court.

§ 3B:15-4. Bond when property unsafe or in danger of waste

If a fiduciary has not previously furnished a bond and proof is made to the satisfaction of the court that the property in his hands is unsafe, insecure, or in danger of being wasted, the court may, at the instance of any person interested, including creditors, in the decedent's estate or the estate held by the fiduciary, require the fiduciary to furnish a bond with sureties to the Superior Court in a sum to be fixed by the court conditioned for the faithful performance of the fiduciary's duty.

§ 3B:15-5. Conditions of bond on grant of intestate administration

The bond of an administrator of the estate of a person dying intestate shall be conditioned substantially as follows:
a. If required by the court or if an exemption is to be set off as required in chapter 16 of this title, to make a true and perfect inventory of the real and personal property of the decedent which has or shall come to his hands, possession or knowledge or into the hands of any other person for him, and to cause an appraisal to be made of the real and personal property and to file the inventory and appraisal in the office of the clerk of the Superior Court or of the surrogate of the proper county, as the case may be, within the time so required;
b. To faithfully discharge all of the duties imposed upon him according to law;
c. To make a just and true account of his administration of the estate and, if required by court, to settle his account therein within the time so required;
d. To deliver and pay to the distributees entitled thereto by law the surplus property of the decedent as may remain pursuant to the account; and
e. To deliver his letters of administration to the proper court, when required so to do, if a will of the decedent is found and exhibited to it and by it admitted to probate.

§ 3B:15-6. Conditions of bonds on certain grants of administration

In the case of the grant of letters of administration durante minori aetate, durante absentia, pendente lite, cum testamento annexo and other grants of administration, the conditions of the fiduciary's bond shall be substantially as provided in N.J.S. 3B:15-5 with changes as shall be appropriate in view of the nature of the respective grants.

§ 3B:15-7. Bond required of guardian of minor or person who is incapacitated

The bond required of a guardian of a minor or a person who is incapacitated shall be conditioned substantially as follows:

a. To administer the ward's estate to the best of the guardian's ability, and to take proper care of the ward if the guardian is the guardian of the ward's person;

b. To make a just and true account of the administration of the guardianship, and, if required by the court, to settle the accounts therein within the time so required.

§ 3B:15-8. Allowance of expense of procuring surety bond of fiduciary, receiver or assignee

A fiduciary, receiver or assignee for the benefit of creditors required by law or order of court to give a bond, may include as a part of the lawful expense of executing his trust a reasonable sum, not exceeding, however, 1% per annum on the amount of the bond, paid a company authorized under the laws of this State so to do, for becoming his surety on the bond, as may be allowed by the court.

Article 2. Separate and Additional Security

§ 3B:15-9. Additional surety when original sureties and bond insufficient

If it appears that the security given by a fiduciary at the time of his appointment was insufficient or has become insufficient or the sureties appear to be in failing circumstances or insufficient for the security of the estate, the court may order the fiduciary to give other or further security to the Superior Court, by bond in the usual form, and other sureties as the court, after hearing persons interested, including creditors, shall approve.

§ 3B:15-10. When fiduciary required to account and give separate security to surety

When the surety on the bond of a fiduciary discovers that the fiduciary is wasting or mismanaging the estate, so that the surety may become liable to loss or damage, the court may, in an action by the surety, and upon sufficient reason therefor, require the fiduciary to render an account of the performance of his office to the surety. If it shall appear that the fiduciary has embezzled, wasted, misapplied, mismanaged or insufficiently secured the estate, the court shall direct the fiduciary to give separate security to the surety for the true payment of the balance in his hands to be paid according to the trust.

Article 3. Deposit in Lieu of Full Security of Bond

§ 3B:15-11. When deposit permitted

If the value of an estate or fund is so great that the court in which the fiduciary received his letters or appointment deems it inexpedient to require security in the full amount prescribed by law, or if the estate or fund is in cash or is invested in securities in which a fiduciary may by law invest money intrusted to him in his fiduciary capacity without special order of any court, the court may direct that any securities for the payment of money belonging to the estate or fund be deposited in a savings bank, savings institution or trust company incorporated under the laws of this State, or in a national bank, having safe deposit boxes for the use of private individuals, and that any money belonging to the estate or fund be deposited in a savings bank, savings institution or trust company incorporated under the laws of this State or in a national bank, which depository shall be approved by the court when it directs the making of the deposit.

§ 3B:15-12. Bond after deposit

After deposit has been made pursuant to N.J.S. 3B:15-11, the court may fix the amount of the bond with respect to the value of the remainder only of the estate or fund, or in case all of the estate or fund is so deposited, then in an amount as the court shall determine to be sufficient under the circumstances.

§ 3B:15-13. How deposits made and withdrawn

Deposits authorized under N.J.S. 3B:15-11 shall be made in the name of the fiduciary and shall be withdrawn from the custody of the depository only upon the direction of the court which authorized the deposit and no part of the principal of securities so deposited shall be received or collected by the fiduciary without a like direction.

§ 3B:15-14. Additional bond upon withdrawals

A fiduciary shall not be permitted by the court to collect or receive the principal of securities on deposit or to withdraw a deposit pursuant to N.J.S. 3B:15-13 unless an additional bond has been given by him, or unless there is proof that the estate or fund has been so reduced by payments or otherwise, that the amount of the bond originally given will be sufficient in amount to secure the estate or fund.

§ 3B:15-15. Depository to issue duplicate deposit certificates

A depository receiving a deposit pursuant to N.J.S. 3B:15-11 shall issue a certificate in duplicate and deliver one certificate to the clerk of the court authorizing the deposit and the other to the fiduciary. The certificates shall set forth the amount and nature of the securities, or amount of money, deposited.

§ 3B:15-16. Deposit and investment

Where the estate of a minor for whom a guardian has been or is to be appointed by a surrogate, consists of or is likely to consist of the proceeds of a judgment recovered in favor of the minor in any court of this State, the court, on application of the guardian or a person entitled to be appointed as guardian, by its order may dispense with the giving of a bond by the guardian where the order directs that the moneys be paid into the Superior Court for the benefit of the minor and that the moneys, or any part thereof, shall be deposited to the credit of the court in an interest-bearing account in, or in interest-bearing certificates of deposit of, a responsible bank, savings bank or trust company, or in an account in, or in interest-bearing certificates of deposit of, any savings and loan association of this State or any other state, or any federal savings and loan association within the United States, the accounts of which are insured by the Federal Deposit Insurance Corporation, designated by the court.

§ 3B:15-17. Investment by surrogate

The court may direct that the moneys, or any part thereof, shall be invested by the surrogate of the county, where the guardian has been or shall be appointed, in United States Savings Bonds in the name of the minor, and in the event of the maturity of the bonds during the period of minority, the court may order the surrogate to reinvest the proceeds in other United States Savings Bonds having later maturity dates. The custody of the bonds shall be retained by the surrogate, and the moneys or bonds shall be subject to any order in respect thereto as may be made by the court. The moneys shall be paid out or the bonds surrendered by the surrogate only by order of the court.

§ 3B:15-17.1. Payment at age 18

Where the estate of a minor consists of the proceeds of a judgment recovered in favor of the minor in any court of this State and the funds recovered are placed under the control of the county surrogate, the funds shall be paid over to the person when the person reaches the age of 18 years, unless the court finds the person to be incapacitated.

Article 4. Discharge of Surety; Reduction of Bonds

§ 3B:15-18. Discharge of surety from liability for future acts of fiduciary, receiver or assignee

The court shall discharge a surety on the bond of a fiduciary, receiver or assignee for the benefit of creditors from liability for all his acts and omissions occurring after the granting of the discharge, if he accounts and files a new bond duly approved or, in default of an accounting and the filing of the bond, if the trust property shall be found or made good and paid over or properly secured.

§ 3B:15-19. Discharge of surety for fiduciary or assignee after final account

At any time 3 months after the entry of a final judgment of distribution made after the allowance of the final account of a fiduciary or assignee for the benefit of creditors, the court shall, in an action by any person interested, and upon proof to the satisfaction of the court that the entire estate has been distributed according to law, and that no appeal from the judgment of distribution is pending, discharge the sureties of the principal from any and every liability by reason of having become sureties.

§ 3B:15-20. Effect of discharge of surety

After discharge of a surety pursuant to this article, all his liability by virtue of his undertaking shall cease, but the personal liability of the principal in the bond shall remain.

§ 3B:15-21. Reduction of fiduciary's bond; discharge of original sureties

When it shall appear upon the allowance of a fiduciary's intermediate account that the fiduciary's bond is in a greater sum than is necessary for the proper protection of property and assets of the estate remaining in his hands, the court may, in an action for that purpose, allow the fiduciary to give a new bond in a lesser sum as the court may deem sufficient.

When the new bond, with conditions and sureties duly approved, is filed, the court by its order may discharge the sureties upon the original bond from all liability thereunder after the date of the order.

§ 3B:15-22. Discharge of fiduciary from liability on bond without surety

Whenever a fiduciary which is a bank, trust company, savings bank or national bank, has heretofore given or hereafter gives a bond without surety and it shall appear to the satisfaction of the court, that the person entitled to take the assets of the estate or trust administered by the fiduciary has received the estate or trust, and has by release or other instrument released the fiduciary from liability, the court, with notice or without notice if it be so directed, may cancel the bond given by the fiduciary and discharge it from all liability on the bond.

§ 3B:15-23. Proof of order to limit creditors required in certain cases

An order of discharge shall not be made in cases in which the fiduciary is an executor, administrator with the will annexed, substituted administrator with the will annexed, administrator or substituted administrator except upon proof that nine months have elapsed after the entry of an order to limit creditors pursuant to N.J.S. 3B:22-4, and that there are not any unpaid or pending claims of creditors of the decedent presented to the fiduciary pursuant to chapter 22 of this title.

Article 5. Prosecution of Bonds

§ 3B:15-24. Prosecution of fiduciaries' bonds

Except as otherwise provided by law, when the bond of a fiduciary given to a court or to a judicial officer or clerk of a court, for the faithful performance, by him, of the duties of his office as fiduciary, is forfeited, the bond may, without leave of court, be prosecuted in any court of record by, and at the expense of, an aggrieved party and in the name of the State at the relation of the aggrieved party.

§ 3B:15-25. Court in which to bring proceedings to assess damages, to satisfy judgment or to discontinue action

The moneys found due on the fiduciary's bond shall be applied toward making good the damage sustained by reason of the nonperformance of the conditions of the bond. Proceedings for that purpose, proceedings under N.J.S. 3B:15-26 to N.J.S. 3B:15-29 for the satisfaction of the judgment on the bond, and proceedings under N.J.S. 3B:15-30 and N.J.S. 3B:15-31 for the discontinuance of the action on the bond shall be taken in the Superior Court.

§ 3B:15-26. Proceedings to satisfy judgment on bond; notice to claimants

If any bond given by a fiduciary is forfeited and prosecuted to judgment in any court of record, and it is made to appear to the Superior Court, by a complaint filed by any surety against whom judgment has been rendered upon the bond, that the damages sustained by the nonperformance of the condition of the bond, together with costs of action and execution fees thereon, have been fully satisfied so far as the surety shall have been able to ascertain the damages, the court may make an order directing the surety to give public notice to all persons aggrieved by the forfeiture of the bond, to bring in their debts, demands and claims against the estate in charge of the fiduciary, under oath within 3 months from the date of the order. The notice shall be advertised, commencing within 20 days of the date of the order, for 6 weeks successively, once in each week, in one or more of the newspapers of this State, as may be directed in the order. Further notice shall also be given if the court deems it necessary.

§ 3B:15-27. Presentation of claims

Debts, claims and demands ordered to be brought in, pursuant to this article, shall be presented by the respective claimants in writing, verified by oath, setting forth the amount and particulars thereof, or they shall be of no effect.

§ 3B:15-28. Exceptions; trial

The surety may except to any claim, debt or demand, and thereupon the same shall be tried as the court may direct, and the court may disallow and reject it if it is not established.

§ 3B:15-29. Satisfaction of judgment

After expiration of the time limited in the order the court may order satisfaction of the judgment to be entered pursuant to law upon proof to its satisfaction that notice has been advertised as directed and that no claims, debts or demands have been presented or that all claims, debts or demands presented and allowed have been fully paid and satisfied by the surety.

§ 3B:15-30. Application to have action on bond discontinued

In any action on the bond of a fiduciary, the surety before judgment may apply to have the action discontinued. The application shall be made to the Superior Court as provided in N.J.S. 3B:15-25. The court shall thereupon appoint a time and place to hear the application and direct what notice, if any, of the application be given to the persons aggrieved by the forfeiture of the bond.

§ 3B:15-31. Discontinuance of action on bond

If it shall appear on the hearing that all damages sustained by reason of the forfeiture of the bond have been paid so far as the surety shall have been able to ascertain, the court may direct that the action be discontinued upon payment of taxed costs of the suit.

§ 3B:15-32. Unsatisfied claims

If the claim of any person aggrieved by the forfeiture of the bond shall remain unsatisfied after the discontinuance of the action, the person may reprosecute the bond, in the same manner as if the action had not been instituted on the bond.

§ 3B:15-33. Bonds not invalidated because of abolition of certain offices or courts

No bond heretofore given by any fiduciary for the faithful performance, by him, of the duties of his office as a fiduciary, to any court or to any judicial officer, or clerk of any court abolished by the Constitution of 1947, as amended, shall be invalidated by reason of the abolition of any court, judicial or clerical office, but the bond shall remain in full force and effect, and if forfeited, may be prosecuted in accordance with the provisions of this article.

Chapter 16. Inventories

§ 3B:16-1. General requisites

An inventory shall not be received nor admitted to be proved which is not full and specific in its details.

§ 3B:16-2. Inventory and appraisal to be made and filed

A personal representative may or, if required by the court or if the exemption for the benefit of the family of the decedent is to be set off as allowed by N.J.S. 3B:16-5, shall make and file a true and perfect inventory of the real and personal property of his decedent, which has come to his hands, possession or knowledge or into the hands of any other person for him, and cause a just appraisal thereof to be made by two discreet and impartial persons.

The court shall not require an inventory and appraisal to be filed until 3 months after the grant of letters, except that if an exemption is to be set off, the inventory and appraisal shall be made within the 3 months.

§ 3B:16-3. Appointment of appraisers

If an inventory and appraisal is to be filed, the appraisers shall be chosen by the personal representative subject to the approval of the Superior Court or surrogate, except in cases where it shall be necessary to set off the exemption for the benefit of the family of the decedent as allowed by N.J.S. 3B:16-5, in which event the personal representative shall apply to the surrogate of the county wherein the decedent resided at his death, or to the Superior Court, as the case may be, for the appointment of two persons as appraisers who are neither interested in the estate nor related to the decedent's widow or child. The appraisers shall, before entering upon the duties of their appointment, be severally sworn before the surrogate, or a person authorized to administer oaths, to faithfully, honestly and impartially appraise the property according to its true and intrinsic value without reference to what the property might bring at a public sale.

§ 3B:16-4. Property to be included in inventory and appraisal

The appraisers shall make an inventory and appraisement of all the real and personal property of which the decedent died seized and possessed.

§ 3B:16-5. Exemption for benefit of decedent's family

The wearing apparel of any person who shall die leaving a family residing in this State, and his personal property to the value of $5,000.00, shall be reserved to and for the use of his family against all creditors, and before any distribution or other disposition thereof. This section and N.J.S. 3B:16-3 and N.J.S. 3B:16-7 of this title shall not be permitted to conflict with the will of the decedent. Every person residing in this State at the time of his death and leaving surviving him a widow or child who shall reside in his family at his death, shall be deemed to have left a family entitled to the benefits of this section.

§ 3B:16-6. Proof of inventory and exempt list

The inventory of a personal representative which is to be filed, shall be proved by his oath that it is just and true, and by the oath of the appraisers, or one of them, that the real and personal property specified in the inventory was appraised at its just and true values according to their or his best judgment. If only one of the appraisers be sworn it shall be added that the other appraiser was present at the same time and consented to the valuation and appraisal. The oaths shall be taken before any person qualified to administer oaths in this State and shall be indorsed on the inventory filed with the surrogate or clerk of the Superior Court, as the case may be. If personal property of the decedent shall have been set off for the benefit of the family, the executor or administrator shall also verify by his oath the list of property selected and file the list with the inventory.

§ 3B:16-7. Selection of property to be exempted

From the completed inventory, the widow of the decedent, or his personal representative may select personal property to the value of $5,000.00 and a list of the property selected shall be annexed to the inventory. Personal property so selected shall thereupon become the property of the family and remain for their use.

§ 3B:16-8. Guardian to file inventory of estate of minor or person who is incapacitated

Every guardian of the estate of a minor or a person who is incapacitated may, and if required by the court shall, file with the surrogate of the proper county or the clerk of the Superior Court an inventory, under oath, of all the real and personal property which is in the control, possession, or knowledge of the guardian or any other person on the guardian's behalf. The court shall not require an inventory and appraisal to be filed until three months have elapsed after the grant of letters.

Chapter 17. Accounting

Article 1. When Unnecessary

§ 3B:17-1. Filing of release or discharge

A fiduciary need not render or settle an account if the fiduciary files with the court a release or discharge from the beneficiary, ward, or cestui que trust who has reached majority and is not incapacitated.

The release or discharge shall be executed and acknowledged as provided for deeds of real estate to be recorded.

Article 2. Requirements

§ 3B:17-2. Accounts of personal representatives

A personal representative may settle his account or be required to settle his account in the Superior Court. Unless for special cause shown, he shall not be required to account until after the expiration of 1 year after his appointment.

§ 3B:17-3. Accounts of guardians and trustees

A guardian or trustee shall settle his account in the Superior Court at intervals as the court may require. A guardian or trustee may settle his first account within 1 year after his appointment or as soon thereafter as may be practicable.

§ 3B:17-4. Account and bond required of cofiduciary

Upon good cause shown, the Superior Court may order each cofiduciary to account for all assets which may have come into his hands.

The Superior Court may also require a fiduciary to give bond, in a sum and with sureties to be approved by the court, to each of his cofiduciaries to indemnify them against loss due to his neglect, default or breach of trust or to give a like bond to the Superior Court, conditioned for the faithful performance of his duties as a fiduciary and the proper disposition of all assets then in, or thereafter to come into, his hands.

§ 3B:17-5. Account by representative of deceased fiduciary

When a fiduciary dies without having filed an account or having fully settled and obtained an allowance of an account of the administration of the estate that has come into his hands, his legal representative may settle the account.

§ 3B:17-6. Examination of accountant on exceptions to account

On exceptions to an account of a fiduciary, the court or any party interested therein may examine the accountant, on oath, concerning the truth and fairness of the account.

§ 3B:17-7. Statements or information regarding assets as part of account

When, in an account, or in a complaint in an action for the settlement of an account, or in any writing annexed to the complaint or account, there appear lists of or statements or information as to the investments or other assets in a fiduciary's hands at the close of, or during, the period covered by the account or as to changes made in investments or other assets during that period, or there appear allegations or information as to other matters done or omitted by the fiduciary during the period, the complaint and the writing, statements, lists, information and allegations shall be deemed to be part of the account.

§ 3B:17-8. Effect of judgment allowing account

A judgment allowing an account, including a guardian's intermediate account, after due notice, shall be res adjudicata as to all exceptions which could or might have been taken to the account, and shall constitute an approval of the correctness and propriety of the account, the legality and propriety of the investments and other assets, the legality and propriety of the changes in investments or other assets, and the legality and propriety of other matters, and also shall exonerate and discharge the fiduciary from all claims of all interested parties and of those in privity with or represented by interested parties except:

a. For the investments and other assets in the fiduciary's hands at the close of the period covered by the account, and assets which may come into his hands after the close of the account;
b. Insofar as exceptions to the account shall be taken and sustained; and
c. As relief may be had from a judgment in any civil action.

Article 3. Nontestamentary Trustees

§ 3B:17-9. Nontestamentary trustee defined

As used in this article, "nontestamentary trustee" means any owner of real or personal property who holds title thereto subject to equitable duties to deal with the property for the benefit of another or others arising from an express intention to create those duties manifested in writing otherwise than by a will or other testamentary disposition of property.

§ 3B:17-10. Settling accounts in the Superior Court

A nontestamentary trustee shall have the right, in addition to and not in limitation of any other remedy now or hereafter provided, from time to time to settle his intermediate and final accounts in the Superior Court.

§ 3B:17-11. Surrogate's fees

The surrogate and the Clerk of the Superior Court shall receive for filing, auditing, and reporting to the court the accounts of nontestamentary trustees the same fees as are now or may hereafter be provided by law in the case of accountings by other fiduciaries.

Article 4. Authority for Certain Expenditures

§ 3B:17-12. Fiduciary, receiver or assignee; rental of safe deposit box; expenses of safe-keeping of securities

A fiduciary, receiver or assignee for the benefit of creditors may include as a part of the lawful expense of executing his trust a reasonable sum paid to a bank, trust company or safe deposit company organized under the laws of this State, or to a national bank doing business in this State, for safe deposit box rental for the safe-keeping or custody of the securities of the trust, as may be allowed by the court. A fiduciary, receiver or assignee for the benefit of creditors who holds under a lease or owns a vault within this State may include as a part of the lawful expense of executing his trust a reasonable sum for the safe-keeping of the securities and other property of the trust in the vault as may be allowed by the court.

§ 3B:17-13. Effect of nonjudicial settlement or waiver of account

Unless the governing instrument expressly provides otherwise, an instrument settling or waiving an account, executed by all persons whom it would be necessary to join as parties in a proceeding for the judicial settlement of the account, shall be binding and conclusive on all other persons who may have a future interest in the property to the same extent as that instrument binds the person who executed it.

Chapter 18. Commissions

Article 1. In General

§ 3B:18-2. Commissions of nontestamentary trustee

On the settlement of the account of a nontestamentary trustee, as defined in N.J.S. 3B:17-9, the court shall allow him the compensation as may have been agreed upon by the instrument creating the trust; and in the absence of any express provision concerning compensation, shall allow him commissions in accordance with this chapter.

§ 3B:18-3. Provision in will for specific compensation

Where provision is made in a will for specific compensation to a fiduciary, the compensation shall be deemed full payment for services in lieu of commissions provided by this chapter, unless the fiduciary shall in writing filed with the surrogate or clerk of the Superior Court renounce the specific compensation.

§ 3B:18-4. Disputes between fiduciaries as to apportionment

When a difference arises between fiduciaries concerning the apportionment of commissions between them, the Superior Court shall determine the apportionment of commissions, having regard to their respective services.

§ 3B:18-5. Fiduciary removed from office; forfeiture of commissions

Where a fiduciary is removed for any cause, the Superior Court may direct that his commissions be forfeited.

§ 3B:18-6. Legal fees for attorney also serving as fiduciary

If the fiduciary is a duly licensed attorney of this State and shall have performed professional services in addition to his fiduciary duties, the court shall, in addition to the commissions provided by this chapter, allow him a just counsel fee. If more than one fiduciary shall have performed the professional services, the court shall apportion the fee among them according to the services rendered by them respectively.

§ 3B:18-7. Annual statement relating to corpus commissions taken

A trustee under a will or a guardian shall, within 60 days after the end of each tax year of the trust or guardianship furnish to each beneficiary currently receiving income, and to any other beneficiary interested in the income and to any person interested in the principal of the trust or guardianship who shall make a demand therefor, a statement showing any corpus commissions taken during the tax year and the basis upon which those commissions were computed, including the inventory value and value as of the date the commissions were computed.

Article 2. Certain Fiduciaries; Additional Compensation

§ 3B:18-8. Definitions

As used in this article:

a. "Fiduciary" means executor, administrator with the will annexed, substituted administrator with the will annexed, administrator, substituted administrator, or trustee or substituted trustee under a will of a decedent;

b. "Property" means any property, real or personal, tangible or intangible, or any interest or estate therein, which does not come into the hands of a fiduciary as part of a decedent's estate, and which, by operation of law or otherwise, has been received or is receivable by anyone other than the fiduciary, and which a taxing authority attempts to tax or does tax, as a decedent's taxable estate, or as part of a decedent's taxable estate, for the purposes of Federal estate tax, New Jersey estate tax, other state or foreign estate taxes, or New Jersey or other state or foreign transfer inheritance, legacy or succession taxes.

§ 3B:18-9. Additional compensation

The court upon the settlement and allowance of a fiduciary's accounts, in addition to the compensation as may otherwise be allowable, may allow reasonable compensation to the fiduciary for services required by law to be rendered by the fiduciary in connection with or arising out of any property as defined in N.J.S. 3B:18-8, including, but not by way of limitation, services rendered in connection with apportionment of any taxes specified in N.J.S. 3B:18 8 between a decedent's estate and the recipient of the property, or between the decedent's estate and the property, and in collecting or attempting to collect, the apportionment of the taxes applicable to the property.

§ 3B:18-10. Notice to recipient of property

The court shall prescribe the notice to be given to the recipient of the property of the fiduciary's application for additional compensation.

§ 3B:18-11. Manner of payment of additional compensation

The additional compensation of the fiduciary shall be payable by the recipient of the property if the recipient is within the jurisdiction of the court, or if the recipient is not within the jurisdiction of the court, shall be payable out of the property, if the property is within the jurisdiction of the court. If the recipient of the property is not within the jurisdiction of the court and if the property is not within the jurisdiction of the court, or if the fiduciary does not succeed in collecting the additional fiduciary's compensation from the recipient of the property or out of the property, the court may order the fiduciary's additional compensation to be paid out of the corpus of the decedent's estate which comes into the hands of the fiduciary.

Article 3. Commissions; Executors, Administrators and Certain Fiduciaries

§ 3B:18-12. Definition of fiduciary

As used in this article "fiduciary" means personal representative and fiduciaries appointed under chapter 26 of this title for absentees.

§ 3B:18-13. Income commissions

Commissions in the amount of 6% may be taken without court allowance on all income received by the fiduciary. For the purposes of this section, income which is withheld from payment to a fiduciary or fiduciaries pursuant to any law of this State, or of the United States, or any other state, country or sovereignty, or of any political subdivision or governmental unit of any of the foregoing, requiring the withholding for income tax or other tax purposes, shall be deemed to be income received by the fiduciary, and shall be subject to income commissions as provided in this section in the same manner as if actually received by the fiduciary.

§ 3B:18-14. Corpus commissions

Commissions on all corpus received by the fiduciary may be taken as follows:

5% on the first $200,000 of all corpus received by the fiduciary;

3.5% on the excess over $200,000 up to $1,000,000;
2% on the excess over $1,000,000; and
1% of all corpus for each additional fiduciary provided that no one fiduciary shall be entitled to any greater commission than that which would be allowed if there were but one fiduciary involved.

Such commissions may be reduced by the court having jurisdiction over the estate only upon application by a beneficiary adversely affected upon an affirmative showing that the services rendered were materially deficient or that the actual pains, trouble and risk of the fiduciary in settling the estate were substantially less than generally required for estates of comparable size.

§ 3B:18-16. Corpus commissions; unusual or extraordinary services

The court may, on an intermediate or the final settlement of the fiduciary's accounts, allow corpus commissions in addition to those hereinabove provided, on a showing that unusual or extraordinary services have been rendered by the fiduciary for which the fiduciary should receive extra compensation.

§ 3B:18-17. Taking annual amounts on account of corpus commissions

Fiduciaries may annually, without court allowance, take sums as follows on account of corpus commissions: if there is but one fiduciary, the amount so taken may equal one-fifth of 1% of the value of the corpus and, if there are two or more fiduciaries, the amount so taken may equal the commissions which may be taken pursuant to this section when there is but one fiduciary, plus one-fifth of the commissions for each fiduciary more than one.

§ 3B:18-18. Value of assets for computing commissions taken annually

In computing the amount of commissions which may be taken annually pursuant to N.J.S. 3B:18-17, the value of any item of corpus at the time when the item is received by the fiduciary, referred to in this section as the "presumptive value" of the item, may be used as the value of the item, or, at the option of the fiduciary, the value of the item at the end of the period for which the commissions are taken may be used.

§ 3B:18-19. Failure to take commissions annually shall not constitute a waiver thereof

The failure of a fiduciary to take commissions in any year as provided in N.J.S. 3B:18-17 shall not constitute a waiver of the right of the fiduciary to take in a subsequent year the commissions not taken for that year.

§ 3B:18-20. Corpus commissions taken annually subject to review

Commissions taken as provided in N.J.S. 3B:18-17 shall be subject to review on intermediate and final accountings, and to the extent that aggregate commissions so taken exceed the commissions allowable under N.J.S. 3B:18-14 and N.J.S. 3B:18-15, they may be disallowed.

§ 3B:18-21. Burden of proving value

In the event of a dispute as to the value of corpus on the settlement of the account of a fiduciary, the burden of proving that the value of any item of corpus differs from the presumptive value of the item shall be upon the fiduciary or other party claiming the difference.

§ 3B:18-22. When rates for corpus commissions taken annually effective

With respect to a fiduciary's annual corpus commissions, the rates set forth in this article shall apply for all yearly periods ending after February 29, 1980.

Article 4. Commission of Trustees Under Will and Guardians

§ 3B:18-23. "Fiduciary" defined

As used in this article "fiduciary" means a trustee acting under a will, a nontestamentary trustee as defined in N.J.S. 3B:17-9 or a guardian.

§ 3B:18-24. Income commissions

Commissions in the amount of 6% may be taken without court allowance on all income received by the fiduciary. For the purposes of this section, income which is withheld from payment to the fiduciary pursuant to any law of this State, or of the United States, or any other state, country or sovereignty or of any political subdivision or governmental unit of any of the foregoing, for income tax or other tax purposes, shall be deemed to be income received by the fiduciary, and shall be subject to income commissions as if actually received by the fiduciary.

§ 3B:18-25. Fiduciaries may take annual commissions on corpus

a. Fiduciaries may annually, without court allowance, take commissions on corpus (including accumulated income which has been invested by the fiduciary) in the amount of $5.00 per thousand dollars of corpus value on the first $400,000.00 of value of corpus and $3.00 per thousand dollars of the corpus value in excess of $400,000.00.

b. Notwithstanding the provisions of subsection a. of this section, if the fiduciary is a banking institution, foreign bank or savings and loan association authorized to exercise fiduciary powers, the fiduciary shall be entitled to such commissions as may be reasonable.

c. Notwithstanding the provisions of subsection a. of this section, a fiduciary may take a minimum commission of $100.00 annually.

d. The value of the corpus for the purpose of this section shall be the "presumptive value" as defined in N.J.S. 3B:18-18 or, at the option of the fiduciary, the value at the end of the period.

e. Upon application of a person interested in the trust or guardianship, a court may review the reasonableness of the commissions of the fiduciary, provided, however, the fiduciary shall be entitled to receive at least the compensation provided for all fiduciaries as set forth in subsections a. and c. of this section.

§ 3B:18-25.1. Taking annual amount on accounts of corpus commissions: two or more fiduciaries

Taking annual amount on accounts of corpus commissions: two or more fiduciaries. If there are two or more fiduciaries, the amount of the annual commissions taken pursuant to N.J.S. 3B:18-25 may equal the commissions which may be taken pursuant to that section when there is but one fiduciary, plus one-fifth of the commissions for each fiduciary more than one. No one fiduciary shall be entitled to any greater commission than that which would be allowed if there were but one fiduciary involved.

§ 3B:18-25.2. Powers of qualified bank; duties of agent

a. Notwithstanding any law to the contrary, a qualified bank acting in any capacity authorized pursuant to section 28 of P.L. 1948, c. 67 (C. 17:9A-28) on behalf of a trust or estate may employ and pay reasonable compensation to any person, including attorneys, auditors, investment advisers or other agents, even if they are affiliated or associated with the qualified bank, to advise or assist the qualified bank in the performance of any of its administrative duties, whether or not discretionary, and to act without independent investigation upon their recommendation, so long as the qualified bank exercises care, skill, and caution in: selecting the agent; establishing the scope and terms of the agent's duties consistent with the purpose and terms of the governing trust instrument; and periodically reviewing the agent's actions in order to monitor the agent's performance. A qualified bank that delegates investment functions to an investment adviser shall also comply with the requirements of sections 8 and 10 of P.L. 1997, c. 26 (C. 3B:20-11.8 and 3B:20-11.10).

b. In performing any agency function, the agent shall owe to the qualified bank and the beneficiaries the same duties as the qualified bank and shall be held to the same fiduciary standards as the qualified bank.

c. In the absence of express contrary provisions in the trust instrument, a qualified bank which employs an agent other than an investment adviser or investment manager, may pay the agent from the fiduciary fund if the qualified bank reasonably believes in the exercise of its discretion that such an arrangement is in the best interests of all interested persons and will improve the efficiency of the administration of the fiduciary fund. In the absence of express contrary provisions in the trust instrument, a qualified bank which delegates investment and trust asset management functions to an investment adviser or an investment manager shall comply with the cost control and other requirements of sections 8 and 10 of P.L. 1997, c. 26 (C. 3B:20-11.8 and 3B:20-11.10).

d. A qualified bank which substantially complies with the requirements of subsections a. and c. of this section shall not be liable to the beneficiaries or to the trust or estate for the decisions or actions of the agent, and shall not, solely by reason of the delegation, be deemed to engage in acts of self-dealing or a conflict of interest.

e. By accepting an appointment as agent from a qualified bank acting as a fiduciary of a trust or estate that is subject to the law of New Jersey, the agent submits to the jurisdiction of the courts of New Jersey, even if the agency agreement provides otherwise.

§ 3B:18-26. Failure to take commissions annually shall not constitute a waiver thereof

The failure of a fiduciary to take commissions in any year shall not constitute a waiver by the fiduciary to take in a subsequent year the commissions not taken for that year.

§ 3B:18-27. Commissions taken annually subject to review

Commissions taken as provided in N.J.S. 3B:18-25 shall be subject to review on intermediate and final accountings, and to the extent that aggregate commissions so taken exceed the commissions allowable under this article, they may be disallowed.

§ 3B:18-28. Corpus commissions on termination of trust, guardianship or upon distribution of assets

In addition to the annual commissions on corpus, upon termination of the trust or guardianship, or upon distribution of assets from the trust or guardianship, the fiduciary may take a commission on corpus distributed, including accumulated income which has been invested by the fiduciary. The value of the corpus for the purpose of computing the commissions shall be the "presumptive value" or, at the option of the fiduciary, the value at the time of distribution, as defined in N.J.S. 3B:18-18. The amounts of the commissions to be taken are as follows:

a. If the distribution of corpus occurs within 5 years of the date when the corpus is received by the fiduciary, an amount equal to the annual commissions on corpus authorized pursuant to N.J.S. 3B:18-25, but not actually taken by the fiduciary, plus an amount equal to 2% of the value of the corpus distributed;

b. If distribution of the corpus occurs between 5 and 10 years of the date when the corpus is received by the fiduciary, an amount equal to the annual commissions on corpus authorized pursuant to N.J.S. 3B:18-25, but not actually received by the fiduciary, plus an amount equal to 1 ½ % of the value of the corpus distributed;

c. If the distribution of corpus occurs more than 10 years after the date the corpus is received by the fiduciary, an amount equal to the annual commissions on corpus authorized pursuant to N.J.S. 3B:18-25, but not actually received by the fiduciary, plus an amount equal to 1% of the value of the corpus distributed; and

d. If there are two or more fiduciaries, their corpus commissions shall be the same as for a single fiduciary plus an additional amount of one-fifth of the commissions for each additional fiduciary.

§ 3B:18-29. Corpus commissions; unusual or extraordinary services

The court may, on an intermediate or the final settlement of fiduciaries' accounts, allow corpus commissions in addition to those provided in this article, on a showing that unusual or extraordinary services have been rendered by the fiduciary for which he should receive additional compensation.

§ 3B:18-30. Burden of proving value

In the event of a dispute as to the value of corpus on the settlement of the account of a fiduciary, the burden of proving that the value of any item of corpus differs from the presumptive value of the item shall be upon the party claiming the difference.

§ 3B:18-31. Authorization in testator's will as to commissions exceeding legal rates

No commissions in excess of those authorized in this article shall be paid to a fiduciary acting as a trustee under a will unless the testator, in his last will acknowledges that he is aware of the commissions specified in this article and expressly authorizes payment of commissions in excess thereof. The absence of an express authorization to pay excess commissions shall not preclude the court from allowing commissions as provided in N.J.S. 3B:18-29.

§ 3B:18-32. When rates for corpus commissions taken annually effective

With respect to fiduciaries' annual corpus commissions, the rates set forth in this article shall apply for all annual periods ending after February 29, 1980.

§ 3B:18-33. When rates of corpus commissions on termination of trusts or guardianship effective

With respect to the computation of corpus commissions pursuant to N.J.S. 3B:18-28 as to all corpus held by a fiduciary on February 29, 1980, the commissions which may be taken shall be the greater of (i) the commission permitted by law effective prior to February 29, 1980, or (ii) the commission computed pursuant to N.J.S. 3B:18-28; provided that the "annual commissions authorized" to be take for yearly periods ending prior to February 29, 1980, shall be at the rate authorized by the applicable law in effect during that yearly period.

Chapter 19. Principal and Income [Repealed]

§ 3B:19-1. Repealed by L. 1991, c. 257, § 1, eff. Aug. 13, 1991.

§ 3B:19-2. Repealed by L. 1991, c. 257, § 1, eff. Aug. 13, 1991.

§ 3B:19-3. Repealed by L. 1991, c. 257, § 1, eff. Aug. 13, 1991.

§ 3B:19-4. Repealed by L. 1991, c. 257, § 1, eff. Aug. 13, 1991.

§ 3B:19-5. Repealed by L. 1991, c. 257, § 1, eff. Aug. 13, 1991.

§ 3B:19-6. Repealed by L. 1991, c. 257, § 1, eff. Aug. 13, 1991.

§ 3B:19-7. Repealed by L. 1991, c. 257, § 1, eff. Aug. 13, 1991.

§ 3B:19-8. Repealed by L. 1991, c. 257, § 1, eff. Aug. 13, 1991.

§ 3B:19-9. Repealed by L. 1991, c. 257, § 1, eff. Aug. 13, 1991.

§ 3B:19-10. Repealed by L. 1991, c. 257, § 1, eff. Aug. 13, 1991.

§ 3B:19-11. Repealed by L. 1991, c. 257, § 1, eff. Aug. 13, 1991.

§ 3B:19-12. Repealed by L. 1991, c. 257, § 1, eff. Aug. 13, 1991.

§ 3B:19-13. Repealed by L. 1991, c. 257, § 1, eff. Aug. 13, 1991.

§ 3B:19-14. Repealed by L. 1991, c. 257, § 1, eff. Aug. 13, 1991.

§ 3B:19-15. Repealed by L. 1991, c. 257, § 1, eff. Aug. 13, 1991.

§ 3B:19-16. Repealed by L. 1991, c. 257, § 1, eff. Aug. 13, 1991.

§ 3B:19-17. Repealed by L. 1991, c. 257, § 1, eff. Aug. 13, 1991.

§ 3B:19-18. Repealed by L. 1991, c. 257, § 1, eff. Aug. 13, 1991.

§ 3B:19-19. Repealed by L. 1991, c. 257, § 1, eff. Aug. 13, 1991.

§ 3B:19A-19. Repealed by L. 2001, ch. 212, § 32, eff. Jan. 1, 2002

Chapter 19B. Uniform Principal and Income Act

§ 3B:19B-1. Short title

This act shall be known and may be cited as the "Uniform Principal and Income Act of 2001."

§ 3B:19B-2. Definitions

As used in this act:

"Accounting period" means a calendar year unless another 12-month period is selected by a fiduciary. The term includes a portion of a calendar year or other 12-month period that begins when an income interest begins or ends when an income interest ends.

"Beneficiary" includes, in the case of a decedent's estate, an heir, legatee and devisee and, in the case of a trust, an income beneficiary and a remainder beneficiary.

"Fiduciary" means a personal representative or a trustee. The term includes an executor, administrator, successor personal representative, special administrator and a person performing substantially the same function.

"Income" means money or property that a fiduciary receives as current return from a principal asset. The term includes a portion of receipts from a sale, exchange or liquidation of a principal asset, to the extent provided in sections 10 through 23 of this act.

"Income beneficiary" means a person to whom net income of a trust is or may be payable.

"Income interest" means the right of an income beneficiary to receive all or part of net income, whether the terms of the trust require it to be distributed or authorize it to be distributed in the trustee's discretion.

"Mandatory income interest" means the right of an income beneficiary to receive net income that the terms of the trust require the fiduciary to distribute.

"Net income" means the total receipts allocated to income during an accounting period minus the disbursements made from income during the period, plus or minus transfers under this act to or from income during the period.

"Person" means an individual, corporation, business trust, estate, trust, partnership, limited liability company, association, joint venture, government, governmental subdivision, agency or instrumentality, public corporation or any other legal or commercial entity.

"Principal" means property held in trust for distribution to a remainder beneficiary when the trust terminates.

"Remainder beneficiary" means a person entitled to receive principal when an income interest ends.

"Terms of a trust" means the manifestation of the intent of a settlor or decedent with respect to the trust, expressed in a manner that admits of its proof in a judicial proceeding, whether by written or spoken words or by conduct.

"Trustee" includes an original, additional or successor trustee, whether or not appointed or confirmed by a court.

§ 3B:19B-3. Fiduciary duties; general principles

a. In allocating receipts and disbursements to or between principal and income, and with respect to any matter within the scope of sections 5 through 9 of this act, a fiduciary:

(1) shall administer a trust or estate in accordance with the terms of the trust or the will, even if there is a different provision in this act;

(2) may administer a trust or estate by the exercise of a discretionary power of administration given to the fiduciary by the terms of the trust or the will, even if the exercise of the power produces a result different from a result required or permitted by this act;

(3) shall administer a trust or estate in accordance with this act if the terms of the trust or the will do not contain a different provision or do not give the fiduciary a discretionary power of administration; and

(4) shall add a receipt or charge a disbursement to principal to the extent that the terms of the trust and this act do not provide a rule for allocating the receipt or disbursement to or between principal and income.

b. A fiduciary shall administer a trust or estate impartially, based on what is fair and reasonable to all of the beneficiaries, except to the extent that the terms of the trust or the will clearly manifest an intention that the fiduciary shall or may favor one or more of the beneficiaries.

§ 3B:19B-4. Trustee's power to adjust

a. A trustee may adjust between principal and income if the terms of the trust describe the amount that may or shall be distributed to a beneficiary by referring to the trust's income and the trustee determines, after applying the rules in subsection a. of section 3 [C.3B:19B-3] of this act, that the trustee is unable to comply with subsection b. of section 3 of this act. A decision by a trustee to adjust the distribution to the income beneficiary or beneficiaries in any accounting period to an amount not less than three percent nor more than five percent, or in accordance with such other percentages as may be approved for trust distribution adjustment purposes from time to time by the United States Department of the Treasury or the Internal Revenue Service, of the net fair market value of the trust assets on the first business day of that accounting period shall be presumed to be fair and reasonable to all of the beneficiaries. Any adjustment by a trustee between income and principal with respect to any accounting period shall be made during that accounting period or within 65 days after the end of that period.

This subsection shall apply to a trust that is administered in New Jersey under New Jersey law unless contrary to the provisions of the governing instrument.

b. In deciding whether and to what extent to exercise the power conferred by subsection a. of this section, a trustee shall consider all factors relevant to the trust and its beneficiaries, including the following factors to the extent they are relevant:

(1) the nature, purpose and expected duration of the trust;

(2) the intent of the settlor;

(3) the identity and circumstances of the beneficiaries;

(4) the needs for liquidity, regularity of income and preservation and appreciation of capital;

(5) the assets held in the trust; the extent to which they consist of financial assets, interests in closely held enterprises, tangible and intangible personal property or real property; the extent to which an asset is used by a beneficiary; and whether an asset was purchased by the trustee or received from the settlor;

(6) the net amount allocated to income under the other sections of this act and the increase or decrease in the value of the principal assets, which the trustee may estimate as to assets for which market values are not readily available;

(7) whether and to what extent the terms of the trust give the trustee the power to invade principal or accumulate income or prohibit the trustee from invading principal or accumulating income, and the extent to which the trustee has exercised a power from time to time to invade principal or accumulate income;

(8) the actual and anticipated effect of economic conditions on principal and income and effects of inflation and deflation;

(9) the shifting of economic interests or tax benefits between income beneficiaries and remainder beneficiaries that arise from elections and decisions regarding tax matters, the imposition of an income or other tax on the fiduciary or a beneficiary as a result

of a transaction involving a distribution from the estate or trust, or the ownership of an interest in an entity whose taxable income, whether or not distributed, is includable in the taxable income of the estate, trust or a beneficiary; and

(10) the anticipated tax consequences of an adjustment.

c. A trustee shall not make an adjustment:

(1) that diminishes the income interest in a trust that requires all of the income to be paid at least annually to a spouse and for which an estate tax or gift tax marital deduction would be allowed, in whole or in part, if the trustee did not have the power to make the adjustment;

(2) that reduces the actuarial value of the income interest in a trust to which a person transfers property with the intent to qualify for a gift tax exclusion;

(3) that changes the amount payable to a beneficiary as a fixed annuity or a fixed fraction of the value of the trust assets;

(4) from any amount that is permanently set aside for charitable purposes under a will or the terms of a trust unless both income and principal are so set aside;

(5) if possessing or exercising the power to make an adjustment causes an individual to be treated as the owner of all or part of the trust for income tax purposes, and the individual would not be treated as the owner if the trustee did not possess the power to make an adjustment;

(6) if possessing or exercising the power to make an adjustment causes all or part of the trust assets to be included for estate tax purposes in the estate of an individual who has the power to remove a trustee or appoint a trustee, or both, and the assets would not be included in the estate of the individual if the trustee did not possess the power to make an adjustment;

(7) if the trustee is a beneficiary of the trust; or

(8) that satisfies the trustee's obligation of support or other legal obligation.

d. If paragraph (5), (6), (7) or (8) of subsection c. of this section applies to a trustee and there is more than one trustee, a co-trustee to whom the provision does not apply may make the adjustment unless the exercise of the power by the remaining trustee or trustees is not permitted by the terms of the trust.

e. A trustee may release the entire power conferred by subsection a. of this section or may release only the power to adjust from income to principal or the power to adjust from principal to income if the trustee is uncertain about whether possessing or exercising the power will cause a result described in paragraphs (1) through (6) or (8) of subsection c. of this section, or if the trustee determines that possessing or exercising the power will or may deprive the trust of a tax benefit or impose a tax burden not described in subsection c. of this section. The release may be permanent or for a specified period, including a period measured by the life of an individual.

f. Terms of a trust that limit the power of a trustee to make an adjustment between principal and income do not affect the application of this section unless it is clear from the terms of the trust that the terms are intended to deny the trustee the power of adjustment conferred by subsection a. of this section.

§ 3B:19B-5. *Determination and distribution of net income*

After a decedent dies, in the case of an estate or after an income interest in a trust ends, the following rules apply:

a. A fiduciary of an estate or of a terminating income interest shall determine the amount of net income and net principal receipts received from property specifically devised to a beneficiary under the rules in sections 7 through 28 of this act which apply to trustees and the rules in subsection e. of this section. The fiduciary shall distribute the net income and net principal receipts to the beneficiary who is to receive the specific property.

b. A fiduciary shall determine the remaining net income of a decedent's estate or a terminating income interest under the rules in sections 7 through 28 of this act which apply to trustees and by:

(1) including in net income all income from property used to discharge liabilities; and

(2) paying from principal all disbursements made or incurred in connection with the settlement of a decedent's estate or the winding up of a terminating income interest, expenses of administration, including fees of attorneys, accountants and fiduciaries, court costs, debts, funeral expenses, disposition of remains, family allowances and death taxes and related penalties that are apportioned to the estate or terminating income interest by the will, the terms of the trust or applicable law.

c. A fiduciary shall distribute to a beneficiary who receives a pecuniary amount outright the interest or any other amount provided by the will, the terms of the trust or applicable law from net income determined under subsection b. of this section or from principal to the extent that net income is insufficient. If a beneficiary is to receive a pecuniary amount outright from a trust after an income interest ends and no interest or other amount is provided for by the terms of the trust or applicable law, the fiduciary shall distribute the interest or other amount to which the beneficiary would be entitled under applicable law if the pecuniary amount were required to be paid under a will.

d. A fiduciary shall distribute the net income remaining after distributions required by subsection c. of this section in the manner described in section 6 of this act to all other beneficiaries, excluding a beneficiary who receives a pecuniary amount outright or in trust.

e. A fiduciary shall not reduce principal or income receipts from property described in subsection a. of this section because of a payment described in section 24 or 25 of this act to the extent that the will, the terms of the trust, or applicable law requires the fiduciary to make the payment from assets other than the property or to the extent that the fiduciary recovers or expects to recover the payment from a third party. The net income and principal receipts from the property are determined by including all of the amounts the fiduciary receives or pays with respect to the property, whether those amounts accrued or became due before, on or after the date of a decedent's death or an income interest's terminating event, and by making a reasonable provision for amounts that the fiduciary believes the estate or terminating income interest may become obligated to pay after the property is distributed.

§ 3B:19B-6. Distribution to residuary and remainder beneficiaries

a. Each beneficiary described in subsection d. of section 5 of this act is entitled to receive a portion of the net income equal to the beneficiary's fractional interest in undistributed principal assets, using values as of the distribution date. If a fiduciary makes more than one distribution of assets to beneficiaries to whom this section applies, each beneficiary, including one who does not receive part of the distribution, is entitled, as of each distribution date, to the net income the fiduciary has received after the date of death or terminating event or earlier distribution date but has not distributed as of the current distribution date.

b. In determining a beneficiary's share of net income, the following rules apply:

(1) The beneficiary is entitled to receive a portion of the net income equal to the beneficiary's fractional interest in the undistributed principal assets immediately before the distribution date, including assets that later may be sold to meet principal obligations.

(2) The beneficiary's fractional interest in the undistributed principal assets shall be calculated without regard to property specifically given to a beneficiary and property required to pay pecuniary amounts not in trust.

(3) The beneficiary's fractional interest in the undistributed principal assets shall be calculated on the basis of the aggregate value of those assets as of the distribution date without reducing the value by any unpaid principal obligation.

(4) The distribution date for purposes of this section may be the date as of which the fiduciary calculates the value of the assets if that date is reasonably near the date on which assets are actually distributed.

c. If a fiduciary does not distribute all of the collected but undistributed net income to each person as of a distribution date, the fiduciary shall maintain appropriate records showing the interest of each beneficiary in that net income.

d. A fiduciary may apply the rules in this section, to the extent that the fiduciary considers it appropriate, to net gain or loss realized after the date of death or terminating event or earlier distribution date from the disposition of a principal asset if this section applies to the income from the asset.

§ 3B:19B-7. When right to income begins and ends

a. An income beneficiary is entitled to net income from the date on which the income interest begins. An income interest begins on the date specified in the terms of the trust or, if no date is specified, on the date an asset becomes subject to a trust or successive income interest.

b. An asset becomes subject to a trust:

(1) on the date it is transferred to the trust in the case of an asset that is transferred to a trust during the transferor's life;

(2) on the date of a testator's death in the case of an asset that becomes subject to a trust by reason of a will, even if there is an intervening period of administration of the testator's estate; or

(3) on the date of an individual's death in the case of an asset that is transferred to a fiduciary by a third party because of the individual's death.

c. An asset becomes subject to a successive income interest on the day after the preceding income interest ends, as determined under subsection d. of this section, even if there is an intervening period of administration to wind up the preceding income interest.

d. An income interest ends on the day before an income beneficiary dies or another terminating event occurs, or on the last day of a period during which there is no beneficiary to whom a trustee may distribute income.

§ 3B:19B-8. Apportionment of receipts and disbursements when decedent dies or income interest begins

a. A trustee shall allocate an income receipt or disbursement, other than one to which subsection a. of section 5 of this act applies, to principal if its due date occurs before a decedent dies in the case of an estate or before an income interest begins in the case of a trust or successive income interest.

b. A trustee shall allocate an income receipt or disbursement to income if its due date occurs on or after the date on which a decedent dies or an income interest begins and it is a periodic due date. An income receipt or disbursement shall be treated as accruing from day to day if its due date is not periodic or it has no due date. The portion of the receipt or disbursement accruing before the date on which a decedent dies or an income interest begins shall be allocated to principal and the balance shall be allocated to income.

c. An item of income or an obligation is due on the date the payer is required to make a payment. If a payment date is not stated, there is no due date for the purposes of this act. Distributions to shareholders or other owners from an entity to which section 10 of this act applies are deemed to be due on the date fixed by the entity for determining who is entitled to receive the distribution or, if no date is fixed, on the declaration date for the distribution. A due date is periodic for receipts or disbursements that are to be paid at regular intervals under a lease or an obligation to pay interest or if an entity customarily makes distributions at regular intervals.

§ 3B:19B-9. Apportionment when income interest ends

a. As used in this section, "undistributed income" means net income received before the date on which an income interest ends. The term does not include an item of income or expense that is due or accrued or net income that has been added or is required to be added to principal under the terms of the trust.

b. When a mandatory income interest ends, the trustee shall pay to a mandatory income beneficiary who survives that date, or the estate of a deceased mandatory income beneficiary whose death causes the interest to end, the beneficiary's share of the undistributed income that is not disposed of under the terms of the trust, unless the beneficiary has an unqualified power to revoke more than five percent of the trust immediately before the income interest ends. In the latter case, the undistributed income from the portion of the trust that may be revoked shall be added to principal.

c. When a trustee's obligation to pay a fixed annuity or a fixed fraction of the value of the trust's assets ends, the trustee shall prorate the final payment if and to the extent required by applicable law to accomplish a purpose of the trust or its settlor relating to income, gift, estate or other tax requirements.

§ 3B:19B-10. Character of receipts

a. As used in this section, "entity" means a corporation, partnership, limited liability company, regulated investment company, real estate investment trust, common trust fund or any other organization in which a trustee has an interest other than a trust or estate to which section 11 of this act applies, a business or activity to which section 12 of this act applies or an asset-backed security to which section 23 of this act applies.

b. Except as otherwise provided in this section, a trustee shall allocate to income money received from an entity.

c. A trustee shall allocate the following receipts from an entity to principal:

(1) property other than money;
(2) money received in one distribution or a series of related distributions in exchange for part or all of a trust's interest in the entity;
(3) money received in total or partial liquidation of the entity; and
(4) money received from an entity that is a regulated investment company or a real estate investment trust if the money distributed is a capital gain dividend for federal income tax purposes.

d. Money is received in partial liquidation:

(1) to the extent that the entity, at or near the time of a distribution, indicates that it is a distribution in partial liquidation; or
(2) if the total amount of money and property received in a distribution or series of related distributions is greater than 20 percent of the entity's gross assets, as shown by the entity's year-end financial statements immediately preceding the initial receipt.

e. Money is not received in partial liquidation, nor may it be taken into account under paragraph (2) of subsection d. of this section, to the extent that it does not exceed the amount of income tax that a trustee or beneficiary must pay on taxable income of the entity that distributes the money.

f. A trustee may rely upon a statement made by an entity about the source or character of a distribution if the statement is made at or near the time of distribution by the entity's board of directors or other person or group of persons authorized to exercise powers to pay money or transfer property comparable to those of a corporation's board of directors.

§ 3B:19B-11. Distribution from trust or estate

A trustee shall allocate to income an amount received as a distribution of income from a trust or an estate in which the trust has an interest other than a purchased interest, and shall allocate to principal an amount received as a distribution of principal from such a trust or estate. If a trustee purchases an interest in a trust that is an investment entity, or a decedent or donor transfers an interest in such a trust to a trustee, section 10 or 23 of this act applies to a receipt from the trust.

§ 3B:19B-12. Business and other activities conducted by trustee

a. If a trustee who conducts a business or other activity determines that it is in the best interest of all the beneficiaries to account separately for the business or activity instead of accounting for it as part of the trust's general accounting records, the trustee may maintain separate accounting records for its transactions, whether or not its assets are segregated from other trust assets.

b. A trustee who accounts separately for a business or other activity may determine the extent to which its net cash receipts are to be retained for working capital, the acquisition or replacement of fixed assets and other reasonably foreseeable needs of the business or activity, and the extent to which the remaining net cash receipts are accounted for as principal or income in the trust's general accounting records. If a trustee sells assets of the business or other activity, other than in the ordinary course of the business or activity, the trustee shall account for the net amount received as principal in the trust's general accounting records to the extent the trustee determines that the amount received is no longer required in the conduct of the business.

c. Activities for which a trustee may maintain separate accounting records include:

(1) retail, manufacturing, service and other traditional business activities;
(2) farming;
(3) raising and selling livestock and other animals;
(4) management of rental properties;
(5) extraction of minerals and other natural resources;
(6) timber operations; and
(7) activities to which section 22 of this act applies.

§ 3B:19B-13. Principal receipts

A trustee shall allocate to principal:

a. To the extent not allocated to income under this act, assets received from a transferor during the transferor's lifetime, a decedent's estate, a trust with a terminating income interest or a payer under a contract naming the trust or its trustee as beneficiary;

b. Money or other property received from the sale, exchange, liquidation or change in form of a principal asset, including realized profit, subject to sections 10 through 23 of this act;

c. Amounts recovered from third parties to reimburse the trust because of disbursements described in paragraph (9) of subsection a. of section 25 of this act or for other reasons to the extent not based on the loss of income;

d. Proceeds of property taken by eminent domain, but a separate award made for the loss of income with respect to an accounting period during which a current income beneficiary had a mandatory income interest is income;

e. Net income received in an accounting period during which there is no beneficiary to whom a trustee may or shall distribute income; and

f. Other receipts as provided in sections 17 through 23 of this act.

§ 3B:19B-14. Rental property

To the extent that a trustee accounts for receipts from rental property pursuant to this section, the trustee shall allocate to income an amount received as rent of real or personal property, including an amount received for cancellation or renewal of a lease. An amount received as a refundable deposit, including a security deposit or a deposit that is to be applied as rent for future periods, shall be added to principal and held subject to the terms of the lease and is not available for distribution to a beneficiary until the trustee's contractual obligations have been satisfied with respect to that amount.

§ 3B:19B-15. Obligation to pay money

a. An amount received as interest, whether determined at a fixed, variable or floating rate, on an obligation to pay money to the trustee, including an amount received as consideration for prepaying principal, shall be allocated to income without any provision for amortization of premium.

b. A trustee shall allocate to principal an amount received from the sale, redemption or other disposition of an obligation to pay money to the trustee more than one year after it is purchased or acquired by the trustee, including an obligation whose purchase price or value when it is acquired is less than its value at maturity. If the obligation matures within one year after it is purchased or acquired by the trustee, an amount received in excess of its purchase price or its value when acquired by the trust shall be allocated to income.

c. This section does not apply to an obligation to which section 17, 18, 19, 20, 22 or 23 of this act applies.

§ 3B:19B-16. Insurance policies and similar contracts

a. Except as otherwise provided in subsection b. of this section, a trustee shall allocate to principal the proceeds of a life insurance policy or other contract in which the trust or its trustee is named as beneficiary, including a contract that insures the trust or its trustee against loss for damage to, destruction of or loss of title to a trust asset. The trustee shall allocate dividends on an insurance policy to income if the premiums on the policy are paid from income, and to principal if the premiums are paid from principal.

b. A trustee shall allocate to income proceeds of a contract that insures the trustee against loss of occupancy or other use by an income beneficiary, loss of income or, subject to section 12 of this act, loss of profits from a business.

c. This section does not apply to a contract to which section 17 of this act applies.

§ 3B:19B-17. Deferred compensation, retirement benefits, annuities, and similar payments

a. As used in this section, "payment" means a payment that a trustee may receive over a fixed period of time or during the life of one or more individuals because of services rendered or property transferred to the payer in exchange for future payments. The term includes a payment made in money or property from the payer's general assets or from a separate fund created by the payer or by another, including a private or commercial annuity, an individual retirement account and a pension, profit-sharing, stock-bonus, or stock-ownership plan.

b. To the extent that a trustee can readily ascertain the part of a payment from a separate fund held for the benefit of the trust that represents the then undistributed net income of the fund realized since the trust acquired its interest in the fund, a trustee shall allocate that part to income. The trustee shall allocate to principal the balance of the payment.

c. If no part of a payment is allocated to income under subsection b. of this section, and all or part of the payment is required to be made, a trustee shall allocate to income 10 percent of the part that is required to be made during the accounting period and the balance to principal. If no part of a payment is required to be made or the payment received is the entire amount to which the trustee is entitled, the trustee shall allocate the entire payment to principal. For purposes of this subsection, a payment is not "required to be made" to the extent that it is made because the trustee exercises a right of withdrawal.

d. If, to obtain an estate tax or gift tax marital deduction for a trust, the trustee must allocate more of a payment to income than provided for by this section, the trustee shall allocate to income the additional amount necessary to obtain the marital deduction.

e. This section does not apply to payments to which section 18 of this act applies.

§ 3B:19B-18. Liquidating asset

a. As used in this section, "liquidating asset" means an asset whose value will diminish or terminate because the asset is expected to produce receipts for a period of limited duration. The term includes a leasehold, patent, copyright, royalty right and right to receive payments during a period of more than one year under an arrangement that does not provide for the payment of interest on the unpaid balance. The term does not include a payment subject to section 17 of this act, resources subject to section 19 of this act, timber subject to section 20 of this act, an activity subject to section 22 of this act, an asset subject to section 23 of this act, or any asset for which the trustee establishes a reserve for depreciation under section 26 of this act.

b. A trustee shall allocate to income 10 percent of the receipts from a liquidating asset and the balance to principal.

§ 3B:19B-19. Minerals, water and other natural resources

a. To the extent that a trustee accounts for receipts from an interest in minerals or other natural resources pursuant to this section, the trustee shall allocate them as follows:

(1) if received as nominal delay rental or nominal annual rent on a lease, a receipt shall be allocated to income;

(2) if received from a production payment, a receipt shall be allocated to income if and to the extent that the agreement creating the production payment provides a factor for interest or its equivalent. The balance shall be allocated to principal;
(3) if an amount received as a royalty, shut-in-well payment, take-or-pay payment, bonus or delay rental is more than nominal, 90 percent shall be allocated to principal and the balance to income;
(4) if an amount is received from a working interest or any other interest not provided for in paragraph (1), (2) or (3) of this subsection a., 90 percent of the net amount received shall be allocated to principal and the balance to income.
b. An amount received on account of an interest in water that is renewable shall be allocated to income. If the water is not renewable, 90 percent of the amount shall be allocated to principal and the balance to income.
c. This act applies whether or not a decedent or donor was extracting minerals, water or other natural resources before the interest became subject to the trust.
d. If a trust owns an interest in minerals, water, or other natural resources on the effective date of this act, the trustee may allocate receipts from the interest as provided in this act or in the manner used by the trustee before the effective date of this act. If the trust acquires an interest in minerals, water or other natural resources after the effective date of this act, the trustee shall allocate receipts from the interest as provided in this act.

§ 3B:19B-20. Timber

a. To the extent that a trustee accounts for receipts from the sale of timber and related products pursuant to this section, the trustee shall allocate the net receipts:
(1) to income to the extent that the amount of timber removed from the land does not exceed the rate of growth of the timber during the accounting periods in which a beneficiary has a mandatory income interest;
(2) to principal to the extent that the amount of timber removed from the land exceeds the rate of growth of the timber or the net receipts are from the sale of standing timber;
(3) to or between income and principal if the net receipts are from the lease of timberland or from a contract to cut timber from land owned by a trust, by determining the amount of timber removed from the land under the lease or contract and applying the rules in paragraphs (1) and (2) of this subsection a.; or
(4) to principal to the extent that advance payments, bonuses and other payments are not allocated pursuant to paragraph (1), (2) or (3) of this subsection a.
b. In determining net receipts to be allocated pursuant to subsection a. of this section, a trustee shall deduct and transfer to principal a reasonable amount for depletion.
c. This section applies whether or not a decedent or transferor was harvesting timber from the property before it became subject to the trust.
d. If a trust owns an interest in timberland on the effective date of this act, the trustee may allocate net receipts from the sale of timber and related products as provided in this act or in the manner used by the trustee before the effective date of this act. If the trust acquires an interest in timberland after the effective date of this act, the trustee shall allocate net receipts from the sale of timber and related products as provided in this act.

§ 3B:19B-21. Property not productive of income

a. If a marital deduction is allowed for all or part of a trust whose assets consist substantially of property that does not provide the spouse with sufficient income from or use of the trust assets, and if the amounts that the trustee transfers from principal to income under section 4 of this act and distributes to the spouse from principal pursuant to the terms of the trust are insufficient to provide the spouse with the beneficial enjoyment required to obtain the marital deduction, the spouse may require the trustee to make property productive of income, convert property within a reasonable time or exercise the power conferred by subsection a. of section 4 of this act. The trustee may decide which action or combination of actions to take.
b. In cases not governed by subsection a. of this section, proceeds from the sale or other disposition of an asset are principal without regard to the amount of income the asset produces during any accounting period.

§ 3B:19B-22. Derivatives and options

a. As used in this section, "derivative" means a contract or financial instrument or a combination of contracts and financial instruments which gives a trust the right or obligation to participate in some or all changes in the price of a tangible or intangible asset or group of assets, or changes in a rate, an index of prices or rates or other market indicator for an asset or a group of assets.
b. To the extent that a trustee does not account under section 12 of this act for transactions in derivatives, the trustee shall allocate to principal receipts from and disbursements made in connection with those transactions.
c. If a trustee grants an option to buy property from the trust, whether or not the trust owns the property when the option is granted, grants an option that permits another person to sell property to the trust or acquires an option to buy property for the trust or an option to sell an asset owned by the trust, and the trustee or other owner of the asset is required to deliver the asset if the option is exercised, an amount received for granting the option shall be allocated to principal. An amount paid to acquire the option shall be paid from principal. A gain or loss realized upon the exercise of an option, including an option granted to a settlor of the trust for services rendered, shall be allocated to principal.

§ 3B:19B-23. Asset-backed securities

a. As used in this section, "asset-backed security" means an asset whose value is based upon the right it gives the owner to receive distributions from the proceeds of financial assets that provide collateral for the security. The term includes an asset that gives the owner the right to receive from the collateral financial assets only the interest or other current return or only the proceeds other than interest or current return. The term does not include an asset to which section 10 or 17 of this act applies.

b. If a trust receives a payment from interest or other current return and from other proceeds of the collateral financial assets, the trustee shall allocate to income the portion of the payment which the payer identifies as being from interest or other current return and shall allocate the balance of the payment to principal.

c. If a trust receives one or more payments in exchange for the trust's entire interest in an asset-backed security in one accounting period, the trustee shall allocate the payments to principal. If a payment is one of a series of payments that will result in the liquidation of the trust's interest in the security over more than one accounting period, the trustee shall allocate 10 percent of the payment to income and the balance to principal.

§ 3B:19B-24. Disbursements from income

A trustee shall make the following disbursements from income to the extent that they are not disbursements to which paragraph (1) or (2) of subsection b. of section 5 of this act applies:

a. commissions allowed by law to a trustee on income receipts, if properly chargeable to the trust;

b. one-half of the fees paid to banks and other financial institutions for custodial services to the fiduciary if properly chargeable to the trust;

c. all of the other ordinary expenses incurred in connection with the administration, management, or preservation of trust property and the distribution of income, including interest paid by the trustee, including interest on death taxes, regularly recurring taxes assessed against any portion of the principal, water rates, bond premiums, and the expenses, including court costs, attorneys' fees, and accountants' fees, of an accounting, judicial proceeding or other matter that concerns primarily the income interest, unless the court directs otherwise; and

d. recurring premiums on insurance covering the loss of a principal asset or the loss of income from or use of the asset.

§ 3B:19B-25. Disbursements from principal

a. A trustee shall make the following disbursements from principal:

(1) commissions allowed by law to a trustee on principal receipts or distributions or on termination of the trust estate;

(2) the remaining one-half of the fees paid to banks and other financial institutions for custodial services, if properly chargeable to the trust;

(3) fees paid to banks and other financial institutions and registered investment advisors for investment advisory or investment management services, if properly chargeable to the trust;

(4) costs of investing and reinvesting principal and payments on the principal of an indebtedness, including a mortgage or security interest amortized by periodic payments of principal;

(5) extraordinary repairs or expenses incurred in making a capital improvement, including special assessments, and disbursements made to prepare property for sale;

(6) court costs, attorneys' fees, accountants' fees and other fees, incurred on an accounting or judicial proceeding or in maintaining or defending any action to construe a will or a trust, protect it or the trust estate, or assure the title of any property, unless properly chargeable to income under subsection c. of section 24 of this act or the court otherwise directs;

(7) premiums paid on an insurance policy not described in subsection d. of section 24 of this act of which the trust is the owner and beneficiary;

(8) estate, inheritance and other transfer taxes, including penalties apportioned to the trust;

(9) disbursements related to environmental matters, including reclamation, assessing environmental conditions, remedying and removing environmental contamination, monitoring remedial activities and the release of substances, preventing future releases of substances, collecting amounts from persons liable or potentially liable for the cost of those activities, penalties imposed under environmental laws or regulations and other payments made to comply with those laws or regulations, statutory or common law claims by third parties and defending claims based on environmental matters; and

(10) if an estate or inheritance tax is levied in respect of a trust in which both an income beneficiary and remainderman have an interest, any amount apportioned to the trust, including penalties, even though the income beneficiary also has rights in the principal.

b. If a principal asset is encumbered with an obligation that requires income from that asset to be paid directly to the creditor, the trustee shall transfer from principal to income an amount equal to the income paid to the creditor in reduction of the principal balance of the obligation.

§ 3B:19B-26. Transfers from income to principal for depreciation

a. As used in this section, "depreciation" means a reduction in value due to wear, tear, decay, corrosion or gradual obsolescence of a fixed asset having a useful life of more than one year.

b. A trustee may transfer to principal a reasonable amount of the net cash receipts from a principal asset that is subject to depreciation, but may not transfer any amount for depreciation:

(1) of that portion of real property used or available for use by a beneficiary as a residence or of tangible personal property held or made available for the personal use or enjoyment of a beneficiary;

(2) during the administration of a decedent's estate; or

(3) under this section if the trustee is accounting under section 12 of this act for the business or activity in which the asset is used.

c. An amount transferred to principal need not be held as a separate fund.

§ 3B:19B-27. Transfer from income to reimburse principal

a. If a trustee makes or expects to make a principal disbursement described in this section, the trustee may transfer an appropriate amount from income to principal in one or more accounting periods to reimburse principal or to provide a reserve for future principal disbursements.
b. Principal disbursements to which subsection a. of this section applies include the following, but only to the extent that the trustee has not been and does not expect to be reimbursed by a third party:
(1) an amount chargeable to income but paid from principal because it is unusually large, including extraordinary repairs;
(2) disbursements made to prepare property for rental, including tenant allowances, leasehold improvements and broker's commissions; and
(3) periodic payments on an obligation secured by a principal asset to the extent that the amount transferred from income to principal for depreciation is less than the periodic payments.
c. If the asset whose ownership gives rise to the disbursements becomes subject to a successive income interest after an income interest ends, a trustee may continue to transfer amounts from income to principal as provided in subsection a. of this section.

§ 3B:19B-28. Income taxes

a. A tax required to be paid by a trustee based on receipts allocated to income shall be paid from income.
b. A tax required to be paid by a trustee based on receipts allocated to principal shall be paid from principal, even if the tax is called an income tax by the taxing authority.
c. A tax required to be paid by a trustee on the trust's share of an entity's taxable income shall be paid proportionately:
(1) from income to the extent that receipts from the entity are allocated to income; and
(2) from principal to the extent that:
(a) receipts from the entity are allocated to principal; and
(b) the trust's share of the entity's taxable income exceeds the total receipts described in paragraph (1) and subparagraph (a) of this paragraph (2).
d. For purposes of this section, receipts allocated to principal or income shall be reduced by the amount distributed to a beneficiary from principal or income for which the trust receives a deduction in calculating the tax.

§ 3B:19B-29. Uniformity of application and construction

In applying and construing this act, consideration shall be given to the fact that this is a uniform act, and there is a need to promote uniformity of the act with respect to its subject matter among states that enact it.

§ 3B:19B-30. Application of act to existing and future trusts and estates

This act applies to every trust or decedent's estate existing on or after the effective date of this act, except as otherwise expressly provided in the will or terms of the trust or in this act.

§ 3B:19B-31. Judicial control of discretionary powers

a. A court shall not change a fiduciary's decision to exercise or not to exercise a discretionary power conferred by this act unless it determines that the decision was an abuse of discretion. A court shall not determine that a fiduciary abused its discretion merely because the court would have exercised the discretion in a different manner or would not have exercised the discretion.
b. The decisions to which subsection a. of this section applies include:
(1) A determination under subsection a. of section 4 of this act of whether and to what extent an amount should be transferred from principal to income or from income to principal.
(2) A determination of the factors that are relevant to the trust and its beneficiaries, the extent to which they are relevant, and the weight, if any, to be given to the relevant factors in deciding whether and to what extent to exercise the powers conferred by subsection a. of section 4 of this act.
c. If a court determines that a fiduciary has abused its discretion, the remedy is to restore the income and remainder beneficiaries to the position they would have occupied if the fiduciary had not abused its discretion, according to the following rules:
(1) To the extent that the abuse of discretion has resulted in no distribution to a beneficiary or a distribution that is too small, the court shall require the fiduciary to distribute from the trust to the beneficiary an amount that the court determines will restore the beneficiary, in whole or in part, to his appropriate position.
(2) To the extent that an abuse of discretion has resulted in a distribution to a beneficiary that is too large, the court shall restore the beneficiaries, the trust, or both, in whole or in part, to their appropriate position by requiring the fiduciary to withhold an amount from one or more of future distributions to the beneficiary who received the distribution that was too large or requiring that beneficiary to return some or all of the distribution to the trust.
(3) To the extent that the court is unable, after applying paragraphs (1) and (2) of this subsection to restore the beneficiaries, the trust, or both, to the position they would have occupied if the fiduciary had not abused its discretion, the court may require the fiduciary to pay an appropriate amount from its own funds to one or more of the beneficiaries or the trust or both.
d. Upon a petition by the fiduciary, the court having jurisdiction over the trust or estate shall determine whether a proposed exercise or nonexercise by the fiduciary of a discretionary power conferred by this act will result in an abuse of the fiduciary's discretion. If the petition describes the proposed exercise or nonexercise of the power and contains sufficient information to inform the beneficiaries of the reasons for the proposal, the facts upon which the fiduciary relies, and an explanation of how the income

and remainder beneficiaries will be affected by the proposed exercise or nonexercise of the power, a beneficiary who challenges the proposed exercise or nonexercise has the burden of establishing that it will result in an abuse of discretion.

Chapter 20. Investments

Article 1. In General

§ 3B:20-1. Definitions

As used in this chapter:

a. "Trust instrument" means and includes a will, deed, agreement, court order or other instrument pursuant to which money or other property is entrusted to a fiduciary;

b. "Fiduciary" means an individual or corporation that is authorized to act as or acts as a trustee, personal representative, conservator, guardian, and every other individual or corporation charged with the duty of administering a trust estate;

c. "Trust estate" or "trust assets" means money or other property entrusted to a fiduciary;

d. (Deleted by amendment, P.L.1997, c.26.)

e. "Beneficiary" means an individual or corporation for whose benefit a fiduciary acts or is authorized to act.

§ 3B:20-2. Repealed by L. 1997, c. 26

§ 3B:20-3. Corporate fiduciary may register securities in name of nominee without disclosing fiduciary capacity

Any bank may, when acting as sole fiduciary or when acting as cofiduciary, with the consent of a cofiduciary or cofiduciaries, cause any certificates for shares of stock, bonds, debentures, notes or other securities, herein denominated "securities", held in fiduciary capacities, to be registered and held in the name of a nominee of the corporate fiduciary without disclosing the fiduciary capacity in which the securities are held; provided, that

a. The records of the fiduciary or fiduciaries and all accounts rendered by it or them shall at all times clearly show the ownership of the securities so registered,

b. The securities shall at all times be kept separate and apart from the assets of the fiduciary or fiduciaries, and

c. The nominee shall not have possession of or access to the securities.

§ 3B:20-4. Corporate fiduciary liable for loss caused by acts of nominee

The fiduciary or fiduciaries shall be liable for any loss caused by the acts of the nominee with respect to securities registered as provided in N.J.S. 3B:20-3.

§ 3B:20-5. Limitation on authority to register securities in name of nominee

A fiduciary or fiduciaries may not register securities in the name of a nominee where any will, trust instrument or any order appointing or relating to any fiduciary or fiduciaries prohibits securities from being registered in the name of a nominee.

§ 3B:20-6. Repealed by L. 1997, c. 26

§ 3B:20-7. Directions of court concerning the sale, conversion or retention of investments

When securities or other property come into possession of a fiduciary as part of the assets of the trust estate the fiduciary is to administer or manage, the fiduciary may apply to the court for direction as to the sale, conversion or retention of the securities or property.

The court shall make an order as it shall deem most advantageous to the trust estate and the interests of persons entitled to share therein.

§ 3B:20-8. Protection afforded fiduciary continuing investments under court order

A fiduciary shall not be held accountable for any loss by reason of continuing to hold the trust assets in accordance with an order pursuant to N.J.S.3B:20-7.

§ 3B:20-9. Application to court upon change in conditions

If, as a result of a change in conditions which occurs or which may be reasonably foreseen, the objects of the trust estate may be defeated in whole or in part by the investment or retention of investments of the trust estate in property to which the fiduciary is limited by the trust instrument, the fiduciary or any beneficiary of the trust may apply to the court to secure authority permitting or directing the fiduciary to invest all or any part of the trust estate in accordance with the provisions of N.J.S.3B:20-1 et seq.

§ 3B:20-10. Investments by court order upon change in conditions

If the court finds that by reason of a change in conditions which has occurred since the creation of the trust or which may be reasonably foreseen, the objects of the trust estate may be defeated in whole or in part by the investment or retention of the trust estate in property to which the fiduciary is limited by the trust instrument and that the objects of the trust estate and those interested in it would be promoted by the investment of all or part of the trust estate otherwise, the court shall authorize or direct the fiduciary to invest the whole of the trust estate or that part of it as shall be designated, in accordance with the provisions of N.J.S.3B:20-1 et seq.

§ 3B:20-11. Repealed by L. 1997, c. 26

§ 3B:20-11.1. Short title

Sections 1 through 12 of this 1997 amendatory and supplementary act shall be known and may be cited as the "Prudent Investor Act."

§ 3B:20-11.2. Compliance by fiduciary with prudent investor rule

a. Except as provided in subsection b. of this section, a fiduciary who invests and manages trust assets owes a duty to the beneficiaries of the trust to comply with the prudent investor rule, as set forth in this act.

b. The prudent investor rule is a default rule that may be expanded, restricted, eliminated, or otherwise altered by express provisions of the trust instrument. A fiduciary is not liable to a beneficiary to the extent that the fiduciary acted in reasonable reliance on those express provisions. Nothing herein shall affect the jurisdiction of the Superior Court to order or authorize a fiduciary to deviate from the express terms or provisions of a trust instrument for the causes, in the manner, and to the extent otherwise provided by law.

§ 3B:20-11.3. Investments, management of trust assets by fiduciary

a. A fiduciary shall invest and manage trust assets as a prudent investor would, by considering the purposes, terms, distribution requirements, and other circumstances of the trust. In satisfying this standard, the fiduciary shall exercise reasonable care, skill, and caution.

b. A fiduciary's investment and management decisions respecting individual assets shall not be evaluated in isolation, but in the context of the trust portfolio as a whole and as a part of an overall investment strategy having risk and return objectives reasonably suited to the trust.

c. Subject to the standards established in this act, a fiduciary may invest in any kind of property or type of investment. No specific investment or course of action is inherently imprudent.

d. Among the circumstances that the fiduciary shall consider in investing and managing trust assets are those of the following as are relevant to the trust and its beneficiaries:

(1) general economic conditions;
(2) the possible effect of inflation or deflation;
(3) the expected tax consequences of investment decisions or strategies;
(4) the role that each investment or course of action plays within the overall trust portfolio;
(5) the expected total return from income and the appreciation of capital;
(6) other resources of the beneficiaries;
(7) the need for liquidity, for regularity of income, and for preservation or appreciation of capital; and
(8) an asset's special relationship or special value, if any, to the purposes of the trust or to one or more of the beneficiaries as, for example, an interest in a closely-held enterprise, tangible and intangible personalty, or real estate.

e. The fiduciary shall take reasonable steps to verify facts relevant to the investment and management of trust assets and may rely and be fully protected in relying upon statistical, financial, corporate or other information as to a particular investment, and upon ratings or other opinion as to the financial or other status thereof, contained in or offered by any financial, statistical, investment, rating or other publication or service published for the use of and accepted as reliable by investors in like investments or upon a copy of the prospectus prepared and filed with the Securities and Exchange Commission in connection with a new issue.

f. A fiduciary who has special skills or expertise, or is named fiduciary in reliance upon representations of special skills or expertise, has a duty to use those special skills or expertise.

§ 3B:20-11.4. Diversification of investments

A fiduciary shall diversify the investments of the trust unless the fiduciary reasonably determines that, because of special circumstances, the purposes of the trust are better served without diversifying.

§ 3B:20-11.5. Assets to be managed in interest of beneficiaries

A fiduciary shall invest and manage the trust assets solely in the interest of the beneficiaries.

§ 3B:20-11.6. Impartiality of fiduciary

If a trust has two or more beneficiaries, the fiduciary shall act impartially in investing and managing the trust assets, taking into account any differing interests of the beneficiaries.

§ 3B:20-11.7. Review of trust assets

Within six months after accepting trust assets, the fiduciary shall review the trust assets and shall make and implement decisions concerning the retention and disposition of assets received at the inception of the trust, in order to bring the trust portfolio into compliance with the provisions of the trust instrument or with the requirements of this act.

§ 3B:20-11.8. Incurrence of costs by fiduciary

In investing and managing trust assets, a fiduciary may only incur costs that are appropriate and reasonable in relation to the assets, the purposes of the trust, and the skills of the fiduciary. A fiduciary who delegates investment and management functions pursuant to section 10 of P.L.1997, c.26 (C.3B:20-11.10) shall control the overall costs of the delegation, including making a reduction in the amount of corpus commissions otherwise allowable to the fiduciary with respect to the trust assets for which investment responsibility has been delegated, which reduction shall take account of the duties and responsibilities retained by the fiduciary with respect to such assets.

§ 3B:20-11.9. Rule expresses standard of conduct

The prudent investor rule expresses a standard of conduct, not outcome. Compliance with the rule is determined in light of the facts and circumstances existing at the time of the fiduciary's decision or action.

§ 3B:20-11.10. Delegation of investment, management functions by fiduciary

a. A fiduciary may delegate investment and management functions that a prudent fiduciary of comparable skills could properly delegate under the circumstances. The fiduciary shall exercise reasonable care, skill, and caution in:

(1) selecting an agent with special investment skills and expertise and of sound financial standing;

(2) establishing the scope and terms of the delegation consistent with the purpose and terms of the trust instrument; and

(3) periodically reviewing the agent's actions in order to monitor the agent's performance and compliance with the scope and terms of the delegation.

b. In performing a delegated function, the agent shall owe to the trustee and the beneficiaries the same duties as the fiduciary and shall be held to the same standards as the fiduciary.

c. The fiduciary who complies with the requirements of subsection a. of this section shall not be liable to the beneficiaries or to the trust for the decisions or actions of the agent to whom the function was delegated.

d. By accepting the delegation of a trust function from the fiduciary of a trust that is subject to the law of New Jersey, the agent submits to the jurisdiction of the courts of New Jersey, even if the delegation agreement provides otherwise.

e. If there are two or more fiduciaries serving, only one of whom has special investment and management skills or expertise or has been named in reliance upon representations of such special skills or expertise, then the fiduciary or fiduciaries not possessed of such special skills or expertise may, pursuant to this section, delegate investment and management functions to the other fiduciary as if such other fiduciary were an agent selected in accordance with this section and subject to the provisions of this section.

f. A fiduciary shall provide reasonable advance written notice on each occasion upon which the fiduciary intends to delegate investment and management functions pursuant to this section, including the identity of the agent, to the beneficiary or beneficiaries eligible to receive income from the trust on the date of the intended delegation. Upon providing such notice, the fiduciary shall be authorized to delegate investment and management functions pursuant to this section.

§ 3B:20-11.11. Construction of terms

The following terms or comparable language in a trust instrument, unless otherwise limited or modified by that instrument, shall be construed as authorizing any investment or strategy permitted under this act: "investments permissible by law for investment of trust funds," "legal investment," "authorized investments," "using the judgment and care under the circumstances then prevailing that persons of prudence, discretion, and intelligence exercise in the management of their own affairs, not in regard to speculation but in regard to the permanent disposition of their funds, considering the probable income as well as the probable safety of their capital," "prudent man rule," "prudent trustee rule," "prudent person rule," and "prudent investor rule."

§ 3B:20-11.12. Applicability of act

This act shall apply to and govern trusts existing on and created after its effective date. As applied to trusts existing on its effective date, this act governs only actions or omissions occurring after that date.

Article 2. Prudent Investment Law [Repealed]

§ 3B:20-13. Repealed by L. 1997, c. 26

§ 3B:20-14. Repealed by L. 1997, c. 26

§ 3B:20-15. Repealed by L. 1997. c. 26

§ 3B:20-16. Repealed by L. 1997, c. 26

§ 3B:20-17. Repealed by L. 1997, c. 26

Article 3. Exchange or Conversion of Securities upon Merger, Recapitalization, Consolidation or Reorganization of Issuing Corporation

§ 3B:20-18. Authority to exchange or convert securities

Except as otherwise provided in the trust instrument, a fiduciary who holds securities in a trust estate issued by a corporation which has been recapitalized or reorganized, or which has been a party to a merger or consolidation, may exchange or convert the securities so held for or into other securities issued by the corporation as an incident of its recapitalization, reorganization, merger or consolidation, or issued by the corporation's successor corporation as an incident of the merger or consolidation.

§ 3B:20-19. Fiduciary as issuing corporation

An exchange or conversion of securities may be made pursuant to this article notwithstanding that the fiduciary which holds the securities in a trust estate is the same corporation which issued the securities.

§ 3B:20-20. Repealed by L. 1997, c. 26

Article 4. Exchange and Conversion of Bank Shares for Shares of Bank Holding Company

§ 3B:20-21. Definitions

As used in this article:

a. "Banking institution" includes State chartered banks and national banking associations;

b. "Bank holding company" means a bank holding company as defined in the Bank Holding Company Act of 1956 (Act of May 9, 1956, 70 Stat. 1933, 12 U.S.C. 1841 et seq.) as amended by the Bank Holding Company Act Amendments of 1970 (Act of December 31, 1970, 84 Stat. 1760).

§ 3B:20-22. Authority to exchange or convert

When a bank holding company which is a corporation acquires 80% or more of the outstanding capital stock of a banking institution, any shares of the capital stock of the banking institution held in a trust estate by a fiduciary may be exchanged for or converted into the capital stock of the bank holding company as an incident of the company's acquisition of the shares.

§ 3B:20-23. Banking institution acting as fiduciary

An exchange or conversion of shares may be made pursuant to this article notwithstanding that the fiduciary which holds the shares in the trust estate is the banking institution which issued them.

§ 3B:20-24. Repealed by L. 1997, c. 26

§ 3B:20-25. Application of article

This article shall not apply where a trust instrument contains provisions inconsistent with or contrary to the provisions of this article.

Article 5. Clearing Corporations; Deposit of Securities

§ 3B:20-26. Short title

This article shall be known and may be cited as the "Clearing Corporation Deposit Law of 1973."

§ 3B:20-27. Definitions

As used in this article:

a. (Deleted by amendment, P.L.1997, c.26).

b. "Securities" means instruments which are commonly dealt with on securities exchanges or markets or commonly recognized in any area in which they are issued or dealt with as a medium for investment, and which are subject to the provisions of chapter 8, "Uniform Commercial Code-Investment Securities" (chapter 8, Title 12A of the New Jersey Statutes);

c. "Clearing corporation" means a corporation as defined in N.J.S.12A:8-102.

§ 3B:20-28. Deposit of securities by fiduciary

Notwithstanding any other provision of law, a fiduciary holding securities in a trust estate, or any banking institution holding securities as a custodian or managing agent, or as custodian for a fiduciary, is authorized to deposit or arrange for the deposit of the securities in a clearing corporation.

§ 3B:20-29. Merger of certificates deposited

When securities are deposited, certificates representing securities of the same class of the same issuer may be merged and held in bulk in the name of the nominee of the clearing corporation with any other securities deposited in the clearing corporation by any person regardless of the ownership of the securities, and certificates of small denomination may be merged into one or more certificates of larger denomination.

§ 3B:20-30. Records of securities deposited

The records of the fiduciary and the records of a banking institution acting as custodian, as managing agent or as custodian for a fiduciary, shall at all times show the name of the party for whose account the securities are deposited.

§ 3B:20-31. Transfer of ownership in securities deposited

Ownership of, and other interests in, securities deposited may be transferred by bookkeeping entry on the books of the clearing corporation without physical delivery of certificates representing the securities.

§ 3B:20-32. Rules and regulations governing banking institutions

A banking institution depositing securities pursuant to this article shall be subject to rules and regulations as, in the case of State chartered institutions the Commissioner of the Department of Banking and, in the case of national banks, the Comptroller of the Currency may from time to time issue.

§ 3B:20-33. Certification of securities deposited

A banking institution acting as custodian for a fiduciary shall, on demand by the fiduciary, certify in writing to the fiduciary securities deposited by the banking institution in a clearing corporation for the account of the fiduciary. A fiduciary shall, on demand by any party to a judicial proceeding for the settlement of the fiduciary's account or on demand by the attorney for the party, certify in writing to the party the securities deposited by the fiduciary in the clearing corporation for its account as the fiduciary.

§ 3B:20-34. Application of article

This article shall apply to any fiduciary holding securities in its fiduciary capacity, and to any banking institution holding securities as a custodian, managing agent or custodian for a fiduciary, acting on January 2, 1974, or who thereafter may act regardless of the date of the trust instrument by which the fiduciary is appointed and regardless of whether or not the fiduciary or the banking institution acting as custodian, managing agent or custodian for a fiduciary owns capital stock of the clearing corporation.

§ 3B:20-35. Construction of article

Nothing contained in this article shall be construed as relieving a fiduciary depositing securities as authorized herein from the duty to account for all securities so deposited.

Chapter 21. Transfer of Property Out of State

§ 3B:21-1. Removal of property from the State

When a ward or a cestui que trust, or all the cestuis que trustent in esse, is or, all of them, are nonresidents of this State and is or are entitled to personal or real property in this State and the guardian or trustee received his letters from, or is subject to the jurisdiction of, a court of another state or country, the Superior Court may authorize the guardian or trustee, if it is in the interest of the persons in interest, to demand, collect, sue for, receive and remove from this State all or any part of the personal property and the rents, issues and profits of the real property, or authorize the personal property, and the rents, issues and profits of the real property to be transferred to the custody of the proper court of that state, jurisdiction or country.

§ 3B:21-2. Meaning of term "personal property"

The term "personal property" as used in this chapter shall include, but without limitation, property or money or any devise or distributive share, interest, trust fund or trust property in the hands of a fiduciary residing or acting in this State, moneys in the hands of a receiver appointed by any court, moneys in the hands of a commissioner, officer, fiduciary or other person constituting the proceeds from the sale of real estate under any judicial proceeding, or pursuant to the provisions of any will or instrument of trust, or awarded as damages for the taking of lands under legislative authority, moneys or funds deposited in any court of this State, whether arising from the sale of lands or otherwise, and moneys or property in the custody or under the control or subject to the directions of any court.

§ 3B:21-3. Proof of authority of, and giving of security by, guardian or trustee

In any action brought pursuant to N.J.S. 3B:21-1, the court shall be satisfied by proof that the guardian or trustee is authorized and qualified to act in the state or country to which the money or other property is to be removed. The court shall require him to give bond, in double the amount or value of the moneys or other property to be removed, or in any other sum and with an obligee, conditions and sureties as the court may determine. A bond need not be required if the court is satisfied that he has given security satisfactory to the court in that state or country or is not required to furnish security under the laws thereof.

§ 3B:21-4. When removal will be denied

Property belonging to any cestui que trust or ward shall not be removed or transferred where it would conflict with the terms, limitations or conditions attending his right to the property, whether they are created by will, trust or any other instrument, or where the interests of a citizen of this State with respect to the property would thereby be prejudiced.

§ 3B:21-5. Effect of judgment for removal and transfer

The delivery, transfer or payment of property or money pursuant to a judgment entered in accordance with this chapter shall be a legal discharge and acquittance for the delivery, transfer or payment of property or money, but if the court deems it advisable, it may require receipts or releases or refunding bonds to be given and recorded.

Chapter 22. Rights and Remedies of Creditors of Decedents

Article 1. In General

§ 3B:22-1. Waiver of statutes of limitations

Unless an estate is insolvent the personal representative may, but only with the consent of all successors, waive any defense of limitations available to the estate. If the defense is not waived, no claim which was barred by any statute of limitations at the time of the decedent's death shall be allowed or paid.

§ 3B:22-2. Order of priority of claims when assets insufficient

If the applicable assets of the estate are insufficient to pay all claims in full, the personal representative shall make payment in the following order:
a. Reasonable funeral expenses;
b. Costs and expenses of administration;
c. Debts for the reasonable value of services rendered to the decedent by the Office of the Public Guardian for Elderly Adults;
d. Debts and taxes with preference under federal law or the laws of this State;
e. Reasonable medical and hospital expenses of the last illness of the decedent, including compensation of persons attending him;
f. Judgments entered against the decedent according to the priorities of their entries respectively;
g. All other claims.

No preference shall be given in the payment of any claim over any other claim of the same class, and a claim due and payable shall not be entitled to a preference over claims not due. The commencement of an action against the personal representative for the recovery of a debt or claim or the entry of a judgment thereon against the personal representative shall not entitle such debt or claim to preference over others of the same class.

§ 3B:22-3. Abatement for purpose of paying claims and debts

The property of a decedent's estate shall abate for the purposes of paying debts and claims in the order prescribed in N.J.S. 3B:23-12.

§ 3B:22-4. Limitation of time to present claims of creditors to personal representative; discharge of personal representative where claim is not duly presented before distribution

Creditors of the decedent shall present their claims to the personal representative of the decedent's estate in writing and under oath, specifying the amount claimed and the particulars of the claim, within nine months from the date of the decedent's death. If a claim is not so presented to the personal representative within nine months from the date of the decedent's death, the personal representative shall not be liable to the creditor with respect to any assets which the personal representative may have delivered or paid in satisfaction of any lawful claims, devises or distributive shares, before the presentation of the claim.

§ 3B:22-5. Liquidated claims payable in future

A liquidated claim, not due and payable, but payable in the future, may be presented for allowance, a reasonable rebate of interest being made when interest is not accruing thereon. If the claim is disputed and action is brought thereon, the plaintiff shall not fail in the action because the claim is payable in the future, if the claim is otherwise valid.

§ 3B:22-6. Payment of claim not legally presented; effect; allowance in personal representative's account

If a personal representative in good faith pays a claim presented to him which is not verified as required, and, on or before final accounting, it is proved to the court or surrogate that the claim was owed by the decedent and was a just claim against the estate, the court shall allow in the personal representative's account the full amount of the claim if the estate is sufficient to pay the debts of equal degree with the claim in full. If the estate is not sufficient for that purpose, he shall be allowed the pro rata amount the creditor would have been entitled to receive if the claim had been presented verified as required.

§ 3B:22-7. Allowance or rejection of claims within 3 months

Within 3 months after the presentation to him of a claim, the personal representative shall allow or dispute it or allow it in part and dispute it in part, and give notice in writing to the creditor, his agent or attorney, of that which he allows or disputes.

§ 3B:22-8. Commencement of action by creditor on disputed claim within 3 months after notice

Within 3 months after receiving notice that a claim or a part of it has been disputed, the creditor shall commence an action to recover on the claim or so much of it as is disputed; otherwise the personal representative shall not be liable to the creditor with respect to any assets which he may have delivered or paid in satisfaction of any lawful claims, devises or distributive shares before the commencement of the action.

Article 3. Remedies of Creditors; Failure to Present Claims Within Time Limits

§ 3B:22-10. Presentation of claim

Where the assets of an estate exceed the amount needed to pay claims presented within the time limited pursuant to N.J.S. 3B:22-4, a claimant, who has failed to present his claim within the time so limited, may present the claim, in the form required by that section, to the personal representative at any time before the remaining assets of the estate shall have been distributed or paid over pursuant to law.

§ 3B:22-11. Acceptance or rejection of claim

The personal representative shall, if satisfied that the claim is correct and should be paid, pay the claim or so much thereof as the amount of the assets available for distribution will permit. If not satisfied with the correctness thereof, the personal representative shall notify the claimant, his agent or attorney, to proceed forthwith to establish the disputed claim, or part thereof, by judgment. In that case the personal representative shall retain from the assets available for distribution a sum sufficient to pay the amount of the claim, together with interest and costs, until the claimant shall have had an opportunity to establish his claim by judgment.

§ 3B:22-12. Action on unrejected claim

If a personal representative fails to pay a claim presented pursuant to N.J.S. 3B:22-11, the claimant may bring an action against the personal representative to recover on his claim in any court of competent jurisdiction.

§ 3B:22-13. Failure to sue after notice to perfect claim; claim debarred

If a creditor fails to commence an action upon his claim within 1 month after being notified to establish the claim by judgment, as provided by N.J.S. 3B:22-11, he shall be thereafter forever barred from any action against the personal representative to recover on the claim.

§ 3B:22-14. Direction of court before paying claims not presented within 9-month period

A personal representative may not be compelled to pay any claim not presented within the period limited pursuant to N.J.S. 3B:22-4, unless the court shall, for good cause shown, so direct or until his account has been settled by the court and the court has authorized or directed him to make the payment.

§ 3B:22-15. Failure to file refunding bond; presumption that devise or distributive share remains unpaid

In an action by a creditor against a personal representative, for the payment of a ratable proportion of his debt, it shall be presumed that the assets of the estate due a devisee or heir have not been paid over to him, if no refunding bond from the devisee or heir is on file. However, the presumption may be rebutted by proof that the devise or distributive share was actually paid over to him.

§ 3B:22-16. Action upon refunding bond of devisee or heir

A claimant against an estate who has failed to present his claim in due form within the time required, may bring an action in his own name without leave of court on a refunding bond given by a devisee or heir and recover the proportion of his claim which ought to be paid out of the devise or distributive share for which the bond was given.

Recovery on a refunding bond shall in no case exceed the amount actually received by the devisee or heir furnishing the bond.

§ 3B:22-17. Defense to action on fiduciary's bond in certain cases

A fiduciary, who has received a devise or distributive share from a personal representative and has given a refunding bond therefor, may set up in absolute bar to an action on the bond, that he has lawfully paid out and distributed the devise or distributive share to the person entitled thereto, and has taken a refunding bond therefor from that person. If the fiduciary has paid out a part only of the devise or distributive share and has taken a similar refunding bond therefor, he may defend in like manner as to the part so paid or distributed.

§ 3B:22-18. Action on refunding bond of ultimate devisee or heir

A creditor may sue on a bond taken by a fiduciary pursuant to N.J.S. 3B:22-17, in the same manner and with like effect as if the original personal representative had made payment or distribution directly and had taken the bond himself.

Article 4. Estate Administration in More than One State

§ 3B:22-19. Assets being administered here subject to claims established wherever personal representative appointed

All assets of estates being administered in this State are subject to all claims and charges existing or established against the personal representative wherever appointed.

§ 3B:22-20. Payment of claims where assets insufficient

If the estate either in this State or as a whole is insufficient to cover all claims and prior charges, each claimant whose claim has been allowed either in this State or elsewhere in administrations of which the personal representative is aware, is entitled to receive payment of an equal proportion of his claim. If a preference or security in regard to a claim is allowed in another jurisdiction but not in this State, the creditor so benefited is to receive dividends from local assets only upon the balance of his claim after deducting the amount of the benefit.

§ 3B:22-21. Payment of claims allowed in this State out of local assets; delivery of surplus assets to domiciliary personal representative

In case the claims and prior charges of the entire estate exceed the total value of the portions of the estate being administered separately and this State is not the state of the decedent's last domicile, the claims allowed in this State shall be paid their proportion if local assets are adequate for the purpose, and the balance of local assets shall be transferred to the domiciliary personal representative. If local assets are not sufficient to pay all claims allowed in this State the amount to which they are entitled, local assets shall be marshaled so that each claim allowed in this State is paid its proportion as far as possible, after taking into account all dividends on claims allowed in this State from assets in other jurisdictions.

Article 5. Real Property Liability for Debts

§ 3B:22-22. Real property liable only 1 year for debts

The real property of any person who shall die seized thereof or entitled thereto shall be and remain liable for the payment of his debts for 1 year after his decease, but may be sold free from liability for payment of debts by his personal representative upon application to the court upon terms and conditions as the court may direct for the protection of creditors, any alienation or encumbrance made or attempted to be made by his heirs or devisee to the contrary notwithstanding. Nothing herein contained shall affect any right of dower or curtesy in the real property.

§ 3B:22-23. Time not extended by general words in will

The period of 1 year fixed in N.J.S. 3B:22-22, shall not be deemed to be extended by any directions in a will that just debts be paid. Any charge upon real property created by any directions in a will that just debts be paid shall not attach to the real property beyond the period of 1 year fixed in that section, unless the will contains express language to the effect that the debts shall remain a lien upon the real property for a longer period.

§ 3B:22-24. Article not to affect liability of heirs or devisees

Nothing contained in this article shall affect any liability of heirs and devisees under article 8 of this chapter.

Article 6. Payment of Debts by Sale of Property Subject to Escheat

§ 3B:22-25. Sale of property subject to escheat to pay debts

In any case where property may be subject to escheat to the State, proceedings to sell the property to pay debts may be taken as provided in this article.

§ 3B:22-26. Direction of court as to sale

If it shall appear to the satisfaction of the court that property of which a decedent died seized or possessed is subject to escheat to the State and that it is necessary to sell the property in order to pay debts of the decedent, the court shall direct the personal representative of the decedent's estate to sell the property or so much thereof as may be necessary for that purpose.

§ 3B:22-27. Estate passed by sale or conveyance

A sale or conveyance of property directed to be sold by the court, as provided in N.J.S. 3B:22-26, when made by a personal representative, shall vest in the purchaser all the estate of which the decedent was seized or possessed at the time of his death.

§ 3B:22-28. Effect of confirmation

When property is sold pursuant to N.J.S. 3B:22-26 and the sale is confirmed by the court directing the sale, the judgment or order confirming the sale or a certified copy thereof shall be conclusive evidence in all courts of the validity of the proceedings for sale and of the fulfillment of statutory requirements.

The judgment or order may be set aside or reversed by appropriate proceedings for that purpose; but the proceedings shall not affect a bona fide purchaser, and the purchaser, his heirs and assigns, shall hold the property so purchased, notwithstanding the setting aside or reversal and notwithstanding any defect in the proceedings for sale.

§ 3B:22-29. Accounting; surplus from sale payable to State Treasurer

After accounting duly made by the personal representative and after the payment of debts and just expenses, fees and commissions of every sort, if no heirs at law of the decedent, to whom distribution may be made pursuant to the provisions of law, have made claim to any surplus remaining from the sale, the court shall order the surplus to be paid over to the State Treasurer. Upon receiving the State Treasurer's receipt therefor, the personal representative shall have no further obligation with respect to the surplus.

§ 3B:22-30. Distribution by State Treasurer; proof of claim required of claimants

After payment to the State Treasurer, no distribution of the surplus shall be made to any heir or other person interested in the property from the sale of which the surplus so paid over to the State Treasurer arose, unless the heir or other person shall have secured a judgment under the "Uniform Declaratory Judgments Act" (Article 9 of chapter 16 of Title 2A, of the New Jersey Statutes) establishing his right thereto. Upon receipt of a certified copy of the judgment, the State Treasurer shall distribute the surplus to the person or persons entitled thereto according to their respective interests. Payment shall be made by the State Treasurer upon proof by the person as to his identity and right to payment under the judgment.

§ 3B:22-31. Payment of share to established claimant; State Treasurer released as to subsequent claimants; recovery by claimant from distributee

After the State Treasurer has made payment to any person or persons in accordance with the declaratory judgment, as provided in N.J.S. 3B:22-30, no recovery may be had against the State Treasurer by any other person who may thereafter establish in any court proceeding his contrary interest in the surplus or the property from the sale of which the surplus arose. However, any other person who may thereafter establish in any court proceeding his contrary interest therein shall, as to the portion of the surplus remaining in the State Treasurer's hands, be entitled to his proportionate share thereof and, in addition thereto, may bring an action at law against the persons to whom distribution has been made by the State Treasurer, to recover his proportionate share of that portion of the surplus so distributed by the State Treasurer.

Article 7. Insolvent Estates

§ 3B:22-32. Distribution among creditors to be pro rata; preferred debts excepted

If the estate of a decedent is insufficient to pay his debts, his estate shall be applied to the preferred expenses and debts in accordance with N.J.S. 3B:22-2, and the balance shall be distributed among his creditors in proportion to the sum due to each.

§ 3B:22-33. Claims not presented in time barred; exception; extension of time

If an estate is adjudged insolvent, any creditor who fails to exhibit his claim to the personal representative within the time limited and prescribed by N.J.S. 3B:22-4 shall be forever barred from prosecuting or recovering thereon unless the estate shall prove sufficient, after all claims exhibited and allowed are fully satisfied, or the creditors shall find some other asset not accounted for by the personal representative before distribution, in which case the creditor shall receive his ratable proportion therefrom. However, the court, before distribution made, may upon the application of any creditor of any insolvent decedent and after notice to the personal representative, extend the time within which claims may be presented by creditors of the decedent upon terms as the court may deem just.

§ 3B:22-34. Authority of court to pass upon claims against the estate and upon amount and value of estate

In an action to have an estate adjudged insolvent, the court may adjudicate upon and determine the amount and value of the estate and the liability of the estate on claims made against it.

§ 3B:22-35. Judgment of insolvency; sale of assets

If upon an adjudication and determination, it appears to the court that the estate is insufficient to pay the debts, or whenever it appears to the satisfaction of the court, upon consideration of the claims of creditors and the amount of estate and the value thereof that the estate is insufficient to pay the debts and that the estate is likely to be insolvent, the court may enter judgment to this effect, and direct the personal representative to proceed as if the estate were insolvent, and to make sale of the whole or any part of the estate of his decedent, from time to time, as may appear expedient.

§ 3B:22-36. Proceeds; distribution

Proceeds of the estate which come to the hands of the personal representative shall be distributed under direction of the court, from time to time, as may be found convenient and just.

§ 3B:22-37. Residue after debts to go to heirs or devisees

If full payment of debts and claims is made, and there remains a residue, the residue shall be divided among the heirs of an intestate in the proportions as provided by law, or in case of a will, to the devisees as the will directs.

§ 3B:22-38. Certain actions against personal representative saved

Nothing contained in this article shall prevent a person from maintaining an action against the personal representative for, or in respect of, waste or misapplication of the estate of his decedent.

§ 3B:22-39. "Heirs and devisees" defined

As used in this article, heirs and devisees shall include the heirs and devisees of a deceased debtor and the heirs and devisees of any of them, who shall have died before the commencement of the action, authorized by this article, to whom any of the real or personal property, of which the debtor died seized or possessed, descended or was devised.

§ 3B:22-40. Heirs and devisees liable for debt of decedent

Every creditor, whether by simple contract or specialty, and whether or not the heirs or devisees are mentioned therein, shall have and may maintain by virtue of this article an action against the heirs and devisees of his deceased debtor dying seized or possessed of any real or personal property. The heirs or devisees shall be liable to pay the debt by reason of the descent or devise of the real or personal property to them in the manner provided in this article. In all actions creditors shall be preferred as in actions against personal representatives.

§ 3B:22-41. Joinder of parties

The action shall be brought against all of the heirs and devisees of the deceased debtor who can be found within the State.

§ 3B:22-42. General judgment; special judgment

If the debt be found due, the judgment against any heir or devisee shall be general for the full amount found due, unless the heir or devisee shall admit in the action the descent or devise of the estate to him, specifically describing it, in which case the judgment shall be special against him to be made out of the estate so descended and devised alone.

§ 3B:22-43. Liability in case of sale or transfer of estate

In the event an estate descended or devised to any heir or devisee has been bona fide sold or transferred prior to the commencement of the action, it shall not be liable for the debt or for any judgment obtained in an action against him. In that event, if in an action against him the debt be found due, the judgment against him shall be general for the full amount thereof, unless he shall admit in the action the descent or devise of the estate to him, specifically describing it, in which case the judgment shall be general for the amount so found due, but only to the value of the estate descended or devised, and sold or transferred.

§ 3B:22-44. Contribution between heirs and devisees liable

Contribution between heirs and devisees liable under this article may be had as heretofore.

Chapter 23. Distributive Shares and Devises

Article 1. Distribution: in Kind

§ 3B:23-1. Distribution of assets in kind

Except where a will authorizes distribution to be made in cash or in kind, the distributable assets of an intestate's estate or testator's estate shall be distributed in kind to the extent reasonably possible through application of the following provisions:

a. A specific devisee is entitled to distribution of the thing devised to him;

b. Any devise payable in money or an intestate share may be satisfied by value in kind provided:

(1) The person entitled to the payment has not demanded payment in cash;

(2) The property distributed in kind is valued at fair market value as of the date of its distribution; and

(3) No residuary devisee has requested that the asset in question remain a part of the residue of the estate.

§ 3B:23-2. Valuation of assets

For the purpose of valuation under subsection b. of N.J.S. 3B:23-1 securities regularly traded on recognized exchanges, if distributed in kind, are valued at the price for the last sale of like securities traded on the business day prior to distribution, or if there was no sale on that day, at the mean between amounts bid and offered at the close of that day. Assets consisting of sums owed the decedent or the estate by solvent debtors as to which there is no known dispute or defense are valued at the sum due with accrued interest or discounted to the date of distribution. For assets which do not have readily ascertainable value, a valuation as of a date not more than 30 days prior to the date of distribution, if otherwise reasonable, controls. For purposes of facilitating distribution, the personal representative may ascertain the value of the assets as of the time of the proposed distribution in any reasonable way, including the employment of qualified appraisers, even if the assets may have been previously appraised.

§ 3B:23-3. Method of distribution

If the personal representative of either a testate or an intestate estate has, in the exercise of good faith and reasonable discretion, continued to hold in kind the distributable assets of an intestate estate or of the residue of a testate estate, the assets shall be distributed in kind if there is no objection to the proposed distribution and it is practicable to distribute undivided interests, otherwise those assets shall be converted into cash for distribution.

§ 3B:23-4. Proposal of distribution; contents; time to object

After the probable charges against the estate are known, the personal representative may mail or deliver a proposal for distribution to all persons who have a right to object to the proposed distribution. The proposal shall notify all persons who have a right to object to the proposal of their right to object and that their objection must be in writing and received by the personal representative within 30 days after the mailing or delivery of the proposal. The right of any distributee to object to the proposed distribution on the basis of the kind or value of asset he is to receive, if not waived earlier in writing, terminates if he fails to object in writing received by the personal representative within 30 days after mailing or delivery of the proposal.

§ 3B:23-5. Instrument of distribution

If distribution in kind is made, the personal representative may and, if requested, shall execute an instrument or deed of distribution assigning, transferring or releasing the assets to the distributee as evidence of the distributee's title to the property.

§ 3B:23-6. Proof of delivery of instrument of distribution conclusive evidence of distributee's receipt of assets; exception

Proof that a distributee has received an instrument or deed of distribution of assets in kind or payment in distribution, from a personal representative, is conclusive evidence that the distributee has succeeded to the interest of the estate in the distributed assets, as against all persons interested in the estate, except that the personal representative may recover the assets or their value if the distribution was improper.

§ 3B:23-7. Protection of purchaser from or lender to distributee

If property distributed in kind or a security interest therein is acquired for value by a purchaser from or lender to a distributee who has received an instrument or deed of distribution from the personal representative, or is so acquired by a purchaser from or lender to a transferee from the distributee, the purchaser or lender takes title free of rights of any interested person in the estate and incurs no personal liability to the estate, or to any interested person, whether or not the distribution was proper or supported by court order or the authority of the personal representative was terminated before execution of the instrument or deed. This section protects a purchaser from or lender to a distributee who, as personal representative, has executed a deed of distribution to himself, as well as a purchaser from or lender to any other distributee or his transferee. To be protected under this provision, a purchaser or lender need not inquire whether a personal representative acted properly in making the distribution in kind, even if the personal representative and the distributee are the same person, or whether the authority of the personal representative had terminated before the distribution. Any recorded instrument described in this section on which a State documentary fee is noted pursuant to section 3 of P.L.1968, c. 49 (C. 46:15-7) shall be prima facie evidence that the transfer was made for value.

§ 3B:23-8. Partition for purpose of distribution

When two or more heirs or devisees are entitled to distribution of undivided interests in any real or personal property of the estate, the personal representative or one or more of the heirs or devisees may institute an action, prior to the formal or informal closing of the estate, for partition. After notice to the interested heirs or devisees, the court shall partition the property in the same manner as provided by law for civil actions of partition. The court may direct the personal representative to sell any property which cannot be partitioned without prejudice to the owners and which cannot conveniently be allotted to any one party.

§ 3B:23-9. Agreement among successors binding on personal representative

Subject to the rights of creditors and taxing authorities, competent successors may agree among themselves to alter the interests, shares, or amounts to which they are entitled under the will of the decedent, or under the laws of intestacy, in any way that they provide in a written contract executed by all who are affected by its provisions. The personal representative shall abide by the terms of the agreement subject to his obligation to administer the estate for the benefit of creditors, to pay all taxes and costs of administration, and to carry out the responsibilities of his office for the benefit of any successors of the decedent who are not parties. Personal representatives of decedents' estates are not required to see to the performance of trusts if the trustee thereof is another person who is willing to accept the trust. Accordingly, trustees of a testamentary trust are successors for the purposes of this section. Nothing herein relieves trustees of any duties owed to beneficiaries of trusts.

§ 3B:23-10. Distribution to guardian

A personal representative may discharge his obligation to distribute to any person under legal disability by distributing to the guardian of his estate.

Article 2. Distribution: Under Will

§ 3B:23-11. Interest on general pecuniary devise

General pecuniary devises shall bear interest beginning one year after the first appointment of a personal representative until payment, unless a contrary intent is indicated by the will or unless the court, for good cause, waives the imposition of interest. The annual rate of interest on general pecuniary devises shall equal the average rate of return, to the nearest whole or one-half percent, for the corresponding preceding fiscal year terminating on June 30, of the State of New Jersey Cash Management Fund (State accounts) as reported by the Division of Investment in the Department of the Treasury.

§ 3B:23-12. Abatement generally

Except as provided in N.J.S. 3B:23-14 and except as provided in connection with the share of a surviving spouse who elects to take an elective share, shares of distributees abate, without any preference or priority as between real and personal property, in the following order:
a. Property passing by intestacy;
b. Residuary devises;
c. General devises;
d. Specific devises; and
e. Abatement within each classification is in proportion to the amount of property each of the beneficiaries would have received if full distribution of the property had been made in accordance with the terms of the will.

§ 3B:23-13. General devise charged upon specific property or fund

For purposes of abatement, a general devise charged on any specific property or fund is a specific devise to the extent of the value of the property on which it is charged, and upon the failure or insufficiency of the property on which it is charged, a general devise to the extent of the failure or insufficiency.

§ 3B:23-14. Where will expresses order of abatement

If the will expresses an order of abatement, or if the testamentary plan or the express or implied purpose of the devise would be defeated by the order of abatement stated in N.J.S. 3B:23-12, shares of the distributees abate as may be found necessary to give effect to the intention of the testator.

§ 3B:23-15. Abatement where subject of specific devise sold

If the subject of a specific devise is sold or used incident to administration, abatement shall be achieved by appropriate adjustments in, or contribution from, other interests in the remaining assets.

§ 3B:23-16. Distribution by order of court

When the account of a personal representative has been allowed by court, the court may direct just distribution, in accordance with the provisions of the will, of what shall remain in the estate or a trust under the will, after all debts and expenses and other charges have been allowed and deducted.

Article 3. Distribution: Intestate Estate

§ 3B:23-17. Judgment for distribution

When the account of a personal representative has been allowed by court, the court may direct just distribution of the property whereof a decedent died intestate which remains in his estate after payment of all debts, expenses and other charges which have been allowed and deducted as provided in chapter 5 of this title.

§ 3B:23-18. Distribution; when made

Distribution of the property of an intestate shall not be made until 1 year after the granting of administration unless an order to limit creditors is entered, in which case distribution may be made 6 months after the order.

§ 3B:23-19. Order for filing claims of unknown distributees

3B:23-19. Order for filing claims of unknown distributees.
a. When it appears in an action for the distribution of the property of which a decedent dies intestate that no heirs to the property can be found or in addition to persons known to have an interest in the estate, there may be others whose names or addresses are unknown who may be entitled to participate in the distribution, the court may order additional actions to identify and locate heirs.
b. If no heirs to the property can be found, the property shall be presumed abandoned and handled in accordance with the "Uniform Unclaimed Property Act (1981)," R.S. 46:30B-1 et seq.
c. If, in addition to persons known to have an interest in the estate, others whose names or addresses are unknown may be entitled to participate in the distribution, the court shall order the part of the estate to which they may be entitled held for a specific period. The court shall set that period as two years beginning at the date of death unless good cause is shown to set another period. If the others cannot be located within the period, the court shall order the property divided among the known heirs in proportions as if the unknown heirs did not exist.

Article 4. Distribution; Devises, Distributive Shares, Trusts, etc.

§ 3B:23-21. Unclaimed estate assets

When a fiduciary states a final account and there remains in the fiduciary's control a balance, devise, distributive share, dividend, or sum of money to be paid to a person and the person, or that person's guardian, if a minor or a person who is incapacitated, fails to claim the balance, devise, distributive share, dividend, or sum of money within the period of time set forth in R.S.46:30B-37.1, then the property shall be disposed of as provided in N.J.S.3B:23-19 if it is part of an intestate estate or otherwise presumed abandoned and handled in accordance with the "Uniform Unclaimed Property Act (1981)," R.S.46:30B-1 et seq.

§ 3B:23-22. Deposit in court of money or other property of devisee, heir or beneficiary of trust in certain cases

Where it shall appear that a devisee, heir or beneficiary of a trust would not have the benefit or use or control of the money or other property due him, or where other special circumstances make it appear desirable that the payment should be withheld or, in the case of a trust where the trustee was appointed other than by a court, the Superior Court, on motion of any person in interest, or, failing such, on motion of the Attorney General, or on the court's own motion, may direct that the money or other property be paid into court for the benefit of the devisee, heir, beneficiary of a trust, or any person or persons who may thereafter appear to be entitled thereto. The money or other property so paid into court shall be paid out only by order of the court.

§ 3B:23-23. Letters of trusteeship required before transfer to trustee

It shall be unlawful for any fiduciary to transfer, pay over or distribute any devise, distributive share or part of the estate or trust in the possession or under the control of the fiduciary to a testamentary trustee or substituted testamentary trustee until letters of trusteeship shall have been issued to the testamentary trustee or substituted testamentary trustee.

Article 5. Bonds of Distributees and Devisees

§ 3B:23-24. Refunding bond of devisee or distributee

A personal representative shall, on paying a devise or distributive share or on delivering an instrument of distribution to the person entitled, take a refunding bond therefor, to be filed in the office of the surrogate of the county wherein he received his letters or in the office of the clerk of the Superior Court, if he received his letters from the Superior Court.

§ 3B:23-25. Amount of bond; form

The bond required under N.J.S. 3B:23-24 or N.J.S. 3B:23-33 shall be in the amount or value of the devise or allotted distributive share and shall be sufficient, if signed by the devisee or distributee, or his guardian, as the case may be, without any sureties whatever.

§ 3B:23-26. Condition of devisee's bond

The bond of a devisee shall be conditioned substantially as follows: That if any part or the whole of the devise shall at any time thereafter be needed to discharge any debt or debts, devise or devises, which the personal representative may not have other assets to pay, he, the devisee, will return his devise or that part thereof as may be necessary for the payment of the debts, or for the payment of a proportional part of the devises.

§ 3B:23-27. Condition of distributee's bond

The bond of a distributee shall be conditioned substantially as follows: That if any debt or debts, truly owing by the intestate, shall be afterwards sued for and recovered or otherwise duly made to appear, and there shall be no other assets to pay, he shall refund and pay back to the administrator his ratable part of the debt or debts, out of the part and share so allotted to him.

§ 3B:23-28. Bonds required of holders of determinable interests; in general

A personal representative shall not be compelled to pay or deliver personal property devised for life, for a term of years or for any other limited period, or upon a condition or any contingency, to the holder of the determinable interest, until security is given to the court in a sum and form as the court may deem sufficient to secure the remainder interest, whenever it shall accrue or vest in possession.

§ 3B:23-29. Bond when remainderman is lineal descendant of holder of determinable estate

Where the person next immediately in remainder is a lineal descendant of the holder of the determinable interest referred to in N.J.S. 3B:23-28, the holder of the determinable interest shall not be required to give security in excess of $50,000.00.

§ 3B:23-30. Bond when the personal representative is holder of a determinable estate

When the personal representative is the holder of a determinable interest referred to in N.J.S. 3B:23-28, he shall, before receiving the personal property into his possession, file a bond with the clerk of the Superior Court or the surrogate of the proper county, as the case may be, unless the will provides that no security shall be required of him.

The bond shall be in the amount of money or the value of the property to be received, with two sufficient sureties, conditioned for the faithful conservation of the property.

Until the bond is filed, the personal representative may not receive the moneys or property, but the court may appoint some other proper person to receive and administer the money or property as trustee upon giving security for the faithful discharge of his duties as the court may deem proper.

Article 6. Actions on Distributive Shares and for Devises

§ 3B:23-31. Actions for distributive shares

If a personal representative fails to pay a distributive share to a person thereto entitled under a judgment made pursuant to N.J.S. 3B:23-17, that person may recover the distributive share in a civil action from the personal representative.

§ 3B:23-32. Limitations on enforcement of devise

Nothing in N.J.S. 3B:23-33 to N.J.S. 3B:23-35 shall be so construed as to permit the enforcement of a devise to the prejudice of creditors of the testator or as giving effect to a will not warranted by law.

§ 3B:23-33. Action for devise

A devisee may bring an action in the Superior Court for his devise.

§ 3B:23-34. Conditions precedent to suit for devise

An action to recover a devise may not be maintained until:
a. The devise becomes due and payable;
b. Reasonable demand for payment is made upon the personal representative; and

c. A refunding bond in substantially the form prescribed in N.J.S.3B:23-26 is tendered to the personal representative by the devisee, or, if the devisee is a minor or a person who is incapacitated, by the guardian of the devisee's estate, and, if not accepted by the personal representative, the refunding bond is filed with the clerk of the court, prior to the commencement of the action.

§ 3B:23-35. Extent of recovery

If it appears in the action that the surplus of assets in the possession of the personal representative over debts of the testator, is sufficient to pay all devises, the full amount of the devise may be recovered with costs; but if the surplus is not sufficient therefor, an abatement shall be made as provided in N.J.S. 3B:23-12 to N.J.S. 3B:23-15.

§ 3B:23-36. Plea of want of assets; procedure

If want of assets to pay debts and devises is pleaded in the action and if the account of the personal representative has not been settled, the court shall require him to account. Judgment shall be entered and execution shall issue only for the proportion ascertained to be payable to plaintiff, but the judgment shall remain a security for the payment of the residue of the devise and costs out of assets which may thereafter come to the possession of the personal representative.

Article 7. Contingent Devises Charged on Real Estate

§ 3B:23-37. Apportionment of certain real estate to pay devise

When a devise, payable on a contingency which has not happened, is or may become a charge, at law or in equity, on real estate devised by will, any person in possession of a part of the real estate may bring a summary action in the Superior Court to set apart, as in an action for partition, a portion of the real estate as may be sufficient for payment of the devise when payable.

§ 3B:23-38. Effect of apportionment; filing and recording papers

If the court approves the partition, the real estate so set apart shall become charged or chargeable with the contingent devise, and the residue of the real estate shall thereupon be entirely discharged from all lien, charge or liability with respect to the devise.

All papers in the action shall be filed and recorded in the office of the county clerk or register of deeds and mortgages, as the case may be, of the county wherein the real estate is situate and shall be plenary evidence of the lien on the real estate so set apart and of the discharge of the residue of the real estate.

§ 3B:23-39. Deposit with court; effect

When a devise charged by will upon real estate is wholly or in part limited over:

a. To minors, persons who are incapacitated, or persons not in esse; or

b. To persons who cannot be ascertained until the happening of an event named in the will; or

c. In a manner that the vesting of the devise may be contingent—

The Superior Court may, in a summary or other action by the executor, or a person interested in the real estate, direct the devise paid into court together with any additional sums as the court may deem reasonable to cover the expense of investing and taking charge of the devise. Upon payment into court, the real estate shall be wholly clear and discharged from the lien created by the will.

§ 3B:23-40. Payment of interest on moneys deposited

When moneys are ordered to be paid into court pursuant to N.J.S. 3B:23-39, the interest thereof, or any part of the interest as the court may direct, shall be paid to or on behalf of the persons who would for the time being be entitled to the interest in proportion to their respective shares therein, and payments of interest shall be made, yearly or half-yearly or otherwise directly to the persons entitled thereto, unless otherwise directed by the court.

Article 8. Miscellaneous Provisions

§ 3B:23-41. Return of devise pro rata

Where there are several devisees and a return of part of a devise shall afterwards appear necessary, each devisee shall only be compelled to return a proportional part of his devise so as to make up the whole sum needed.

§ 3B:23-42. Distribution of nonresident decedent's estate

The estate of a nonresident decedent being administered by a personal representative appointed in this State shall, if there is a personal representative of the decedent's domicile willing to receive it, be distributed to the domiciliary personal representative for the benefit of the successors of the decedent unless:

a. By virtue of the decedent's will, if any, and applicable choice of law rules, the successors are identified pursuant to the local law of this State without reference to the local law of the decedent's domicile; or

b. The personal representative of this State, after reasonable inquiry, is unaware of the existence or identity of a domiciliary personal representative.

In other cases, distribution of the estate of a decedent shall be made in accordance with the law.

§ 3B:23-43. Right of retainer

The amount of a noncontingent indebtedness of a successor to the estate if due, or its present value if not due, shall be offset against the successor's interest; but the successor has the benefit of any defense which would be available to him in a direct proceeding for recovery of the debt.

Chapter 24. Apportionment of New Jersey Estate and Federal Taxes

§ 3B:24-1. Definitions

As used in this chapter:

a. "The tax" means all taxes finally determined to be due and payable by a fiduciary, under the laws of the United States now or hereafter enacted and under the laws of this State now or hereafter enacted, imposing an estate tax;
b. "Gross tax estate" means all property of every description required to be included in computing the tax;
c. "Fiduciary" means any person acting in a fiduciary capacity who is required to pay the tax;
d. "Transferee" means any person to whom the gross tax estate or any part thereof is, or may be, transferred or to whom any benefit therein accrues other than that part of the gross tax estate which passes under the will of decedent, or, if there be no will, comes into the possession of the fiduciary for administration as a part of the gross tax estate of the decedent. The trustee of any inter vivos trust and the executor of, trustee or other fiduciary under, the will of any other decedent holding property included as a part of the gross estate shall be deemed to be a transferee.

§ 3B:24-2. Apportionment of tax among fiduciary and transferees interested in gross tax estate

Whenever a fiduciary has paid or may be required to pay an estate tax under any law of the State of New Jersey or of the United States upon or with respect to any property required to be included in the gross tax estate of a decedent under the provisions of any law, hereinafter called "the tax," the amount of the tax, except in a case where a testator otherwise directs in his will, and except to the extent where by any instrument other than a will, hereinafter called a "nontestamentary instrument," a direction is given for apportionment within the fund of taxes assessed upon the specific fund dealt with in the "nontestamentary instrument," shall be apportioned among the fiduciary and each of the transferees interested in the gross tax estate whether residents or nonresidents of the State, in accordance with the rules of apportionment stated in this chapter, and the transferees shall each contribute to the tax the amounts apportioned against them. Nothing in this chapter shall be taken to require an apportionment of an estate tax inter sese among the devisees and beneficiaries under a will or among those who take as the heirs at law of a person dying intestate, or against the interest of any surviving spouse in any real property which was held by the spouse and the decedent as tenants by the entirety.

§ 3B:24-3. Apportionment of tax where temporary interest is created

Where a trust is created, or other provision made in any nontestamentary instrument whereby any person is given an interest in income, or an estate for years, or for life, or other temporary interest in any property or fund, the tax apportionable against both the temporary interest and the remainder thereafter shall, in the absence of directions to the contrary in the instrument, be charged against and paid out of the corpus of the property or fund without apportionment between remainders and temporary estates. The provisions of this section shall apply notwithstanding that the holder of the temporary interest is given rights to the corpus.

§ 3B:24-4. Apportionment of tax to transferees in absence of directions to contrary

In the absence of directions to the contrary:
a. That part of the tax shall be apportioned to each of the transferees as bears the same ratio to the total tax as the ratio which each of the transferees' property included in the gross tax estate bears to the total property entering into the net estate for purposes of that tax, and the balance of the tax shall be apportioned to the fiduciary, the values as finally determined in the respective tax proceedings being the values to be used as the basis for apportionment of the respective taxes;
b. Any deduction allowed under the law imposing the tax by reason of the relationship of any transferee to the decedent or by reason of the charitable purposes of the gift shall inure to the benefit of the fiduciary or transferee, as the case may be, subject nonetheless to the provisions of N.J.S.3B:24-3;
c. Any deduction for property previously taxed and any credit for gift taxes paid by the decedent shall inure to the benefit of all transferees and the fiduciary and the tax to be apportioned shall be the tax after allowance of the deduction and credit; and
d. Any interest resulting from late payment of the tax shall be apportioned in the same manner as the tax and shall be charged by the fiduciary and any trustee of any inter vivos trust and any other transferee wholly against corpus.

§ 3B:24-5. Limitation on direction for apportionment or nonapportionment of tax

Any direction as to apportionment or nonapportionment of the tax, whether contained in a will or in a nontestamentary instrument, shall be limited in its operation to the property passing thereunder unless the will or instrument otherwise directs.

§ 3B:24-6. Recovery by fiduciary from transferees or others in possession of property included in tax

In all cases in which any property required to be included in the gross tax estate does not come into the possession of the fiduciary, he shall be entitled, and it shall be his duty, to recover from the transferees or from whoever is in possession of the property, the proportionate amounts of the tax and any interest thereon which is or may be payable by the transferees. If the fiduciary cannot recover the amount of the tax and interest thereon apportioned against a transferee, the amount not recoverable shall be dealt with in a manner as the court may determine. Nothing in this chapter shall require a person in possession of property to defer distribution of the property unless and until directed by the court.

§ 3B:24-7. Transfer or distribution of property; duties and liabilities of fiduciary

A person acting in a fiduciary capacity shall not be required to transfer, pay over or distribute to any person, other than the fiduciary charged with the duty to collect and pay the tax, any fund or property with respect to which the tax is or may be imposed, until the amount of the tax and any interest thereon apportioned or which may be apportioned against the fund or property and which may be due from the persons entitled to the fund or property is paid, or, if the tax has not been determined or apportionment made, until adequate security for the payment is furnished to the person acting in a fiduciary capacity. A fiduciary shall not be under any duty to institute any action under this chapter or to make an apportionment thereunder until after the expiration of 3 months following the final determination of the tax. A fiduciary, who within a reasonable time after the expiration of 3 months following the final determination of the tax shall proceed to carry out the duty imposed upon himself by this chapter, shall not be subject to liability or surcharge in case the amount of the tax or any part thereof apportioned or to be apportioned against any transferee or person in possession of property shall be collectible at any time following the death of the decedent but shall thereafter be or become uncollectible.

§ 3B:24-8. Jurisdiction of Superior Court

The Superior Court in a summary action or other action, including any action for the settlement of an account of the fiduciary, may apportion the tax and any interest. In the action the court, insofar as it may acquire jurisdiction over the property or person as the case may be, may charge the apportioned amount due by any transferee against the property of the transferee in the possession of the fiduciary or any other person and may direct all transferees, against whom the tax and any interest thereon have been or may be apportioned or from whom any part of the tax and any interest thereon may be recoverable, to make payment of the apportioned amounts to the fiduciary, and, further, may require the fiduciary to collect the charge and payments. If it shall be ascertained in the action that more than the proportionate amount of the tax and interest thereon due from any transferee has been paid by him or on his behalf, the court may direct reimbursement of the overpayment.

Chapter 25. Exoneration of Property Subject to Mortgage or Security Interest

§ 3B:25-1. Nonexoneration of property subject to mortgage or security interest; exception

When property subject to a mortgage or security interest descends to an heir or passes to a devisee, the heir or devisee shall not be entitled to have the mortgage or security interest discharged out of any other property of the ancestor or testator, but the property so descending or passing to the person shall be primarily liable for the mortgage or secured debt, unless the will of the testator shall direct that the mortgage or security interest be otherwise paid. A general direction in the will to pay debts shall not be deemed a direction to pay the mortgage or security interest.

Chapter 26. Absentees

§ 3B:26-1. Definition of absent person

As used in this chapter, an absent person means any person who has disappeared, or been confined or detained by a foreign power.

§ 3B:26-2. Appointment of trustee for absent person; general duties and powers

If an absent person has property in this State, which property may be wasted or dissipated unless proper management is provided, or where funds are needed for the support, care and welfare of the person or those entitled to be supported by him, and protection is necessary or desirable to obtain or provide funds, the Superior Court may in a summary action appoint one or more trustees to take charge of and manage the property. The trustee shall be under the direction and control of the court and shall have full power over the property and may commence and maintain proceedings for the conservation, protection or disposal of the property, or any part thereof, as the court may deem proper.

§ 3B:26-3. Distribution or other disposition of property

Distribution or any other disposition of the property of an absent person may be made under direction of the court when he is presumed dead under N.J.S. 3B:27-1, or sooner if the death of the absent person is established by evidence satisfactory to the court. If the absent person returns or the need for management or protection ceases before distribution or other disposition, the trustee shall restore to him the property, after deduction of the reasonable expenses of the trust and compensation of the trustees.

§ 3B:26-4. Powers, duties and responsibilities of trustee or court

The trustee shall have all the powers, duties and responsibilities of a guardian of the estate of a minor, and the court shall have all the powers, for the benefit of any person, which it has for the benefit of a minor for whom a guardian has been appointed. The court shall have the same powers, without appointing a trustee, to authorize, direct or ratify any single or more than one transaction necessary or desirable to achieve any security, service, care or protective arrangement, which it has in the case of a minor for whom no general guardian has been appointed.

Chapter 27. Absence for Five Years

Article 1. Presumption of Death

§ 3B:27-1. Death of resident or nonresident presumed after 5 years' absence or exposure to specific catastrophic event

a. A resident or nonresident of this State who absents himself from the place of his last known residence for a continuous period of 5 years, during which he has not been heard from, and whose absence is not satisfactorily explained after diligent search or inquiry, is presumed to be dead. His death is presumed to have occurred at the end of the period unless there is sufficient evidence for determining that death occurred earlier.
b. A resident or nonresident of this State who is exposed to a specific event certified by the Governor as a catastrophic event that has resulted in a loss of life to persons known or unknown and whose absence following that event is not satisfactorily explained after diligent search or inquiry is presumed to be dead. The death is presumed to have occurred at the time of the catastrophic event.
c. Nothing in this section shall be construed to limit or abrogate the special peril doctrine under the common law.

§ 3B:27-2. Restoration and recovery of property upon reappearance of absentee

If an estate or property has been received, recovered or taken into possession by any person by reason of a declaration of death under the provisions of this chapter and in any action or proceeding it is thereafter proved that the person declared dead was alive at the time of the receipt, recovery or taking into possession, the estate or property, or its reasonable value at that time, shall, except as otherwise provided by law, be restored to the person deprived thereof by reason of the declaration, or to his heirs, devisees, personal representative or other persons entitled thereto. He or they may also demand and recover the income, rents and profits therefrom during the time he was or they were deprived thereof.

§ 3B:27-3. Protection of personal representative or trustee making distribution

A personal representative or trustee who pays over or delivers a devise, distributive share or any interest in property held in trust, to which a person declared dead by virtue of this chapter would, if living, be entitled, or which is given to a person so declared dead, for life or otherwise, with a limitation over to take effect in possession or enjoyment at or after the death of that person, shall be fully discharged from any and all liability to the person so declared dead, and to his personal representative and all persons claiming under him, upon filing with the surrogate of the proper county, or the clerk of the Superior Court as the case may be, the releases of the persons who would be entitled to the devise, share or interest if the person so declared to be dead were actually dead, together with their refunding bonds to the fiduciary. The bond shall be in the amount or value of the money or property so distributed, without sureties and upon the condition that the money or property so distributed will be refunded to the fiduciary in the event that the refunding should be required. Any person claiming the devise, share or interest may sue upon the bond as if it had been assigned to him.

Article 2. Sale or Other Disposition of Real Estate

§ 3B:27-4. Real estate transaction in which an absentee has an interest; title

If an absentee, a resident or nonresident of New Jersey, shall be, by virtue of this chapter, declared dead by any court of competent jurisdiction in New Jersey; and if

a. Any real estate in which the absentee had or shall have any interest, divided or not, or contingent or not, as owner, tenant by the entirety, lessee, spouse of an owner, or otherwise, or

b. The interest in the real estate of the absentee has been or shall be sold, conveyed, mortgaged, assigned, leased, devised or otherwise alienated, as though the person were actually dead, then the absentee shall be thereafter forever barred from any claim of title to the real estate or interest therein. The person taking the real estate or interest therein in the transaction, and his heirs, assigns and successors in title, shall have as perfect a right or title therein and thereto, and shall hold the real estate, as though the absentee had actually died on the date he is declared dead.

§ 3B:27-5. Absentee later proved alive entitled to proceeds of transaction

If an absentee should later be proved to have been alive at the time of a transaction referred to in N.J.S. 3B:27-4, then he or any other person taking under him shall be entitled to a just interest in the rents, purchase price, and other proceeds of the transaction, which have not come into the hands of a person who has given value therefor without notice that the absentee was alive.

Article 3. Declaration of Death

§ 3B:27-6. Action to be brought in Superior Court

a. The Superior Court may declare the absentee dead, if it is satisfied that the absentee should be presumed dead under the provisions of N.J.S. 3B:27-1. Under the provisions of subsection a. of N.J.S. 3B:27-1 the Superior Court may, if it concludes from a review of the evidence, both direct and circumstantial, that the earlier death of the absentee has been established and that the death occurred prior to the institution of the proceeding before the court, fix the date of death earlier than the expiration of the 5-year period set forth therein. Under the provisions of subsection b. of N.J.S. 3B:27-1 the death is presumed to have occurred at the time of the catastrophic event. A declaration with respect to a nonresident shall affect only property located within the State.

b. At the request of an applicant who has obtained a declaration based on subsection b. of N.J.S. 3B:27-1 with respect to a resident of this State, the court shall order the State registrar of vital statistics to issue, at no cost to the applicant, a death certificate. The State registrar may indicate on such certificate that it was issued pursuant to court order in accordance with this section.

Chapter 28. Dower and Curtesy

§ 3B:28-1. Estates of dower and curtesy prior to May 28, 1980

The widow or widower, whether alien or not, of an individual dying intestate or otherwise, shall be endowed for the term of his life of one half of all real property of which the decedent, or another to the decedent's use, was seized of an estate of inheritance at any time during marriage prior to May 28, 1980, unless the widow or widower shall have relinquished her right of dower or his right of curtesy in the manner provided by P.L.1953, c.352 (C.37:2-18.1) or such right of dower or such right of curtesy otherwise shall have been extinguished by law.

§ 3B:28-2. No right of dower or curtesy created on or after May 28, 1980

No right of dower or curtesy in real property shall arise if, on or after May 28, 1980, an individual shall become married, or such person or another to his use, shall become seized of an estate of inheritance.

§ 3B:28-3. Right of joint possession of principal matrimonial residence where no dower or curtesy applies; alienation

a. During life every married individual shall be entitled to joint possession with his spouse of any real property which they occupy jointly as their principal matrimonial residence and to which neither dower nor curtesy applies. One who acquires an estate or interest in real property from an individual whose spouse is entitled to joint possession thereof does so subject to such right of possession, unless such right of possession has been released, extinguished or subordinated by such spouse or has been terminated by order or judgment of a court of competent jurisdiction or otherwise.

b. Nothing contained herein shall be construed to prevent the release, subordination or extinguishment of the right of joint possession by either spouse, by premarital agreement, separation agreement or other written instrument.

c. The right of joint possession shall be extinguished by the consent of both parties, by the death of either spouse, by judgment of divorce, separation or annulment, by other order or judgment which extinguishes same, or by voluntary abandonment of the principal matrimonial residence.

§ 3B:28-3.1. Joint occupancy of principal matrimonial residence; mortgage lien

The right of joint possession to the principal matrimonial residence as provided in N.J.S.3B:28-3 is subject to the lien of a mortgage, irrespective of the date when the mortgage is recorded, provided:

a. The mortgage is placed upon the matrimonial residence prior to the time that title to the residence was acquired by the married individual; or

b. The mortgage is placed upon the matrimonial residence prior to the marriage; or

c. The mortgage is a purchase money mortgage; or

d. The parties to the marriage have joined in the mortgage; or

e. The right of joint possession has been subordinated, released or extinguished by subsection b. or c. of N.J.S.3B:28-3.

Article 2. Acts Saved from Repeal

Chapter 29. Repealer

§ 3B:29-1. Laws repealed

The following are repealed:
R.S. 3:2-12 (saved from repeal by N.J.S. 3A:3-32);
R.S. 3:2-45 (saved from repeal by N.J.S. 3A:3-30);
N.J.S. 3A:2-1 to 3A:2-8 inclusive;
N.J.S. 3A:3-4, 3A:3-5, 3A:3-12, 3A:3-15, 3A:3-16, 3A:3-17 to 3A:3-21 inclusive, 3A:3-23 to 3A:3-33 inclusive;
N.J.S. 3A:4-8 and 3A:4-12;
N.J.S. 3A:5-1 to 3A:5-8 inclusive;
N.J.S. 3A:6-1 to 3A:6-20 inclusive, 3A:6-22 to 3A:6-26 inclusive, 3A:6-28 to 3A:6-30 inclusive, 3A:6-33 to 3A:6-36 inclusive, 3A:6-38 to 3A:6-40 inclusive, 3A:6-43 to 3A:6-68 inclusive;
N.J.S. 3A:7-1 to 3A:7-30 inclusive;
N.J.S. 3A:8-1 to 3A:8-8 inclusive;
N.J.S. 3A:9-1 to 3A:9-12 inclusive;
N.J.S. 3A:10-1 to 3A:10-8 inclusive;
N.J.S. 3A:11-1 to 3A:11-5 inclusive;
N.J.S. 3A:12-1 to 3A:12-6 inclusive, 3A:12-10 to 3A:12-18 inclusive;
N.J.S. 3A:14-1 to 3A:14-4 inclusive;
N.J.S. 3A:15-1 to 3A:15-17 inclusive;
N.J.S. 3A:16-1 to 3A:16-11 inclusive, 3A:16-13 to 3A:16-15 inclusive, 3A:16-18 to 3A:16-20 inclusive;
N.J.S. 3A:17-1;
N.J.S. 3A:18-1 to 3A:18-8 inclusive;
N.J.S. 3A:19-1 to 3A:19-4 inclusive;
N.J.S. 3A:20-5 to 3A:20-8 inclusive;
N.J.S. 3A:21-1 to 3A:21-3 inclusive;
N.J.S. 3A:22-2, 3A:22-4 to 3A:22-6 inclusive;
N.J.S. 3A:23-1 to 3A:23-5 inclusive;
N.J.S. 3A:24-1, 3A:24-3 to 3A:24-49 inclusive;
N.J.S. 3A:25-2 to 3A:25-7 inclusive, 3A:25-9 to 3A:25-11 inclusive, 3A:25-13 to 3A:25-38 inclusive;
N.J.S. 3A:26-1;
N.J.S. 3A:27-1 to 3A:27-5 inclusive;
N.J.S. 3A:28-1 to 3A:28-3 inclusive;
N.J.S. 3A:29-1 to 3A:29-4 inclusive;
N.J.S. 3A:30-1 to 3A:30-6 inclusive;
N.J.S. 3A:31-1 to 3A:31-11 inclusive;
N.J.S. 3A:32-1 to 3A:32-3 inclusive;
N.J.S. 3A:33-1 and 3A:33-2;
N.J.S. 3A:34-1 to 3A:34-14 inclusive;
N.J.S. 3A:35-1 to 3A:35-4 inclusive;
N.J.S. 3A:36-1to 3A:36-5 inclusive; 3A:37-1 to 3A:37-6 inclusive;
N.J.S. 3A:38-1 to 3A:38-7 inclusive;
N.J.S. 3A:39-1 and 3A:39-2;

N.J.S. 3A:40-1 to 3A:40-6 inclusive;
N.J.S. 3A:41-1, 3A:41-2, 3A:41-6 to 3A:41-14 inclusive;
N.J.S. 3A:42-1 and 3A:42-2.
Laws of 1948, c. 364, §§ 17 and 18 (saved from repeal by N.J.S. 3A:3-31 and 3A:3-33);
Laws of 1977, c. 412, §§ 1 to 83 inclusive; (C. 3A:2A-1 to C. 3A:2A-83 inclusive);
Laws of 1979, c. 219, § 1 (C. 3A:2A-29.1);
Laws of 1979, c. 221, 12 to 15 inclusive (C. 3A:2A-6.1, C. 3A:2A-48.1, C. 3A:2A-85 and C. 3A:2A-86);
Laws of 1980, c. 51, § 1 (C. 3A:2A-87);
Laws of 1962, c. 241, §§ 1 to 5 inclusive (C. 3A:3-16.1 to C. 3A:3-16.5 inclusive);
Laws of 1952, c. 221, §§ 1 and 2 (C. 3A:3A-1 and C. 3A:3A-2);
Laws of 1968, c. 270, §§ 1 to 3 inclusive (C. 3A:6-16.1 to C. 3A:16-16.3 inclusive);
Laws of 1979, c. 482, §§ 1 to 5 inclusive, 7, 11 to 18 inclusive, 26 to 34 inclusive (C. 3A:6-16.10 to C. 3A:6-16.32 inclusive);
Laws of 1979, c. 494, §§ 1 and 2 (C. 3A:6-32.1 and C. 3A:6-32.2);
Laws of 1959, c. 132, §§ 1 and 2 (C. 3A:7-14.1 and C. 3A:7-14.2);
Laws of 1979, c. 501, §§ 2 to 4 inclusive (C. 3A:10-2.1 to C. 3A:10-2.3 inclusive);
Laws of 1980, c. 6, § 1 (C. 3A:10-2.4);
Laws of 1952, c. 331, §§ 1 and 2 (C. 3A:10-3.1 and C. 3A:10-3.2);
Laws of 1952, c. 156, §§ 1 to 9 inclusive (C. 3A:14A-1 to C. 3A:14A-9 inclusive);
Laws of 1963, c. 94, §§ 1 to 4 inclusive (C. 3A:15-17.1 to C. 3A:15-17.4 inclusive);
Laws of 1975, c. 25, §§ 1 to 5 inclusive (C. 3A:15-17.5 to C. 3A:15-17.9 inclusive);
Laws of 1973, c. 359, §§ 1 to 5 inclusive (C. 3A:15-30 to C. 3A:15-34 inclusive);
Laws of 1975, c. 337, §§ 1 to 7 inclusive (C. 3A:15-35 to C. 3A:15-41 inclusive);
Laws of 1979, c. 486, §§ 1 to 3 inclusive (C. 3A:20-12 to C. 3A:20-14 inclusive);
Laws of 1979, c. 485, § 1 (C. 3A:35-5);
Laws of 1977, c. 483, §§ 1 to 8 inclusive (C. 3A:38A-1 to C. 3A:38A-8 inclusive);
Laws of 1979, c. 487, §§ 1 and 4 (C. 3A:39-5 and C. 3A:39-6);
Laws of 1971, c. 338, §§ 1 to 8 inclusive (C. 3A:43-1 to C. 3A:43-8 inclusive).

Chapter 30. Uniform Transfer on Death Security Registration Act

§ 3B:30-1. Short title.

This act shall be known and may be cited as the "Uniform TOD Security Registration Act."

§ 3B:30-2. Definitions

As used in the act:

"Beneficiary form" means a registration of a security which indicates the present owner of the security and the intention of the owner regarding the person who will become the owner of the security upon the death of the owner.

"Devisee" means any person designated in a will to receive a disposition of real or personal property.

"Heirs" means those persons, including the surviving spouse or domestic partner, who are entitled under the statutes of intestate succession to the property of a decedent.

"Person" means an individual, a corporation, an organization or other legal entity.

"Personal representative" includes executor, administrator, successor personal representative, special administrator, and persons who perform substantially the same function under the law governing their status.

"Property" includes both real and personal property or any interest therein and means anything that may be the subject of ownership.

"Register" including its derivatives, means to issue a certificate showing the ownership of a certificated security or, in the case of an uncertificated security, to initiate or transfer an account showing ownership of securities.

"Registering entity" means a person who originates or transfers a security title by registration, and includes a broker maintaining security accounts for customers and a transfer agent or other person acting for or as an issuer of securities.

"Security" means a share, participation, or other interest in property, in a business, or in an obligation of an enterprise or other issuer, and includes a certificated security, an uncertificated security, and a security account.

"Security account" means: a reinvestment account associated with a security, a securities account with a broker, a cash balance in a brokerage account, cash, interest, earnings, or dividends earned or declared on a security in an account, a reinvestment account, or a brokerage account, whether or not credited to the account before the owner's death; or a cash balance or other property held for or due to the owner of a security as a replacement for or product of an account security, whether or not credited to the account before the owner's death.

"State" includes any state of the United States, the District of Columbia, the Commonwealth of Puerto Rico, and any territory or possession subject to the legislative authority of the United States.

§ 3B:30-3. Individuals, multiple owners, registration of a security.

Only individuals whose registration of a security shows sole ownership by one individual or multiple ownership by two or more with right of survivorship, rather than as tenants in common, may obtain registration in beneficiary form. Multiple owners of a security registered in beneficiary form hold as joint tenants with right of survivorship, as tenants by the entireties, or as owners of community property held in survivorship for, and not as tenants in common.

§ 3B:30-4. Registration of security in beneficiary form.

A security may be registered in beneficiary form if the form is authorized by this or similar statute of the state of organization of the issuer or registering entity, the location of the registering entity's principal office, the office of its transfer agent or its office making the registration, or by this or a similar statute of the law of the state listed as the owner's address at the time of registration. A registration governed by the law of a jurisdiction in which this or similar legislation is not in force or was not in force when a registration in beneficiary form was made is nevertheless presumed to be valid and authorized as a matter of contract law.

§ 3B:30-5. Designation of beneficiary, registration in beneficiary form

A security, whether evidenced by certificate or account, is registered in beneficiary form when the registration includes a designation of a beneficiary to take the ownership at the death of the owner or the deaths of all multiple owners.

§ 3B:30-6. "Transfer on death," "pay on death"

Registration in beneficiary form may be shown by the words "transfer on death" or the abbreviation "TOD," or by the words "pay on death" or the abbreviation "POD," after the name of the registered owner and before the name of the beneficiary.

§ 3B:30-7. No effect on ownership, cancellation, change permitted

The designation of a TOD beneficiary on a registration in beneficiary form has no effect on ownership until the owner's death. A registration of a security in beneficiary form may be cancelled or changed at any time by the sole owner or all then surviving owners, without the consent of the beneficiary.

§ 3B:30-8. Passage of security to beneficiary, reregistration

On death of a sole owner or the last to die of all multiple owners, ownership of securities registered in beneficiary form passes to the beneficiary or beneficiaries who survive all owners. On proof of death of all owners and compliance with any applicable requirements of the registering entity, a security registered in beneficiary form may be reregistered in the name of the beneficiary or beneficiaries who survived the death of all owners. Until division of the security after the death of all owners, multiple beneficiaries surviving the death of all owners hold their interests as tenants in common. If no beneficiary survives the death of all owners, the security belongs to the estate of the deceased sole owner or the estate of the last to die of all multiple owners.

§ 3B:30-9. Rights of registering entity

a. A registering entity is not required to offer or to accept a request for security registration in beneficiary form. If a registration in beneficiary form is offered by a registering entity, the owner requesting registration in beneficiary form assents to the protections given to the registering entity by this act.

b. By accepting a request for registration of a security in beneficiary form, the registering entity agrees that the registration will be implemented on death of the deceased owner as provided in this act.

c. A registering entity is discharged from all claims to a security by the estate, creditors, heirs, or devisees of a deceased owner if it registers a transfer of a security in accordance with section 8 of this act and does so in good faith reliance on:

(1) the registration;

(2) this act; and

(3) on information provided to it by affidavit of the personal representative of the deceased owner, or by the surviving beneficiary or by the surviving beneficiary's representatives, or other information available to the registering entity.

The protections of this act do not extend to a reregistration or payment made after a registering entity has received written notice from any claimant to any interest in the security objecting to implementation of a registration in beneficiary form. No other notice or other information available to the registering entity affects its right to protection under this act.

d. The protection provided by this act to the registering entity of a security does not affect the rights of beneficiaries in disputes between themselves and other claimants to ownership of the security transferred or its value or proceeds.

§ 3B:30-10. Transfer on death, effectiveness

a. A transfer on death resulting from a registration in beneficiary form is effective by reason of the contract regarding the registration between the owner and the registering entity and this act and is not testamentary.

b. This act does not limit the rights of creditors of security owners against beneficiaries and other transferees under other laws of this State.

§ 3B:30-11. Establishment of terms, conditions by registering entity

a. A registering entity offering to accept registration in beneficiary form may establish the terms and conditions under which it will receive requests for registrations in beneficiary form, and for implementation of registrations in beneficiary form, including requests for reregistration to effect a change of beneficiary. The terms and conditions so established may provide for proving death, avoiding or resolving any problems concerning fractional shares, designating primary and contingent beneficiaries, and substituting a named beneficiary's descendants to take in the place of the named beneficiary in the event of the beneficiary's death. Substitution may be indicated by appending to the name of the primary beneficiary the letters LDPS, standing for "lineal descendants per stirpes." This designation substitutes a deceased beneficiary's descendants who survive the owner for a beneficiary who fails to so survive, the descendants to be identified and to share in accordance with the law of the beneficiary's domicile at the owner's death governing inheritance by decedents of an intestate. Other forms of identifying beneficiaries who are to take on one or more contingencies, and rules for providing proofs and assurances needed to satisfy reasonable concerns by registering entities regarding conditions and identities relevant to accurate implementation of registrations in beneficiary form, may be contained in a registering entity's terms and conditions.

b. The following are illustrations of registrations in beneficiary form which a registering entity may authorize:

(1) sole owner-sole beneficiary: John S. Brown TOD (or POD) John S. Brown Jr.;

(2) multiple owners-sole beneficiary: John S. Brown, Mary B. Brown JT TEN TOD John S. Brown Jr.;

(3) multiple owner-primary and secondary (substituted) beneficiaries: John S. Brown, Mary B. Brown JT TEN TOD John S. Brown Jr. LDPS.

§ 3B:30-12. Construction of act

a. This act shall be liberally construed and applied to promote its underlying purposes and policy and to make uniform the laws with respect to the subject of this act among states enacting it.

b. Unless displaced by the particular provisions of this act, the principles of law and equity supplement its provisions.

Chapter 31. Uniform Trust Code

Article 1. General Provisions and Definitions

§ 3B:31-1. Short title

This act shall be known and may be cited as the "Uniform Trust Code."

§ 3B:31-2. Scope

This act applies to express trusts, charitable or noncharitable, and trusts created pursuant to a statute, judgment, or decree that requires the trust to be administered in the manner of an express trust.

§ 3B:31-3. Definitions

As used in this act:

"Action," with respect to an act of a trustee, includes a failure to act.

"Beneficiary," as it relates to trust beneficiaries, includes a person:

(1) who has any present or future interest, vested or contingent;

(2) who, in a capacity other than that of trustee, holds a power of appointment over trust property;

(3) who is the owner of an interest by assignment or other transfer; and

(4) as it relates to a charitable trust, any person who is entitled to enforce the trust.

"Charitable trust" means a trust, or portion of a trust, created for a charitable purpose described in subsection a. of N.J.S.3B:31-22.

"Environmental law" means a federal, State, or local law, rule, regulation, or ordinance relating to protection of the environment.

"Interests of the beneficiaries" means the beneficial interests provided in the terms of the trust.

"Jurisdiction," with respect to a geographic area, includes a state or country.

"Power of withdrawal" means a presently exercisable general power of appointment other than a power exercisable only upon consent of the trustee or a person holding an adverse interest.

"Property" means anything that may be the subject of ownership, whether real or personal, legal or equitable, or any interest therein.

"Qualified beneficiary" means a beneficiary who, on the date the beneficiary's qualification is determined:

(1) is a distributee or permissible distributee of trust income or principal;

(2) would be a distributee or permissible distributee of trust income or principal if the interests of the distributees described in paragraph (1) terminated on that date; or

(3) would be a distributee or permissible distributee of trust income or principal if the trust terminated on that date.

"Revocable," as applied to a trust, means revocable by the settlor without the consent of the trustee or a person holding an adverse interest.

"Settlor" means a person, including a testator, who creates, or contributes property to, a trust. If more than one person creates or contributes property to a trust, each person is a settlor of the portion of the trust property attributable to that person's contribution except to the extent another person has the power to revoke or withdraw that portion.

"Spendthrift provision" means a term of a trust which restrains both voluntary and involuntary transfer of a beneficiary's interest.

"State" means a State of the United States, the District of Columbia, Commonwealth of Puerto Rico, the United States Virgin Islands, or any territory or insular possession subject to the jurisdiction of the United States. The term includes an Indian tribe or band recognized by federal law or formally acknowledged by a state.

"Terms of a trust" means the manifestation of the settlor's intent regarding a trust's provisions as expressed in the trust instrument or as may be established by other evidence that would be admissible in a judicial proceeding.

"Trust instrument" means an instrument executed by the settlor that contains terms of the trust, including any amendments thereto.

"Trustee," in addition to the definition contained in N.J.S.3B:1-2, includes a corporate entity in its capacity as trustee and a co-trustee where two or more are appointed.

§ 3B:31-4. Knowledge

a. Subject to subsection b. of this section, a person has knowledge of a fact if the person:

(1) has actual knowledge of it;

(2) has received a notice or notification of it; or

(3) from all the facts and circumstances known to the person at the time in question, has reason to know it.

b. An organization that conducts activities through employees has notice or knowledge of a fact involving a trust only from the time the information was received by an employee having responsibility to act for the trust, or would have been brought to the employee's attention if the organization had exercised reasonable diligence. An organization exercises reasonable diligence if it maintains reasonable routines for communicating significant information to the employee having responsibility to act for the trust and there is reasonable compliance with the routines. Reasonable diligence does not require an employee of the organization to communicate information unless the communication is part of the individual's regular duties or the individual knows a matter involving the trust would be materially affected by the information.

§ 3B:31-5. Default and mandatory rules

a. Except as otherwise provided in the terms of the trust, this act governs the duties and powers of a trustee, relations among trustees, and the rights and interests of a beneficiary.

b. The terms of a trust prevail over any provision of this act except:

(1) the requirements for creating a trust;
(2) the duty of a trustee to act in good faith and in accordance with the purposes of the trust;
(3) the requirement that a trust and its terms be for the benefit of its beneficiaries, and that the trust have a purpose that is lawful, not contrary to public policy, and possible to achieve;
(4) the power of the court to modify or terminate a trust under N.J.S.3B:31-26 through N.J.S.3B:31-33;
(5) the effect of a spendthrift provision and the rights of certain creditors and assignees to reach a trust as provided in article 4 of this act;
(6) the power of the court under N.J.S.3B:31-47 to require, dispense with, or modify or terminate a bond;
(7) the duty under subsections a. and b. of N.J.S.3B:31-67 to respond to the request of a qualified beneficiary of an irrevocable trust who has attained the age of 35 years for a copy of the trust instrument or for other information reasonably related to the administration of the trust;
(8) the effect of an exculpatory term under N.J.S.3B:31-77;
(9) the rights under N.J.S.3B:31-79 through N.J.S.3B:31-81 of a person other than a trustee or beneficiary;
(10) periods of limitation for commencing a judicial proceeding; and
(11) the power of the court to take such action and exercise such jurisdiction as may be necessary in the interests of justice.

§ 3B:31-6. Common law of trusts; principles of equity

The common law of trusts and principles of equity supplement this act, except to the extent modified by this act or another statute of this State.

§ 3B:31-7. Governing law

The meaning and effect of the terms of a trust are determined by:

a. the law of the jurisdiction designated in the terms unless the designation of that jurisdiction's law is contrary to a strong public policy of the jurisdiction having the most significant relationship to the matter at issue; or

b. in the absence of a controlling designation in the terms of the trust, the law of the jurisdiction having the most significant relationship to the matter at issue.

§ 3B:31-8. Principal place of administration

a. Without precluding other means for establishing a sufficient connection with the designated jurisdiction, terms of a trust designating the principal place of administration are valid and controlling if:

(1) a trustee maintains a place of business located in or a trustee is a resident of the designated jurisdiction; or
(2) all or part of the administration occurs in the designated jurisdiction.

In the absence of terms of a trust designating the principal place of administration, the initial principal place of administration of a nontestamentary trust shall be this State if the trust is governed by the law of this State, and the principal place of administration of a testamentary trust shall be the jurisdiction in which the decedent was domiciled at the time of death.

b. A trustee is under a continuing duty to administer the trust at a place appropriate to its purposes, its administration, and the interests of the beneficiaries.

c. The trustee, in furtherance of the duty prescribed by subsection b. of this section, may transfer the trust's principal place of administration to another State or to a jurisdiction outside of the United States.

d. The trustee shall notify the qualified beneficiaries of a proposed transfer of a trust's principal place of administration not less than 60 days before initiating the transfer. The notice of proposed transfer shall include:

(1) the name of the jurisdiction to which the principal place of administration is to be transferred;
(2) the address and telephone number at the new location at which the trustee can be contacted;
(3) the date on which the proposed transfer is anticipated to occur; and
(4) the date, not less than 60 days after the giving of the notice, by which the qualified beneficiary is required to notify the trustee of an objection to the proposed transfer.

e. The authority of a trustee under this section to transfer a trust's principal place of administration terminates if a qualified beneficiary notifies the trustee of an objection to the proposed transfer on or before the date specified in the notice, unless the trustee secures judicial approval for the transfer.

f. In connection with a transfer of the trust's principal place of administration, the trustee may transfer some or all of the trust property to a successor trustee designated in the terms of the trust or appointed pursuant to N.J.S.3B:31-49.

§ 3B:31-9. Methods and waiver of notice

a. Notice to a person under this act or the sending of a document to a person under this act shall be accomplished in a manner reasonably suitable under the circumstances and likely to result in receipt of the notice or document. Permissible methods of notice or for sending a document include first-class mail, personal delivery, delivery to the person's last known place of residence or place of business, or a properly directed textual electronic message.

b. Notice otherwise required under this act or a document otherwise required to be sent under this act need not be provided to a person whose identity or location is unknown to and not reasonably ascertainable by the trustee.

c. Notice under this act or the sending of a document under this act may be waived by the person to be notified or sent the document.

d. Notice of a judicial proceeding shall be given as provided in the applicable New Jersey Rules of Court.

§ 3B:31-10. Others treated as qualified beneficiaries

a. Whenever notice to qualified beneficiaries of a trust is required under this act, the trustee shall also give notice to any other beneficiary who has sent the trustee a request for notice.

b. A charitable organization expressly designated to receive distributions under the terms of a charitable trust or a person appointed to enforce a trust created for the care of an animal or another noncharitable purpose as provided in N.J.S.3B:31-24 or N.J.S.3B:31-25 has the rights of a qualified beneficiary under this act.

c. The Attorney General of this State has the rights of a qualified beneficiary with respect to a charitable trust having its principal place of administration in this State.

§ 3B:31-11. Nonjudicial settlement agreements

a. For purposes of this section, "interested persons" means persons whose consent would be required in order to achieve a binding settlement were the settlement to be approved by the court.

b. Except as otherwise provided in subsection c. of this section or any other provision of this chapter, interested persons may enter into a binding nonjudicial settlement agreement with respect to any matter involving a trust.

c. A nonjudicial settlement agreement is valid only to the extent it does not violate a material purpose of the trust and includes terms and conditions that could be properly approved by the court under this act or other applicable law.

d. Matters that may be resolved by a nonjudicial settlement agreement include:
(1) the interpretation or construction of the terms of the trust;
(2) the approval of a trustee's report or accounting;
(3) direction to a trustee to refrain from performing a particular act or the grant to a trustee of any necessary or desirable power;
(4) the resignation or appointment of a trustee and the determination of a trustee's compensation;
(5) transfer of a trust's principal place of administration; and
(6) liability of a trustee for an action relating to the trust.

e. Any interested person may request the court to approve a nonjudicial settlement agreement, to determine whether the representation as provided in article 2 was adequate, and to determine whether the agreement contains terms and conditions the court could have properly approved.

f. A nonjudicial settlement may not be used to produce a result that is contrary to other sections of Title 3B of the New Jersey Statutes, including, but not limited to, terminating or modifying a trust in an impermissible manner.

§ 3B:31-12. Rules of construction

The rules of construction that apply in this State to the interpretation of and disposition of property by will also apply as appropriate to the interpretation of the terms of a trust and the disposition of the trust property.

Article 2. Representation

§ 3B:31-13. Representation: basic effect

a. Notice to a person who may represent and bind another person under this article has the same effect as if notice were given directly to the other person.

b. The consent of a person who may represent and bind another person under this article is binding on the person represented unless the person represented objects to the representation before the consent would otherwise have become effective.

c. Except as otherwise provided in N.J.S.3B:31-27 and N.J.S.3B:31-43, a person who under this article may represent a settlor who lacks capacity may receive notice and give a binding consent on the settlor's behalf.

d. A settlor may not represent and bind a beneficiary under this article with respect to the termination or modification of a trust under subsection a. of N.J.S.3B:31-27.

§ 3B:31-14. Representation by holder of general testamentary power of appointment

a. To the extent there is no conflict of interest between the holder of a general testamentary power of appointment and the persons represented with respect to the particular question or dispute, the holder may represent and bind persons whose interests, as permissible appointees, takers in default, or otherwise, are subject to the power.

b. A holder of a general power of appointment in favor of the holder or holder's estate shall not be deemed to have a conflict with permissible appointees and takers in default.

§ 3B:31-15. Representation by fiduciaries and parents

To the extent there is no conflict of interest between the representative and the person represented or among those being represented with respect to a particular question or dispute:

a. a guardian of the property may represent and bind the estate that the guardian of the property controls;
b. a guardian of the person may represent and bind the ward if no guardian of the property has been appointed;
c. an agent having authority to act with respect to the particular question or dispute may represent and bind the principal;
d. a trustee may represent and bind the beneficiaries of the trust;
e. a personal representative of a decedent's estate may represent and bind persons interested in the estate; and
f. a parent may represent and bind the parent's minor or unborn child if a guardian for the child has not been appointed.

§ 3B:31-16. Representation by person having substantially identical interest

Unless otherwise represented, a minor, incapacitated, or unborn individual, or a person whose identity or location is unknown and not reasonably ascertainable, may be represented by and bound by another having a substantially identical interest with respect to the particular question or dispute, but only to the extent there is no conflict of interest between the representative and the person represented.

§ 3B:31-17. Appointment of representative

a. If the court determines that an interest is not represented under this article or that the otherwise available representation might be inadequate, the court may appoint a guardian ad litem or other representative to receive notice, give consent, and otherwise represent, bind, and act on behalf of a minor, incapacitated, or unborn individual, or a person whose identity or location is unknown. A guardian ad litem or other representative may be appointed to represent several persons or interests.

b. A guardian ad litem or other representative may act on behalf of the individual or person represented with respect to any matter arising under this act, whether or not a judicial proceeding concerning the trust is pending.

c. A guardian ad litem or other representative may consider the benefit accruing to the living members of the individual's family.

Article 3. Creation, Validity, Modification and Termination of Trust

§ 3B:31-18. Methods of creating trust

A trust may be created by:

a. transfer of property under a written instrument to another person as trustee during the settlor's lifetime or by will or other written disposition taking effect upon the settlor's death;
b. written declaration by the owner of property that the owner holds identifiable property as trustee; or
c. written exercise of a power of appointment in favor of a trustee.

§ 3B:31-19. Requirements for creation

a. A trust is created only if:
(1) the settlor has capacity to create a trust;
(2) the settlor indicates an intention to create the trust;
(3) the trust has a definite beneficiary or is:
(a) a charitable trust;
(b) a trust for the care of an animal, as provided in N.J.S.3B:31-24; or
(c) a trust for a noncharitable purpose, as provided in N.J.S.3B:31-25;
(4) the trustee has duties to perform; and
(5) the same person is not the sole trustee and sole beneficiary of all beneficial interests.

b. A beneficiary is definite if the beneficiary can be ascertained now or in the future, subject to the provisions of section 14 of P.L.1999, c.159 (C.46:2F-10) or any other applicable rule against perpetuities.

c. A power in a trustee to select a beneficiary from an indefinite class is valid if exercised within a reasonable time and is not void as provided in section 14 of P.L.1999, c.159 (C.46:2F-10) or any other applicable rule against perpetuities or restraint on alienation. If invalid, the power fails and the property subject to the power passes to the persons who would have taken the property had the power not been conferred.

d. A written instrument which creates a trust or transfers property to a trust shall not be invalid or ineffective because the transferee is identified as the trust rather than the trustee thereof.

§ 3B:31-20. Written trusts created in other jurisdictions

A written trust not created by will is validly created if its creation complies with the law of the jurisdiction in which:

a. the trust instrument was executed;
b. at the time the trust was created, the settlor was domiciled, had a place of abode, or was a national;
c. at the time the trust was created, a trustee was domiciled or had a place of business; or
d. at the time the trust was created, any trust property was located.

§ 3B:31-21. Trust purposes

A trust may be enforced only to the extent its purposes are lawful, not contrary to public policy, and possible to achieve. A trust and its terms shall be for the benefit of its beneficiaries.

§ 3B:31-22. Charitable purposes; enforcement

a. A charitable trust is one that is created for the relief of poverty, the advancement of education or religion, the promotion of health, governmental or municipal purposes, or other purpose the achievement of which is beneficial to the community.

b. f the terms of a charitable trust do not state a particular charitable purpose or beneficiary, and the trustee or other person authorized to state a particular charitable purpose or name a particular charitable beneficiary fails to make a selection, the court may select one or more charitable purposes or beneficiaries. The selection shall be consistent with the settlor's intention to the extent it can be ascertained.

c. A proceeding to enforce a charitable trust may be brought by the settlor, by the Attorney General, by the trust's beneficiaries or by other persons who have standing.

§ 3B:31-23. Creation of trust induced by fraud, duress, or undue influence

A trust is void to the extent its creation was induced by fraud, duress, or undue influence.

§ 3B:31-24. Trust for care of animal

a. A trust may be created to provide for the care of an animal alive during the settlor's lifetime. The trust terminates upon the death of the animal or, if the trust was created to provide for the care of more than one animal alive during the settlor's lifetime, upon the death of the last surviving animal.

b. A trust authorized by this section may be enforced by the settlor or by a person appointed in the terms of the trust or, if no person is so appointed, by a person appointed by the court. A person having an interest in the welfare of the animal may request the court to appoint a person to enforce the trust or to remove a person appointed.

c. Property of a trust authorized by this section may be applied only to its intended use, except to the extent the court determines that the value of the trust property exceeds the amount required for the intended use. Except as otherwise provided in the terms of the trust, property not required for the intended use shall be distributed to the settlor, if then living, otherwise to the settlor's estate.

§ 3B:31-25. Noncharitable trust without ascertainable beneficiary

Except as otherwise provided in N.J.S.3B:31-24 or by another statute, the following rules apply:

a. A trust may be created for a noncharitable but otherwise valid purpose without a definite or definitely ascertainable beneficiary or for a noncharitable but otherwise valid purpose to be selected by the trustee.

b. A trust authorized by this section may be enforced by the settlor or by a person appointed in the terms of the trust or, if no person is so appointed, by a person appointed by the court.

c. Property of a trust authorized by this section may be applied only to its intended use, except to the extent the court determines that the value of the trust property exceeds the amount required for the intended use. Except as otherwise provided in the terms of the trust, property not required for the intended use shall be distributed to the settlor, if then living, otherwise to the settlor's estate.

§ 3B:31-26. Modification or termination of trust; proceedings for approval or disapproval

a. In addition to the methods of termination prescribed by N.J.S.3B:31-27 through N.J.S.3B:31-33, a trust terminates to the extent the trust is revoked or expires pursuant to its terms, no purpose of the trust remains to be achieved, or the purposes of the trust have become unlawful, contrary to public policy of this State, or impossible to achieve.

b. A proceeding to approve or disapprove a proposed modification or termination under N.J.S.3B:31-27 through N.J.S.3B:31-33, or trust combination or division under N.J.S.3B:31-34, may be commenced by a trustee or beneficiary. The settlor of a charitable trust may maintain a proceeding to modify the trust under N.J.S.3B:31-29.

§ 3B:31-27. Modification or termination of noncharitable irrevocable trust by consent

a. A noncharitable irrevocable trust may be modified or terminated upon consent of the trustee and all beneficiaries, if the modification or termination is not inconsistent with a material purpose of the trust.

b. A noncharitable irrevocable trust may be terminated upon consent of all of the beneficiaries if the court concludes that continuance of the trust is not necessary to achieve any material purpose of the trust. A noncharitable irrevocable trust may be modified upon consent of all of the beneficiaries if the court concludes that modification is not inconsistent with a material purpose of the trust.

c. A spendthrift provision in the terms of the trust is not presumed to constitute a material purpose of the trust.

d. Upon termination of a trust under subsection a. or b. of this section, the trustee shall distribute the trust property as agreed by the beneficiaries.

e. If not all of the beneficiaries consent to a proposed modification or termination of the trust under subsection a. or b. of this section, the modification or termination may be approved by the court if the court is satisfied that:

(1) if all of the beneficiaries had consented, the trust could have been modified or terminated under this section; and

(2) the interests of a beneficiary who does not consent will be adequately protected.

§ 3B:31-28 Modification or termination because of unanticipated circumstances or inability to administer trust effectively

a. The court may modify the administrative or dispositive terms of a trust or terminate the trust if, because of circumstances not anticipated by the settlor, modification or termination will further the purposes of the trust. To the extent practicable, the modification shall be made in accordance with the settlor's probable intent.

b. The court may modify the administrative terms of a trust if continuation of the trust on its existing terms would be impracticable or wasteful or impair the trust's administration.

c. Upon termination of a trust under this section, the trustee shall distribute the trust property in a manner consistent with the purposes of the trust.

§ 3B:31-29. Modification or termination of charitable trust (Cy Pres)

a. Except as otherwise provided in subsection b. of this section, if a particular charitable purpose becomes unlawful, impracticable, impossible to achieve, or wasteful:

(1) the trust does not fail, in whole or in part;

(2) the trust property does not revert to the settlor or the settlor's estate; and

(3) the court may modify or terminate the trust by directing that the trust property be applied or distributed, in whole or in part, in a manner consistent with the settlor's charitable purposes.

b. A provision in the terms of a charitable trust that would result in distribution of the trust property to a noncharitable beneficiary prevails over the power of the court under subsection a. of this section.

§ 3B:31-30. Modification or termination of uneconomic trust

a. After notice to the qualified beneficiaries, the trustee of a trust consisting of trust property having a total value less than $100,000 may terminate the trust if the trustee concludes that the value of the trust property is insufficient to justify the cost of administration.

b. The court may modify or terminate a trust or remove the trustee and appoint a different trustee if it determines that the value of the trust property is insufficient to justify the cost of administration.

c. Upon termination of a trust under this section, the trustee shall distribute the trust property in a manner consistent with the purposes of the trust.

d. This section does not apply to an easement for conservation or preservation.

§ 3B:31-31. Reformation to correct mistakes

The court may reform the terms of a trust, even if unambiguous, to conform the terms to the settlor's probable intent if it is proved by clear and convincing evidence that there was a mistake of fact or law, whether in expression or inducement.

§ 3B:31-32. Construction to conform trust terms to probable intent of settlor

Nothing in this act shall prevent the court from construing the terms of a trust, even if unambiguous, to conform to the settlor's probable intent.

§ 3B:31-33. Modification to achieve settlor's tax objectives

To achieve the settlor's tax objectives, the court may modify the terms of a trust in a manner that is not contrary to the settlor's probable intent. The court may provide that the modification has retroactive effect.

§ 3B:31-34. Combination and division of trusts

a. Subject to subsection b. of this section,

(1) the trustees of two or more trusts or parts of trusts may combine the trusts or parts thereof into a single trust, even if such trusts or parts thereof are created by different settlors or under different instruments, and even if the trusts have different trustees; and

(2) the trustees of a single trust may divide the trust into two or more separate trusts, in which case distributions provided by the governing instrument may be made from one or more of the separate trusts.

b. A combination or division under this section may be effected only if the result does not impair rights of any beneficiary or adversely affect the achievement of the purposes of the trust.

Article 4. Creditor's Claims; Spendthrift and Discretionary Trusts

§ 3B:31-35. Rights of beneficiary's creditor or assignee

Except as otherwise provided by law, to the extent a beneficiary's interest is not protected by a spendthrift provision, a creditor or assignee of the beneficiary may reach the beneficiary's interest by attachment of present or future distributions to or for the benefit of the beneficiary, subject to N.J.S.2A:17-50 through N.J.S.2A:17-56 and sections 3 and 4 of P.L.1981, c.203 (C.2A:17-56.1a and C.2A:17-56.6) or other applicable law. The court may limit the award to such relief as is appropriate under the circumstances.

§ 3B:31-36. Spendthrift provision

a. A spendthrift provision is valid only if it restrains both voluntary and involuntary transfer of a beneficiary's interest.

b. A term of the trust providing that the interest of a beneficiary is held subject to a "spendthrift trust," or words of similar import, is sufficient to restrain both voluntary and involuntary transfer of the beneficiary's interest.

c. A beneficiary may not transfer an interest in a trust in violation of a valid spendthrift provision and, except as otherwise provided in this article, a creditor or assignee of the beneficiary may not reach the interest or a distribution by the trustee before its receipt by the beneficiary.

d. A spendthrift provision is valid even though a beneficiary is named as the sole trustee or as a co-trustee of the trust.

e. A valid spendthrift provision does not prevent the appointment of interests through the exercise of a power of appointment.

§ 3B:31-37. Special needs trusts

Even if a trust contains a spendthrift provision, the following shall apply:

a. Special Needs

(1) "Protected person" means a person who is:
(a) an aged, blind, or disabled individual as defined at 42 U.S.C. § 1382c;
(b) developmentally disabled as defined in section 2 of P.L.1979, c.105 (C.30:1AA-2); or
(c) under age 18, or over age 18 and a full-time student, with serious disabilities that reasonably may prevent the individual from being self sufficient as an adult.
(2) "Special needs trust" means an OBRA '93 trust, as defined in subsection a. of section 3 of P.L.2000, c.96 (C.3B:11-37), or trust governed by a written instrument which:
(a) grants a trustee broad discretion to determine whether and when to distribute;
(b) limits distributions during the trust term to distributions to benefit one or more protected persons, although the trust shall have at least one protected person as beneficiary;
(c) provides that the trustee does not have any obligation to pay the protected person's obligations or fund his support;
(d) does not give the protected person any right to require the trustee to distribute at a specific time or for a particular purpose or to assign or encumber interests in the trust; and
(e) evidences the grantor's intent to supplement rather than replace or impair government assistance that the protected person receives or for which he otherwise may be eligible.
b. Notwithstanding any other provision of this act or other law:
(1) trustees of a special needs trust have broad discretion over distributions;
(2) no creditor of a protected person may reach or attach a protected person's interest in a special needs trust and no creditor may require the trustees to distribute to satisfy a protected person's creditor's claim; and
(3) a special needs trust shall terminate at such time as provided in its governing instrument.
c. A special needs trust shall not be required to repay government aid provided to a protected person unless the aid was provided on the basis that the special needs trust would repay the aid when the protected person dies, or the special needs trust terminates sooner and the special needs trust instrument expressly calls for such repayment. This provision does not apply to a first-party, self-settled OBRA '93 trust as defined in subsection a. of section 3 of P.L.2000, c.96 (C.3B:11-37).
d. Notwithstanding N.J.S.3B:31-35 and N.J.S.3B:31-36, trustees of a special needs trust shall exercise their discretion in good faith to further trust purposes and courts may exercise their equity authority to remedy trustee abuses of discretion.

§ 3B:31-38. Discretionary trusts; effect of standard

a. Whether or not a trust contains a spendthrift provision, a creditor of a beneficiary may not compel a distribution that is subject to the trustee's discretion, even if:
(1) The discretion is expressed in the form of a standard of distribution; or
(2) The trustee has abused the discretion.
b. This section does not limit the right of a beneficiary to maintain a judicial proceeding against a trustee for an abuse of discretion or failure to comply with a standard for distribution.
c. With respect to the powers set forth in section 1 of P.L.1996, c.41 (C.3B:11-4.1), the provisions of this section shall apply even though the beneficiary is the sole trustee or a co-trustee of the trust.

§ 3B:31-39. Creditor's claim against settlor

a. Whether or not the terms of a trust contain a spendthrift provision, the following rules apply:
(1) During the lifetime of the settlor, the property of a revocable trust is subject to claims of the settlor's creditors.
(2) With respect to an irrevocable trust, a creditor or assignee of the settlor may reach the maximum amount that can be distributed to or for the settlor's benefit. If a trust has more than one settlor, the amount the creditor or assignee of a particular settlor may reach may not exceed the settlor's interest in the portion of the trust attributable to that settlor's contribution.
(3) After the death of a settlor, and subject to the settlor's right to direct the source from which liabilities will be paid, the property of a trust that was revocable at the settlor's death is subject to claims of the settlor's creditors, costs of administration of the settlor's estate, the expenses of the settlor's funeral and disposal of remains, and to a surviving spouse or partner in a civil union and children to the extent the settlor's probate estate is inadequate to satisfy those claims, costs, expenses.
b. For purposes of this section:
(1) during the period the power may be exercised, the holder of a power of withdrawal is treated in the same manner as the settlor of a revocable trust to the extent of the property subject to the power; and
(2) upon the lapse, release, or waiver of the power, the holder is treated as the settlor of the trust only to the extent the value of the property affected by the lapse, release, or waiver exceeds the greater of the amount specified in section 2041(b)(2) or 2514(e) of the federal Internal Revenue Code of 1986 (26 U.S.C. § 2041(b)(2) or 26 U.S.C. § 2514(e)), or section 2503(b) of the federal Internal Revenue Code of 1986 (26 U.S.C. § 2503(b)), in each case as in effect on the effective date of this act, or as later amended.

§ 3B:31-40. Overdue distribution

a. For the purposes of this section, "mandatory distribution" means a distribution of income or principal that the trustee is required to make to a beneficiary under the terms of the trust, including a distribution upon termination of the trust. The term excludes a distribution subject to the exercise of the trustee's discretion, regardless of whether the terms of the trust (1) include a support or other standard to guide the trustee in making distribution decisions, or (2) provide that the trustee "may" or "shall" make discretionary distributions, including distributions pursuant to a support or other standard.

b. Except as otherwise provided in section 1 of P.L.1996, c.41 (C.3B:11-4.1), whether or not a trust contains a spendthrift provision, a creditor or assignee of a beneficiary may reach a mandatory distribution of income or principal, including a distribution upon termination of the trust, if the trustee has not made the distribution to the beneficiary within a reasonable time after the mandated distribution date.

§ 3B:31-41. Personal obligations of trustee

Trust property is not subject to personal obligations of the trustee, even if the trustee becomes insolvent.

Article 5. Revocable Trusts

§ 3B:31-42. Capacity of settlor of revocable trust

The capacity required to create, amend, revoke, or add property to a revocable trust, or to direct the actions of the trustee of a revocable trust, is the same as that required to make a will.

§ 3B:31-43. Revocation or amendment of revocable trust

a. Unless the terms of a trust expressly provide that the trust is irrevocable, or that it is proved by clear and convincing evidence that the settlor intended for it to be irrevocable, the settlor may revoke or amend the trust. This subsection does not apply to a trust created under an instrument executed before the effective date [July 17, 2016] of this act.
b. If a revocable trust is created or funded by more than one settlor:
(1) to the extent the trust consists of community property, the trust may be revoked by either spouse or partner in a civil union acting alone but may be amended only by joint action of both spouses or partners; and
(2) to the extent the trust consists of property other than community property, each settlor may revoke or amend the trust with regard to the portion of the trust property attributable to that settlor's contribution.
c. The settlor may revoke or amend a revocable trust:
(1) by substantial compliance with a method provided in the terms of the trust; or
(2) if the terms of the trust do not provide a method or the method provided in the terms is not expressly made exclusive, by:
(a) executing a later will or codicil that expressly refers to the trust or specifically devises property that would otherwise have passed according to the terms of the trust; or
(b) any other writing manifesting clear and convincing evidence of the settlor's intent.
d. Upon revocation of a revocable trust, the trustee shall deliver the trust property to the settlor as the settlor directs.
e. A settlor's powers with respect to revocation, amendment, or distribution of trust property may be exercised by an agent under a power of attorney only to the extent expressly authorized by the terms of the trust and the power.
f. A guardian of the property of the settlor may exercise a settlor's powers with respect to revocation, amendment, or distribution of trust property only with the approval of the court supervising the guardianship.
g. A trustee who does not know that a trust has been revoked or amended is not liable to the settlor or settlor's successors in interest for distributions made and other actions taken on the assumption that the trust had not been amended or revoked.

§ 3B:31-44. Settlor's powers

While a trust is revocable, rights of the beneficiaries are subject to the control of, and the duties of the trustee are owed exclusively to, the settlor.

§ 3B:31-45. Limitation on action contesting validity of revocable trust; distribution of trust property

a. A person may commence a judicial proceeding to contest the validity of a trust that was revocable at the settlor's death within the earlier of:
(1) Three years after the settlor's death; or
(2) Four months, in the case of a resident, or six months, in the case of a nonresident, after the trustee sent the person a copy of the trust instrument and a notice informing the person of the trust's existence, of the trustee's name and address, and of the time allowed for commencing a proceeding.
b. Upon the death of the settlor of a trust that was revocable at the settlor's death, the trustee may proceed to distribute the trust property in accordance with the terms of the trust. The trustee is not subject to liability for doing so unless:
(1) the trustee knows of a pending judicial proceeding contesting the validity of the trust; or
(2) a potential contestant has notified the trustee in writing of a possible judicial proceeding to contest the validity of the trust and the trustee has received written notice of a judicial proceeding commenced within 90 days after the contestant sent the notification.
c. A beneficiary of a trust that is determined to have been invalid is liable to return any distribution received.

Article 6. Office of Trustee

§ 3B:31-46. Accepting or declining trusteeship

a. Except as otherwise provided in subsection c. of this section, a person designated as trustee accepts the trusteeship:
(1) in the case of a testamentary trustee or substituted testamentary trustee, as provided in N.J.S.3B:11-2, and
(2) in the case of any other trustee,
(a) by substantially complying with a method of acceptance provided in the terms of the trust; or
(b) if the terms of the trust do not provide a method or the method provided in the terms is not expressly made exclusive, by accepting delivery of the trust property, exercising powers or performing duties as trustee, or otherwise indicating acceptance of the trusteeship.

b. A person designated as trustee who has not yet accepted the trusteeship may renounce the trusteeship. A designated trustee who does not accept the trusteeship within a reasonable time after knowing of the designation is deemed to have renounced the trusteeship.

c. A person designated as trustee, without accepting the trusteeship, may:

(1) act to preserve the trust property if, within a reasonable time after acting, the person sends a renunciation of the trusteeship to the settlor or, if the settlor is dead or lacks capacity, to the qualified beneficiaries and to any designated successor trustee; and

(2) inspect or investigate trust property to determine potential liability under environmental or other law or for any other purpose.

§ 3B:31-47. Trustee's bond

a. A trustee shall give bond to secure performance of the trustee's duties as prescribed by N.J.S.3B:15-1 et seq. if the court finds that a bond is needed to protect the interests of the beneficiaries or is required by the terms of the trust and the court has not dispensed with that requirement.

b. Unless otherwise directed by the court, the cost of the bond is an expense of the trust.

§ 3B:31-48. Co-trustees

a. Co-trustees who are unable to reach a unanimous decision may act by majority decision. A dissenting trustee who joins in carrying out a decision of the majority but expresses his dissent in writing promptly to his co-trustees shall not be liable for the act of the majority.

b. If a vacancy occurs in a co-trusteeship, the remaining co-trustees shall act for the trust unless the trust instrument provides otherwise.

c. A co-trustee shall participate in the performance of a trustee's function unless the co-trustee is unavailable to perform the function because of absence, illness, disqualification under other law, or other temporary incapacity or the co-trustee has properly delegated the performance of the function to another trustee.

d. If a co-trustee is unavailable to perform duties because of absence, illness, disqualification under other law, other temporary incapacity, or a vacancy remains unfilled and prompt action is necessary to achieve the purposes of the trust or to avoid injury to the trust property, the remaining co-trustee or a majority of the remaining co-trustees shall act for the trust.

e. A trustee may not delegate to a co-trustee the performance of a function the settlor reasonably expected the trustees to perform jointly. Unless a delegation was irrevocable, a trustee may revoke a delegation previously made.

f. A trustee who does not join in an action of a co-trustee or co-trustees because of absence, illness, disqualification or other temporary incapacity shall not be liable for that action.

g. Notwithstanding subsection a. or f. of this section, every trustee shall exercise reasonable care to:

(1) prevent a co-trustee from committing a breach of trust; and

(2) compel a co-trustee to redress a breach of trust.

§ 3B:31-49. Vacancy in trusteeship; appointment of successor

a. A vacancy in a trusteeship occurs if:

(1) a person designated as trustee renounces the trusteeship;

(2) a person designated as trustee cannot be identified or does not exist;

(3) a trustee resigns or is discharged;

(4) a trustee is disqualified or removed;

(5) a trustee dies; or

(6) a guardian or conservator is appointed for an individual serving as trustee.

b. If one or more co-trustees remain in office, a vacancy in a trusteeship need not be filled unless the trust instrument provides otherwise. A vacancy in a trusteeship shall be filled if the trust has no remaining trustee.

c. A vacancy in a trusteeship of a noncharitable trust that is required to be filled shall be filled in the following order of priority:

(1) by a person designated pursuant to the terms of the trust to act as successor trustee;

(2) by a procedure established pursuant to the terms of the trust to appoint a successor trustee;

(3) by a person appointed by unanimous agreement of the qualified beneficiaries; or

(4) by a person appointed by the court.

d. A vacancy in a trusteeship of a charitable trust that is required to be filled shall be filled in the following order of priority:

(1) by a person designated pursuant to the terms of the trust to act as successor trustee; or

(2) by a person appointed by the court.

e. Whether or not a vacancy in a trusteeship exists or is required to be filled, the court may appoint an additional trustee or special fiduciary whenever the court considers the appointment desirable for the administration of the trust.

f. A person appointed to fill a vacancy in a trusteeship shall have all the powers and discretions of the original trustee.

§ 3B:31-50. Resignation of trustee

a. A trustee may resign:

(1) upon at least 30 days' notice to the qualified beneficiaries, the settlor, if living, all co-trustees, and the trustee or trustees, if any, designated pursuant to the terms of the trust to succeed the resigning trustee; or

(2) with the approval of the court.

b. In approving a resignation, the court may issue orders and impose conditions reasonably necessary for the protection of the trust property.

c. Any liability of a resigning trustee or of any sureties on the trustee's bond for acts or omissions of the trustee is not discharged or affected by the trustee's resignation.

§ 3B:31-51. Removal of trustee

a. The settlor, a co-trustee, or a beneficiary may request the court to remove a trustee, or a trustee may be removed by the court on its own initiative.

b. The court may remove a trustee for any of the reasons stated in N.J.S.3B:14-21.

c. Pending a final decision on a request to remove a trustee, or in lieu of or in addition to removing a trustee, the court may order such appropriate relief as may be necessary to protect the trust property or the interests of the beneficiaries.

§ 3B:31-52. Delivery of property by former trustee

a. Unless a co-trustee remains in office or the court otherwise orders, and until the trust property is delivered to a successor trustee or other person entitled to it, a trustee who has resigned or been removed has the duties of a trustee and the powers necessary to protect the trust property.

b. A trustee who has resigned or been removed shall proceed expeditiously to deliver the trust property within the trustee's possession to the co-trustee, successor trustee, or other person entitled to it, but a resigning trustee may retain a reasonable reserve for the costs of finalizing that trustee's administration of the trust.

§ 3B:31-53. Reimbursement of expenses

a. In addition to the compensation allowed by N.J.S.3B:18-2 et seq., a trustee is entitled to be reimbursed out of the trust property for:

(1) expenses that were properly incurred in the administration of the trust; and

(2) to the extent necessary to prevent unjust enrichment of the trust, expenses that were not properly incurred in the administration of the trust.

b. An advance by a trustee of money or other property for the protection of the trust gives rise to a lien against trust property to secure reimbursement.

Article 7. Duties and Powers of Trustee

§ 3B:31-54. Duty to administer trust

Upon acceptance of a trusteeship, the trustee shall administer the trust in good faith, in accordance with its terms and purposes and the interests of the beneficiaries, and in accordance with this act and other applicable law.

§ 3B:31-55. Duty of loyalty

a. A trustee shall administer the trust with undivided loyalty to and solely in the best interests of the beneficiaries.

b. Subject to the rights of persons dealing with or assisting the trustee as provided in N.J.S.3B:14-37, a sale, encumbrance, or other transaction involving the investment or management of trust property entered into by the trustee for the trustee's own personal account or which is otherwise affected by a conflict between the trustee's fiduciary and personal interests is voidable by a beneficiary affected by the transaction unless:

(1) the transaction was authorized by the terms of the trust;

(2) the transaction was approved by the court;

(3) the beneficiary did not commence a judicial proceeding within the time allowed by N.J.S.3B:31-74;

(4) the beneficiary consented to the trustee's conduct, ratified the transaction, or released the trustee in compliance with N.J.S.3B:31-78; or

(5) the transaction involves a contract entered into or a claim acquired by the trustee before the person became a trustee.

c. A sale, encumbrance, or other transaction involving the investment or management of trust property is presumed to be affected by a conflict between personal and fiduciary interests if it is entered into by the trustee with:

(1) the trustee's spouse or partner in a civil union;

(2) the trustee's parents, parents' descendants, or the spouse or partner in a civil union of any of the foregoing;

(3) an agent, accountant, or attorney of the trustee; or

(4) a corporation or other person or enterprise in which the trustee, or a person that owns a significant interest in the trustee, has an interest that might affect the trustee's judgment.

d. A transaction between a trustee and a beneficiary that does not concern trust property but that occurs during the existence of the trust or while the trustee retains significant influence over the beneficiary and from which the trustee obtains an advantage attributable to the existence of the trust is voidable by the beneficiary if the beneficiary establishes that the transaction was unfair to the beneficiary.

e. A transaction not concerning trust property in which the trustee engages in the trustee's individual capacity involves a conflict between personal and fiduciary interests if the transaction concerns an opportunity properly belonging to the trust.

f. In voting shares of stock of a corporation or in exercising powers of control over similar interests in other forms of enterprise, the trustee shall act in the best interests of the beneficiaries and shall vote to elect or appoint directors or other managers who will manage the corporation or enterprise in the best interests of the beneficiaries.

g. This section does not preclude the following transactions, if fair to the beneficiaries:

(1) an agreement between a trustee and a beneficiary relating to the appointment or compensation of the trustee;

(2) payment of reasonable compensation to the trustee;

(3) a transaction between the trust and another trust, decedent's estate, guardianship, conservatorship, or other fiduciary relationship of which the trustee is a fiduciary or in which a beneficiary has an interest;
(4) a deposit of trust money in a regulated financial-service institution operated by or affiliated with the trustee; or
(5) an advance by the trustee of money for the protection of the trust.
h. The court may appoint a special fiduciary to make decisions with respect to any proposed transaction that might violate this section if entered into by the trustee.

§ 3B:31-56. Duty of impartiality

If a trust has two or more beneficiaries, the trustee shall act impartially in investing, managing, and distributing the trust property, giving due regard to the beneficiaries' respective interests.

§ 3B:31-57. Duty of prudent administration

A trustee shall administer the trust as a prudent person would, by considering the purposes, terms, distributional requirements, and other circumstances of the trust. In satisfying this standard, the trustee shall exercise reasonable care, skill, and caution.

§ 3B:31-58. Costs of administration

In administering a trust, the trustee may incur only costs that are appropriate and reasonable in relation to the trust property, the purposes of the trust, and the skills of the trustee.

§ 3B:31-59. Duty to use special skills

A trustee who has special skills or expertise, or is named trustee in reliance upon the trustee's representation that the trustee has special skills or expertise, has a duty to use those special skills or expertise.

§ 3B:31-60. Delegation by trustee

a. A trustee may delegate ministerial, administrative and management duties and powers that a prudent trustee of comparable skills could properly delegate under the circumstances.
b. The trustee shall exercise reasonable care, skill, and caution in:
(1) selecting an agent;
(2) establishing in writing the scope and terms of the delegation, consistent with the purposes and terms of the trust; and
(3) periodically reviewing the agent's actions in order to monitor the agent's performance and compliance with the terms of the delegation.
c. A trustee shall provide reasonable written notice to the qualified beneficiaries on each occasion upon which the trustee delegates duties pursuant to this section, including the identity of the agent.
d. A trustee who complies with subsections b. and c. of this section is not liable to the beneficiaries or to the trust for an action of the agent to whom the function was delegated.
e. In performing a delegated function, the agent shall owe to the trustee and the beneficiaries the same duties as the fiduciary and shall be held to the same standards as the fiduciary.
f. By accepting a delegation of powers or duties from the trustee of a trust that is subject to the law of this State, an agent submits to the jurisdiction of the courts of this State, even if the delegation agreement provides otherwise.

§ 3B:31-61. Powers to direct

a. While a trust is revocable, the trustee may follow a direction of the settlor that is contrary to the terms of the trust.
b. If the terms of a trust confer upon a person other than the settlor of a revocable trust the power to direct certain actions of the trustee, the trustee shall act in accordance with a written exercise of the power unless the attempted exercise is contrary to the terms of the trust or the trustee knows the attempted exercise would constitute a breach of a fiduciary duty that the person holding the power owes to the beneficiaries of the trust.
c. The terms of a trust may confer upon a trustee or other person a power to direct the modification or termination of the trust.
d. A person, other than a beneficiary, who holds a power to direct is required to act in good faith with regard to the purposes of the trust and the interests of the beneficiaries. The holder of a power to direct is liable for any loss that results from the holder's failure to act in good faith.

§ 3B:31-62. Powers to direct investment functions

a. When one or more persons are given authority by the terms of a governing instrument to direct, consent to or disapprove a fiduciary's actual or proposed investment decisions, such persons shall be considered to be investment advisers and fiduciaries when exercising such authority unless the governing instrument otherwise provides.
b. If a governing instrument provides that a fiduciary is to follow the direction of an investment adviser, and the fiduciary acts in accordance with such a direction, then except in cases of willful misconduct or gross negligence on the part of the fiduciary so directed, the fiduciary shall not be liable for any loss resulting directly or indirectly from any such act.
c. If a governing instrument provides that a fiduciary is to make decisions with the consent of an investment adviser, then except in cases of willful misconduct or gross negligence on the part of the fiduciary, the fiduciary shall not be liable for any loss resulting directly or indirectly from any act taken or omitted as a result of such investment adviser's failure to provide such consent after having been requested to do so by the fiduciary.
d. For purposes of this section, "investment decision" means with respect to any investment, the retention, purchase, sale, exchange, tender or other transaction affecting the ownership thereof or rights therein and with respect to nonpublicly traded investments, the valuation thereof, and an adviser with authority with respect to such decisions is an investment adviser.

e. Whenever a governing instrument provides that a fiduciary is to follow the direction of an investment adviser with respect to investment decisions, then, except to the extent that the governing instrument provides otherwise, the fiduciary shall have no duty to:
(1) Monitor the conduct of the investment adviser;
(2) Provide advice to the investment adviser or consult with the investment adviser; or
(3) Communicate with or warn or apprise any beneficiary or third party concerning instances in which the fiduciary would or might have exercised the fiduciary's own discretion in a manner different from the manner directed by the investment adviser.
Absent clear and convincing evidence to the contrary, the actions of the fiduciary pertaining to matters within the scope of the investment adviser's authority, such as confirming that the investment adviser's directions have been carried out and recording and reporting actions taken at the investment adviser's direction, shall be presumed to be administrative actions taken by the fiduciary solely to allow the fiduciary to perform those duties assigned to the fiduciary under the governing instrument. Such administrative actions shall not be deemed to constitute an undertaking by the fiduciary to monitor the investment adviser or otherwise participate in actions within the scope of the investment adviser's authority.

§ 3B:31-63. Control and protection of trust property

A trustee shall take reasonable steps to take control of and protect the trust property.

§ 3B:31-64. Recordkeeping and identification of trust property

a. A trustee shall keep adequate records of the administration of the trust.
b. A trustee shall keep trust property separate from the trustee's own property.
c. Except as otherwise provided in subsection d. of this section, a trustee shall cause the trust property to be designated so that the interest of the trust, to the extent feasible, appears in records maintained by a party other than a trustee or beneficiary.
d. If the trustee maintains records clearly indicating the respective interests, a trustee may invest as a whole the property of the trust with other fiduciary accounts maintained by the trustee.

§ 3B:31-65. Duty to enforce and defend claims

A trustee shall take reasonable steps to enforce claims of the trust and to defend claims against the trust.

§ 3B:31-66. Duty to collect trust property and redress breaches of trust

a. A trustee shall take reasonable steps to compel a former trustee or other person to deliver trust property to the trustee.
b. A trustee shall take reasonable steps to redress a breach of trust known to the trustee to have been committed by a former trustee.

§ 3B:31-67. Duty to disclose and discretion to periodically report

a. A trustee shall keep the qualified beneficiaries of the trust reasonably informed about the administration of the trust and of the material facts necessary for them to protect their interests. Unless unreasonable under the circumstances, a trustee shall promptly respond to a beneficiary's request for information related to the administration of a trust.
b. A trustee, upon request of a beneficiary, shall promptly furnish to the beneficiary a copy of the trust instrument.
c. A trustee seeking the protection of N.J.S.3B:31-74 may provide the beneficiaries with a report of the trust property, liabilities, receipts, and disbursements, including the source and amount of the trustee's compensation, a listing of the trust assets, and, if feasible, their respective market values.

§ 3B:31-68. Discretionary powers

Notwithstanding the breadth of discretion granted to a trustee in the terms of the trust, including the use of such terms as "absolute," "sole," or "uncontrolled," the trustee shall exercise a discretionary power in good faith and in accordance with the terms and purposes of the trust and the interests of the beneficiaries.

§ 3B:31-69. General powers of trustee

a. Except as limited by section 1 of P.L.1996, c.41 (C.3B:11-4.1) and other express statutory restrictions, a trustee, without authorization by the court, may exercise:
(1) powers conferred by the terms of the trust; or
(2) except as limited by the terms of the trust:
(a) all powers over the trust property which an unmarried competent owner has over individually owned property;
(b) any other powers appropriate to achieve the proper investment, management, and distribution of the trust property; and
(c) any other powers conferred by this act and by Title 3B of the New Jersey Statutes.
b. The exercise of a power is subject to the fiduciary duties prescribed by this act and by Title 3B of the New Jersey Statutes.

§ 3B:31-70. Distribution upon termination

a. Upon the occurrence of an event terminating or partially terminating a trust, the trustee shall proceed expeditiously to distribute the trust property to the persons entitled to it, subject to the right of the trustee to retain a reasonable reserve for the payment of debts, expenses, and taxes.
b. Upon termination or partial termination of a trust, the trustee may mail or deliver a proposal for distribution to all persons who have a right to object to the proposed distribution. The proposal shall notify all persons who have a right to object to the proposal of their right to object and that their objection is required to be in writing and received by the trustee within 30 days after the mailing or delivery of the proposal. The right of any person to object to the proposed distribution on the basis of the kind or value of asset

he or another beneficiary is to receive, if not waived earlier in writing, terminates if he fails to object in writing received by the trustee within 30 days after mailing or delivery of the proposal.

Article 8. Liability of Trustees and Rights of Persons Dealing with Trustee

§ 3B:31-71. Remedies for breach of trust

a. A violation by a trustee of a duty the trustee owes to a beneficiary is a breach of trust.

b. To remedy a breach of trust that has occurred or may occur, the court may:

(1) compel the trustee to perform the trustee's duties;
(2) enjoin the trustee from committing a breach of trust;
(3) compel the trustee to redress a breach of trust by paying money, restoring property, or other means;
(4) order a trustee to account;
(5) appoint a special fiduciary to take possession of the trust property and administer the trust;
(6) suspend the trustee;
(7) remove the trustee as provided in N.J.S.3B:31-51;
(8) reduce or deny compensation to the trustee;
(9) subject to N.J.S.3B:14-37, void an act of the trustee, impose a lien or a constructive trust on trust property, or trace trust property wrongfully disposed of and recover the property or its proceeds; or
(10) order any other appropriate relief.

§ 3B:31-72. Damages for breach of trust

a. A trustee who commits a breach of trust is liable to the beneficiaries affected for the greater of:

(1) the amount required to restore the value of the trust property and trust distributions to what they would have been had the breach not occurred; or
(2) the profit the trustee made by reason of the breach.

b. Except as otherwise provided in this subsection, if more than one trustee is liable to the beneficiaries for a breach of trust, a trustee is entitled to contribution from the other trustee or trustees based on the comparative degree of culpability for the breach. However, a trustee who committed the breach in bad faith or with reckless indifference to the purposes of the trust or the interests of the beneficiaries is not entitled to contribution from a trustee who was not guilty of such conduct. A trustee who received a benefit from the breach of trust is not entitled to contribution from another trustee to the extent of the benefit received.

§ 3B:31-73. Damages in absence of breach

a. A trustee is accountable to an affected beneficiary for any profit made by the trustee arising from the administration of the trust, even absent a breach of trust, except where the interest in the transaction involved is fully disclosed to the beneficiary and consent is freely given.

b. Absent a breach of trust, a trustee is not liable to a beneficiary for a loss or depreciation in the value of trust property or for not having made a profit.

§ 3B:31-74. Limitation of action against trustee

a. A beneficiary may not commence a proceeding against a trustee for breach of trust more than six months after the date the beneficiary or a representative of the beneficiary was sent a report that adequately disclosed the existence of a potential claim for breach of trust and informed the beneficiary of the time allowed for commencing a proceeding.

b. A report adequately discloses the existence of a potential claim for breach of trust if it provides sufficient information so that the beneficiary or representative knows of the potential claim or should have inquired into its existence.

c. If subsection a. of this section does not apply, a judicial proceeding by a beneficiary against a trustee for breach of trust may be commenced only within five years after the first to occur of:

(1) the removal, resignation, or death of the trustee;
(2) the termination of the beneficiary's interest in the trust; or
(3) the termination of the trust.

Notwithstanding the foregoing, this subsection shall not operate to bar any proceeding by a beneficiary until five years after such beneficiary: (a) has attained majority; (b) has knowledge of the existence of the trust; and (c) has knowledge that such beneficiary is or was a beneficiary of the trust.

d. For purposes of subsection a. of this section, a beneficiary is deemed to have been sent a report if:

(1) in the case of a beneficiary having capacity, it is sent to the beneficiary; or
(2) in the case of a beneficiary who under article 2 of this act may be represented and bound by another person, if it is received by his representative.

e. This section does not preclude an action to recover for fraud or misrepresentation related to the report.

§ 3B:31-75. Reliance on trust instrument

A trustee who acts in reasonable reliance on the terms of the trust as expressed in the trust instrument is not liable to a beneficiary for a breach of trust to the extent the breach resulted from the reliance.

§ 3B:31-76. Event affecting administration or distribution

If the happening of an event, including marriage, divorce, performance of educational requirements, or death, affects the administration or distribution of a trust, a trustee who has exercised reasonable care to ascertain the happening of the event is not liable for a loss resulting from the trustee's lack of knowledge.

§ 3B:31-77. Exculpation of trustee

a. A term of a trust relieving a trustee of liability for breach of trust is unenforceable to the extent that it:
(1) relieves the trustee of liability for breach of trust committed in bad faith or with reckless indifference to the purposes of the trust or the interests of the beneficiaries; or
(2) was inserted as the result of an abuse by the trustee of a fiduciary or confidential relationship to the settlor.
b. An exculpatory term drafted or caused to be drafted by the trustee is invalid as an abuse of a fiduciary or confidential relationship unless the trustee proves that the exculpatory term is fair under the circumstances and that its existence and contents were adequately communicated to the settlor.

§ 3B:31-78. Beneficiary's consent, release, or ratification

A trustee is not liable to a beneficiary for breach of trust if the beneficiary, while having capacity, consented to the conduct constituting the breach, released the trustee from liability for the breach, or ratified the transaction constituting the breach, unless:
a. the consent, release, or ratification of the beneficiary was induced by improper conduct of the trustee; or
b. at the time of the consent, release, or ratification, the beneficiary did not know of the beneficiary's rights or of the material facts relating to the breach.

§ 3B:31-79. Limitation on personal liability of trustee

a. Except as otherwise provided in the contract, a trustee is not personally liable on a contract properly entered into in the trustee's fiduciary capacity in the course of administering the trust if the trustee in the contract disclosed the fiduciary capacity.
b. A trustee is personally liable for torts committed in the course of administering a trust, or for obligations arising from ownership or control of trust property, including liability for violation of environmental law, only if the trustee is personally at fault.
c. A claim based on a contract entered into by a trustee in the trustee's fiduciary capacity, on an obligation arising from ownership or control of trust property, or on a tort committed in the course of administering a trust, may be asserted in a judicial proceeding against the trustee in the trustee's fiduciary capacity, whether or not the trustee is personally liable for the claim.

§ 3B:31-80. Interest as general partner

a. Except as otherwise provided in subsection c. of this section or unless personal liability is imposed in the contract, a trustee who holds an interest as a general partner in a general or limited partnership is not personally liable on a contract entered into by the partnership after the trust's acquisition of the interest if the fiduciary capacity was disclosed in the contract or in a statement previously filed pursuant to the "Uniform Partnership Act (1996)," P.L.2000, c.161 (C.42:1A-1 et seq.) or the "Uniform Limited Partnership Law (1976)," P.L.1983, c.489 (C.42:2A-1 et seq.).
b. Except as otherwise provided in subsection c. of this section, a trustee who holds an interest as a general partner is not personally liable for torts committed by the partnership or for obligations arising from ownership or control of the interest unless the trustee is personally at fault.
c. The immunity provided by this section does not apply if an interest in the partnership is held by the trustee in a capacity other than that of trustee or is held by the trustee's spouse or partner in a civil union or one or more of the trustee's descendants, siblings, or parents, or the spouse or partner in a civil union of any of them.
d. If the trustee of a revocable trust holds an interest as a general partner, the settlor is personally liable for contracts and other obligations of the partnership as if the settlor were a general partner.

§ 3B:31-81. Certification of trust

a. Instead of furnishing a copy of the trust instrument to a person other than a beneficiary, the trustee may furnish to the person a certification of trust containing the following information:
(1) that the trust exists and the date the trust instrument was executed;
(2) the identity of the settlor;
(3) the identity and address of the currently acting trustee;
(4) the powers of the trustee;
(5) the revocability or irrevocability of the trust and the identity of any person holding a power to revoke the trust;
(6) the authority of co-trustees to sign and whether all or less than all are required in order to exercise powers of the trustee; and
(7) the name in which title to trust property may be taken.
b. A certification of trust shall be signed by all persons identified as currently acting as trustee.
c. A certification of trust shall state that the trust has not been revoked, modified, or amended in any manner that would cause the representations contained in the certification of trust to be incorrect.
d. A certification of trust need not contain the dispositive terms of a trust.
e. A recipient of a certification of trust may require the trustee to furnish copies of those excerpts from the original trust instrument and later amendments which designate the trustee and confer upon the trustee the power to act in the pending transaction.
f. A person who acts in reliance upon a certification of trust without knowledge that the representations contained therein are incorrect is not liable to any person for so acting and may assume without inquiry the existence of the facts contained in the

certification. Knowledge of the terms of the trust may not be inferred solely from the fact that a copy of all or part of the trust instrument is held by the person relying upon the certification.

g. A person making a demand for the trust instrument in addition to a certification of trust or excerpts is liable for damages if the court determines that the person did not act in good faith in demanding the trust instrument.

h. This section does not limit the right of a person to obtain a copy of the trust instrument in a judicial proceeding concerning the trust.

Article 9. Miscellaneous Provisions

§ 3B:31-82. Electronic records and signatures

The provisions of this act governing the legal effect, validity, or enforceability of electronic records or electronic signatures, and of contracts formed or performed with the use of such records or signatures, conform to the requirements of section 102 of the "Electronic Signatures in Global and National Commerce Act" (15 U.S.C. § 7002), and supersede, modify, and limit the requirements of that act.

§ 3B:31-83. Severability clause

If any provision of this act or its application to any person or circumstances is held invalid, the invalidity does not affect other provisions or applications of this act which can be given effect without the invalid provision or application, and to this end the provisions of this act are severable.

§ 3B:31-84. Application to existing relationships

a. Except as otherwise provided in this act:
(1) this act applies to all trusts created before, on, or after its effective date [July 17, 2016];
(2) this act applies to all judicial proceedings concerning trusts commenced on or after its effective date;
(3) this act applies to judicial proceedings concerning trusts commenced before its effective date unless the court finds that application of a particular provision of this act would substantially interfere with the effective conduct of the judicial proceedings or prejudice the rights of the parties, in which case the particular provision of this act does not apply and the superseded law applies;
(4) any rule of construction or presumption provided in this act applies to trust instruments executed before the effective date of the act unless there is clear indication of a contrary intent in the terms of the trust; and
(5) an act done before the effective date is not affected by this act.

b. If a right is acquired, extinguished, or barred upon expiration of a prescribed period that has commenced to run under any other statute before the effective date of the act, that statute continues to apply to the right even if that statute has been repealed or superseded by this act.

346.73056 NEW
New Jersey.
 Legislature.
New Jersey Statutes.
 Title 3b

01/18/23

Made in the USA
Middletown, DE
17 August 2022